SPACE, TIME
and
RESURRECTION

SPACE, TIME
and
RESURRECTION

Thomas F. Torrance

T&T CLARK
EDINBURGH

T&T CLARK LTD
59 GEORGE STREET
EDINBURGH EH2 2LQ
SCOTLAND

First published 1976 by The Handsel Press
First published in paperback 1998 by T&T Clark Ltd

ISBN 0 567 08609 7

British Library Cataloguing-in-Publication Data
A catalogue record for this book is available from the British Library

Printed and bound in Great Britain by MPG Books, Bodmin

To

The Very Rev. Professor James S. Stewart

'If Christ is not risen then our preaching is empty and your
faith is vain. We are even found to be misrepresenting God.'

(1 Cor. 15: 14–15.)

CONTENTS

		page
Preface		ix
Introduction		1
1.	The Biblical Concept of the Resurrection	27
2.	The Resurrection and the Person of Christ	46
3.	The Resurrection and the Atoning Work of Christ	61
4.	The Nature of the Resurrection Event	86
5.	The Ascension of Christ	106
6.	The Nature of the Ascension Event	123
7.	The Ascension and the *Parousia* of Christ	143
8.	The Lord of Space and Time	159
Index of Names		195

PREFACE

The last time I saw Karl Barth was at his home in Basel at the end of the summer of 1968. I had not talked with him for ten years and was eager to put a number of questions to him, mostly bearing on the interrelation between theological and natural science, and the relation of his thought to the philosophy and logic of science taught by his old friend and former colleague Heinrich Scholz. Among other things, we discussed the problem of dualism in science and theology with reference to Luther, Newton and Kant, and the implication of the rejection of dualism for the problem of natural theology which had always seemed to come to prominence in an era characterized by a dualist outlook upon the universe, for example, in the middle ages or in the so-called age of reason. I was anxious to get Karl Barth's reaction to the way in which I explained to a Thomist or a physicist his attitude to natural theology by referring to Einstein's account of the relation of geometry to experience, or to physics. I put it this way. With relativity theory Einstein rejected the Newtonian dualism between absolute mathematical space and time and bodies in motion. He argued, therefore, that instead of idealizing geometry by detaching it from experience, and making it an independent conceptual system which was then used as a rigid framework within which physical knowledge is to be pursued and organized, geometry must be brought into the midst of physics where it changes and becomes a kind of natural science (four-dimensional geometry) indissolubly united to physics. Instead of being swallowed up by physics and disappearing, however, geometry becomes the epistemological structure in the heart of physics, although it is incomplete without physics. It is in a similar way, I argued, that Karl Barth treats natural theology when he rejects its status as a *praeambula fidei*, that is, as a preamble of faith, or an independent conceptual system antecedent to actual knowledge of God, which is then used as an epistemological framework within which to interpret and formulate actual empirical knowledge of God, thereby subordinating it to distorting forms of thought. To set aside an *independent* natural theology in that way is demanded by rigorous scientific method, according to which we must allow all our presuppositions and every preconceived framework to be called in question by what is actually disclosed in the process of inquiry. However, instead of rejecting natural theology *tout court*, Barth has transposed it into the material content of theology where in a changed form it constitutes the epistemological structure of our knowledge of God. As such, however, it cannot stand on its own as an independent logical structure detached from the actual subject matter of our knowledge of God, although it is open to philosophical analysis. I referred to Barth's reinterpretation of the Anselmian method worked out with Heinrich Scholz in the summer seminar of 1930 in Bonn, and to the way in which Barth then deployed and developed that epistemological structure in his doctrine of God, especially in *Church Dogmatics*, I/1 and II/1, where a replacing of a dualist with an integrative mode of thought enabled him to reject the Thomist split in the concept of God evident in the separation of a doctrine of the One God from a doctrine of the Triune God. Karl Barth expressed full agreement with my interpretation of his thought, and said, rather characteristically, of the relation of geometry to physics, 'I must have been a blind hen not to have seen that analogy before'.

We went on to talk about his relations with Heinrich Scholz and the question of 'the scientific starting point' in theology which Scholz had early put to Barth, to which Barth had answered that the starting point he had adopted was *the resurrection of Christ*. The reason for that answer Barth had often given: it was from the perspective of the resurrection that the whole of the New Testament presentation of Christ is shaped, and it is still from the event of the resurrection that Jesus Christ and his being and action in his life and death penetrate to us, 'thus becoming truth in their reality, and as truth reality for the world' (*Church Dogmatics*, IV/3, p. 284). Then I ventured to say that unless that starting point was closely bound up with *the incarnation*, it might be only too easy, judging from many of our contemporaries and even some of his former students, to think of the resurrection after all in a rather docetic way, lacking concrete ontological reality. But at that remark, Barth leaned over to me and said with considerable force, which I shall never forget, '*Wohlverstanden, leibliche Auferstehung*' – 'Mark well, bodily resurrection'. Karl Barth died at prayer in that room a few weeks later.

It is with that conversation with my old teacher in mind that I have prepared the following exposition of the resurrection for publication. I have done so without indulging in sleight of hand reinterpretations or reservations, but I have tried to allow a sort of 'theological geometry' and living experience of God through the incarnate and risen Son to operate together, and have therefore offered a theological account of the resurrection in which ground and experience, theoretical and empirical ingredients in the Christian faith, are intrinsically and inseparably interlocked. At the same time I have kept in mind throughout the remarkable transformation of our understanding of the universe which in this decisive form dates from Einstein's early essays in 1905, for it is within that world that we have to read the Bible and use our minds in understanding its message. I have not tried to fit the resurrection into any scientific world-view, for that would only lead to its denial by subsuming it under general conditions and possibilities, but I have tried to think out the epistemological and cosmological implications of the resurrection as it is presented in the New Testament witness and to bring these into discussion with the implications of our modern scientific understanding of the cosmos in a way similar to that which the great Alexandrian theologians attempted in the early Church when they laid the foundations for classical Christian theology and found themselves having to reconstruct even the concepts of space and time.

This book is primarily an attempt to give a *theological* interpretation of the Easter message of the New Testament writers taken *as a whole*, and within the New Testament's own framework of thought which is itself the product of the radical reorientation in our understanding of God and the world grounded upon the incarnation and the resurrection. Here I have also kept in mind, however, the fundamental coherence between the faith of the New Testament and that of the early Church – hence the relevance of the references to patristic literature in what follows. The failure to discern this coherence in some quarters evidently has its roots in the strange gulf, imposed by analytical methods, between the faith of the primitive Church and the historical Jesus. In any case I have always found it difficult to believe that we modern scholars understand the Greek of the New Testament better than the early Greek Fathers themselves!

It was my original intention under this title, *Space, Time and Resurrection*, to produce for publication a shorter and more technical discussion as a sequel to *Space, Time and Incarnation* published in 1969. While the latter was more concerned with the question of *space*, the former was meant to be more concerned with the question of *time*, discussed in the light of the immense change that has come over our understanding of time with relativity theory and its rejection of the dualist cosmologies and epistemologies which have prevailed in modern thought since Galileo, Descartes, Newton and Kant. These questions are taken up more fully in another forthcoming book in which I offer an expanded form of my Harris Lectures in Dundee, under the title of *God and the Universe*. Here, however, I have contented myself with presenting an account of the resurrection and ascension of Christ in a form that has grown out of my teaching in the University of Edinburgh in a set of lectures which presupposes a detailed course in Christology and soteriology – and the book bears clear traces of that kind of communication, for example, in the roughness of its style and in its repetition of central ideas. Some of the important scientific and philosophical questions that bear upon the nature of the resurrection and ascension events are discussed in the Introduction and the last Chapter, but also in the course of the general exposition, especially in Chapters 4 and 6. The main purpose is to give a coherent account of the resurrection in the light of its own intrinsic significance which has thrown its integrating light upon the whole of the New Testament.

Readers of this book whose chief interest lies in the evangelical message of the resurrection may like to omit the rather difficult Introduction and last Chapter, which are really meant for scholars and theologians concerned with hermeneutical and methodological questions, and perhaps turn to them after they have read the substance of the book. I hope scholars and theologians, however, will not be content with reading only the beginning and the end, as here above all, in the doctrine of the resurrection, method and content are not to be separated.

In the preparation of this work I am particularly indebted to my dear friend and colleague, James S. Stewart, who has taught so many people in his inspiring and inimitable way the message of the risen Lord Jesus Christ. His detailed notes on my early draft have been of considerable help and encouragement, but none of its blemishes is to be attributed to him. The dedication of this work to him is a small token of my affection and appreciation. This work also owes not a little to my son Iain for his careful comments and suggested improvements, and for his assistance with the proofs.

Canty Bay   THOMAS F. TORRANCE
East Lothian
August, 1975

PREFACE TO THE NEW EDITION

In an earlier work, *Space, Time and Incarnation*, it was argued that the incarnation is meaningless for us unless its setting within the actual structures of space and time is taken seriously. That was done with special reference to *space*, but in this book concerned with the resurrection, again with relation to space and time, more attention is given to *time*. It seeks to be faithful to the realistic biblical account of the resurrection, and the redemptive significance of the resurrected One as God become man. The empty tomb is entirely consistent with who Jesus was in the whole course of his obedient life and work on earth, and consistent with his full reality as God incarnate for us and our salvation. The resurrection of Jesus is thus understood and treated as of the same nature, in the integration of physical and spiritual existence, as his birth and death. An attempt has been made to elucidate this in the context of scientific inquiry and thought, in such a way as to show that the Gospel message of the risen Lord Jesus is to be taken in its full measure.

Edinburgh
Advent, 1997   T.F.T.

INTRODUCTION

I make no apology for taking divine revelation seriously. If God really is God, the Creator of all things visible and invisible and the Source of all rational order in the universe, I find it absurd to think that he does not actively reveal himself to us but remains inert and aloof, so that we are left to grope about in the dark for possible intimations and clues to his reality which we may use in trying to establish arguments for his existence. I do not deny that there is a proper place for rational argumentation in what is traditionally known as 'natural theology', for I find it contradictory to operate with a deistic disjunction between God and the universe, which presupposes belief in the existence of God but assumes at the same time that he is utterly detached and unknowable. Genuine argumentation must take place within the active interrelation between God and the universe, and is argumentation in which theoretical and empirical components in knowledge operate inseparately together, much as they do in the indissoluble fusion of geometry and physics in a 'relativistic' understanding of the universe. This demands of us, doubtless, a proper natural theology in which form and content, method and subject-matter, are not torn apart – that is, not a 'natural theology' as an *independent* conceptual system, *antecedent* to actual or empirical knowledge of God upon which it is then imposed, quite unscientifically, as a set of necessary epistemological presuppositions! The grounds upon which I find myself forced to accept a proper natural theology, however, are much the same as the grounds on which I find it absurd to think that God does not freely act within the framework of space and time, or the intelligible structures of what he has created, in making himself known to mankind. If God really is God, the living Creator of us all, not only is he intelligibly accessible to our understanding but actively at work within the world in revealing himself in cognitive ways to those whom he has made for communion with himself. Divine revelation and intelligible content belong inseparably together.

That is the kind of divine revelation upon which the Judaeo-Christian Faith is grounded in the Old and New Testaments, for those Scriptures are evidently the inspired product of the community of reciprocity which, in the course of his saving activity in history, God created and maintained between his people and himself, within which and through which he has chosen to make his Word known in articulated communication to mankind. As the new decisive form which that community of reciprocity has taken with the incarnation of God's Word in Jesus Christ, the Christian Church is essentially and necessarily bound up with the unique self-revelation of God in Jesus Christ which, in communicable form, is handed on to us in the apostolic Scriptures of the New Testament. The idea that here we have a non-cognitive revelation, detached from the intelligible structures and the objectivities of space and time within which the Word was made flesh in Jesus Christ, is thus utterly inconsistent with the fundamental substance of the Christian Gospel – as is the idea of faith which is not correlated to an objectivity in the divine revelation rationally accessible to our apprehending and believing.

Yet it is, strangely, some notion of non-cognitive revelation, and correspondingly of non-cognitive faith, deeply embedded in their presuppositions, that appears to govern the approach of many contemporary scholars and theologians, reflecting a fatal deistic disjunction between God and the world which does not allow for any real Word of God to cross the gulf between God and the creature or therefore to permit man in space and time any real knowledge of God as he is in himself. Since it declines to accept any objectively grounded revelation of God or any knowledge of God objectively grounded in himself, biblical and theological interpretation of this kind is regularly trapped within the fallacies of socio-cultural relativism and linguistic nominalism. That is to say, by cutting short the ontological reference of biblical and theological statements to God (at least in respect of any cognitive relation to him) it is forced to interpret them merely culturally in terms of the socio-religious self-understanding of the times, or merely linguistically in terms of the sentential meaning defined through grammatical usage and syntactical complexes – although, admittedly, attempts are made to combine both these approaches. Thus the Bible is treated, and interpreted, in such a way as to bracket off the surface text and the phenomenal events it may describe from the objective, intelligible depth of God's active self-revelation, as though it were not academically respectable to take God or his self-revelation into account! Hence, instead of being regarded as conveying a real Word from God, a biblical writing is automatically held to reflect only what people happened to believe in accordance with the cultural standards of their own time, as if they had no direct access to standards of truth and falsity transcending their time which might limit imaginative construction or subjective fantasies![1] Then it requires to be transposed into our modern cultural context to be reinterpreted under the guidance of our own standards and philosophies if it is to be 'meaningful', 'understandable', or 'relevant' today. But in that event the Bible becomes what the Reformers called 'a nose of wax', which we can bend this way or that to suit our own time-conditioned preconceptions, as is evidently the case, for example, with 'existentialist' interpreters of the biblical message. The lack of ontological objectivity is always fatal in any academic or scientific pursuit, but the Bible without the living, acting, revealing, judging, reconciling God becomes merely an 'academic' concern of the historical and linguistic scholar.

Since I cannot share the obsolete phenomenalist and positivist assumptions upon which much contemporary exegesis depends, I have great difficulty in acknowledging many of its claims for 'assured results'. This is not to say that I disdain in any way careful handling of the biblical texts – far from it – but that my critical mind will not allow me to accept results that are predetermined by uncritical epistemological assumptions;[2] nor does it imply that I have not learned from

---

[1] It is through this pseudo-assumption that all kinds of spurious ideas are easily consecrated in the name of 'historico-critical scholarship'.

[2] R. R. Niebuhr rightly remarks: 'It is because theologians so often try to endow a Christian faith born of the resurrection of Christ with a hetero-

modern New Testament scholars something of the net-work of difficulties and contradictions that must be recognized, for example, in the New Testament presentation of the accounts of the resurrection.[3] But it does mean that I am not prepared (as apparently form-critics have been and now also some redaction-critics) to allow the socially conditioned paradigms of one community to apply as interpretative rules for another, very different in time, place and culture, or to allow a set of theoretical and methodological ideas thrown up out of our own cultural trends and philosophies of life to distort what I read in the ancient texts, but insist that we must be quite ruthless with ourselves in discarding all assumptions of an *a priori* or extraneous derivation, in attempting to penetrate into the conceptual forms and patterns at work in the actual, empirical stream of tradition in which the text being interpreted is to be found. We must do our utmost to allow these texts to bear witness to themselves as far as possible out of themselves and their own inherent demands, and to let them impress upon us the appropriate frame of reference for our understanding of them, so that we may interpret them from within their own natural coherences. That kind of objectivity is not served by assuming from the very start, as for example Rudolf Bultmann insists in his various essays on hermeneutics, that we cannot but operate with an outlook upon the universe as 'a closed continuum of cause and effect', or by setting aside arbitrarily any idea that God's self-utterance in word has left its profound imprint upon the shape and content of the biblical Scriptures,[4] for that is to bring to the task of biblical interpretation an essentially closed mind which can only result in some sort of scientific or sociological reductionism.[5]

---

geneous epistemology that their treatment of the final chapters of the gospels is so pale'. *Resurrection and Historical Reason*, 1957, p. 3. As an outstanding instance (which Niebuhr does not give) one could point to Bultmann's commentary, *The Gospel of John*, which is surely his greatest work.

[3] For discussions of these problems see A. M. Hunter, *The Work and Words of Jesus*, 1950, pp. 123ff.; or G. Bornkamm, *Jesus of Nazareth*, Eng. tr., revised edit., 1963, pp. 180ff.; and, more recently, J. Jeremias, *New Testament Theology*, Eng. tr., 1971, vol. 1, pp. 300ff.

[4] See, for example, 'Is Exegesis without Presuppositions Possible?', in *Existence and Faith*, tr. by S. M. Ogden, 1960, p. 292.

[5] See here the introduction to William Manson, *Jesus and the Christian*,

I make no apology, therefore, for trying to interpret the Bible in the light of the *logos* of God's self-revelation which it conveys and which, in accordance with its own self-witness, created the historical community of reciprocity between God and ancient Israel and God and the apostolic Church, within which the Old and New Testaments arose and took shape as the media through which that *logos* continues to be heard in the obedience of faith.[6] Rigorous scientific procedure makes it incumbent upon us first to essay an interpretation of the Bible within its own distinctive framework, on its own intelligible grounds, and to try to make rational and religious sense of what it has to say about God and the world and his saving activity in history, without prejudging all that from an alien framework of thought, and certainly without automatically excluding its supernatural message as academically unthinkable for 'modern man'. And only then, if it does not yield to appropriate and adequate theological understanding – by which is meant an understanding matched to its objective ground in the realities signified – may we attempt to interpret it in terms of a different set of axioms, but in that case those axioms must be clearly and explicitly spelt out, with nothing taken for granted by way of hidden assumptions, so that they can be tested for appositeness and adequacy in the task to which they are being put, and be rejected if and when they fail to measure up to what is required.[7]

It must be stressed that the theologian handles the New Testament by reflecting on its reports in the light of the reality which they claim to indicate, and tries to understand that reality in its own right, independent of the reports, by letting his mind fall under the power of its intrinsic significance. Only in that way will he be in any position to offer a judgment

---

1957, in which I have tried to summarize the critical principles which my old teacher allowed to guide him in his New Testament studies, pp. 10–14. And see further O. C. Quick's discussion of historical criticism in relation to the incarnation and resurrection, *Doctrines of the Creed*, 1938, 1947 edit., pp. 146–55.

[6] For a fuller exposition of this see *God and Rationality*, 1971, pp. 137ff. and *Theology in Reconstruction*, 1965, pp. 128ff.

[7] For the problems raised here the reader is referred to a forthcoming book, *Integration and Interpretation in Natural and in Theological Science*.

as to the adequacy of those reports, that is, as to how far they succeed in indicating and how far they fall short of the reality they intend. But since he interprets the reports not by subjecting the reality they indicate to the reports but by subjecting the reports to the reality they intend, he takes into account the fact that the reports do inevitably fall short of what they indicate, for they bear witness to what is other than and beyond themselves and which is true, if it is true, apart from them.[8] This does not mean that the theological interpreter pays no attention to the literary and conceptual patterns which the reports assume in fulfilling their intention, for they have an all-important significative role to play, but that he will not allow the realities signified to be reduced to, or resolved into, or equated with, the forms of speech and thought that are employed in the service of their disclosure and apprehension.[9] That kind of nominalist error is, of course, inevitable whenever the ontological reference of biblical statements is broken, or phenomenologically bracketed off, with the result that the significant sequences of the biblical narratives suffer badly from analytical disintegration and considerable loss of meaning.

This is the kind of unfortunate situation in which the biblical scholar and the theologian tend to draw apart, and in which the biblical scholar, particularly if he is epistemologically somewhat blind, finds it difficult to understand why the theologian does not readily accept the 'findings' of his historico-critical analyses as authentic 'data', or 'scientifically established facts', upon which to ground his theology. However, the scholar's 'findings' have often been reached through a process in which the empirical and the theoretical components in the biblical reports have been torn apart, with damage to

[8] Cf. Athanasius, *Contra Arianos*, 2. 3f. (cf. Plato, *Cratylus*, 439B); and Hilary, *De Trinitate*, 4. 14; 5. 7 (cf. P. Lombard, *Sentences*, 1. 5. 1, 25. 2).

[9] Since epistemological questions are inevitably involved here, the theological interpreter must reveal his own position and argue it out in the course of his theological exposition. Here sides have to be taken in which I find myself forced to accept a deeply but critically *realist* position bound up with the inseparability of empirical and theoretical components in knowledge, i.e. with the indissoluble unity of being and form. This will become more and more evident in the course of the book, although the same issue has been fully treated in previous books.

both, which inevitably reduces the range of empirical facts which can be accounted for. Moreover the kerygmatic source-material has been separated from the didactic material with which it is found to be embedded in the biblical witness and tradition, on the assumption that this didactic material derives from editorial additions betraying later ecclesiastical interest, and so it is inevitably reduced to a fragmented and pluralistic condition.[10] Thus it is often the case that the processed 'data', or 'the established facts', presented to the theologian have already been mutilated by being shorn of their intrinsic theological connections, which makes it impossible to erect a theology on such a basis without resort to extrinsic theological connections, and therefore to an artificial framework with no ontological roots, and then the biblical scholar is the first to point out the hiatus between 'kerygma' and 'dogma'. That hiatus will not disappear until both the biblical scholar and the theologian learn to operate with a scientific approach which does not automatically exclude the ontological unity of form and being, or of structure and material content, in their investigation and interpretation of the Holy Scriptures.

It may be useful at this point to say several things in clarification of theological procedure with respect to the received scriptural material which the theologian shares with the biblical scholar.

(1) Christian doctrines or dogmas are not built up from ideas deduced from biblical statements regarded as logical propositions. The assumption that the Scriptures are impregnated with universal, changeless divine truths which can be read off the sentential sequences of the inspired text, provided that it is properly or authoritatively interpreted, is

[10] At this point purely 'dogmatic reasons' tend to be adduced, rather inconsistently, for an historico-critical judgment, e.g. the refusal of so many scholars, irrespective of textual evidence, to accept the commission of the risen Lord to baptize in the Name of the Father and of the Son and of the Holy Spirit as belonging to the original evangelical tradition, not to mention its derivation from Jesus himself. For the theologian the intrinsic theological connection between this and the baptism of Jesus, with the word of the Father to the Son and the descent of the Spirit, is so clear that it argues the other way – but then the theologian may adduce 'dogmatic reasons' consistently, for he does not operate with a false disjunction of the empirical from the theoretical.

admittedly the view that was long held, and often still is held, by Roman Catholic and Protestant fundamentalism alike. This has the effect of putting the Scriptures themselves, with the conceptions they enshrine, into the position of providing the direct objects to which the mind of the interpreter or theologian attends, thereby obscuring the actual realities beyond to which he is referred through them. Here we have implied a view of the biblical language as bearing upon conceptions rather than upon objective realities through conceptions, and a view of truth in which the truth of statement is identified with the truth of being and logical relations are equated with objectively real relations. Such is the nominalism, or extreme realism (for they meet at this point!), inherent in the fundamentalist view that theology is concerned with the systematic connection of propositional truths logically derived from propositional revelation contained in the Holy Scriptures. In a scientific theology, on the contrary, we are concerned not with thinking thoughts, far less with thinking statements themselves, but with thinking realities through thoughts and statements, and with developing an understanding of God from his self-revelation mediated to us by the Holy Scriptures in the Church, in which the connections we think are objectively and ontologically controlled by the intrinsic connections of God's *self*-communication as Father, Son and Holy Spirit.

(2) On the other hand, Christian doctrines or dogmas are not reached by a process of deduction from observational data, regarded as the 'raw' or 'uninterpreted' facts of experience. This is the view that has admittedly prevailed in Neo-Protestantism, and is as such the by-product of the 'observationalist' view of scientific activity dating back to Newton's claim that he did not invent hypotheses but deduced them from appearances or phenomena.[11] That was a radically dualist conception of science which operated with the erroneous belief that the basic data of science are gained from direct observations without any theoretical or interpretative ingredients, the so-called 'raw facts'. Science, it was held, proceeds by deriving concepts abstractively from experience, and then by developing them through working hypotheses or convenient functional arrangements, without claiming that

[11] Isaac Newton, *Principia Mathematica* (ed. by Cajori, 1934), p. 547.

scientific constructs have any real relation to being. However, the more science advanced in this direction through elaborating artificial frames of connection externally imposed upon the analytical particulars resulting from its abstractive methods, the more limited became the areas and aspects of the real world with which it could cope, for it was found to be sacrificing the natural connections and inner organization in the fields of investigation. Such was the matrix which gave shape to the problematic nineteenth-century concept of history as the science of observational investigation (*historia*) concerned with the field of human experience and achievement in which the making and the writing of history are so closely interwoven, but while attempts were made to develop a distinctive method of historical explanation, this became inevitably trapped within the fatal disjunction and artificial connection of the empirical and theoretical components of knowledge.[12] It was out of the consequent historicizing of the human sciences that 'historical criticism' arose largely through the study of biblical and early Christian sources; but while historico-critical examination of those sources is certainly scientifically obligatory, unfortunately it was developed and employed in forms which carried with them the basic errors and limitations that beset nineteenth-century thought from which historical criticism has not yet broken free,[13] even though the ground has been cleared, and the way ahead pointed out, for all scientific study concerned with the structures of space and time, as history certainly is, through recognition of the essential unity of structure and matter in motion. This means that we may grasp the real in all its depth only if we do not

[12] This applies no less to Collingwood than to Dilthey, as a study of the former's *The Idea of History* reveals, for example, in his uneasy juxtaposition of a somewhat positivist notion of natural science with a somewhat idealist notion of history.

[13] Cf. here the fatal dualism which received formalization in Herrmann's distinction between *Geschichte* and *Historie*, *Die Religion im Verhältnis zum Welterkennen und zur Sittlichkeit*, 1879, p. 313; *The Communion of the Christian with God*, 1886, Eng. tr. (of 4th German edit.), 1906, p. 114; cf. also Martin Kähler, *The So-called Historical Jesus and the Historic Biblical Christ* (1892), Eng. tr., 1964. In spite of Kähler's attempt to overcome the problems this involved, it is Bultmann's more radically dualist conception of this distinction which still has a fateful influence.

proceed by abstracting from observational phenomena and thereby carving up the continuous field of experience into analytical particulars, but by penetrating into the interior connections of the field and understanding it out of its own natural dynamic coherences.[14] Since this applies to theological science operating within the intelligible ordering of space and time and indeed of space-time, no less than to the natural sciences, it should be understandable why theologians cannot derive genuine theological concepts by deducing them from analytical particulars, and therefore why they find it so difficult to operate with the kind of 'established facts' or processed 'data' supplied to them by epistemologically and scientifically deficient methods of historical criticism. This is not to deny that valuable results of a certain kind have been, and still are being, established even by nineteenth century methods of historical criticism, but, so far as theology is concerned, only at limited formal levels abstracted from the intrinsic material connections with which theologians have to operate. In the nature of the case, therefore, they are not the kind of results upon which a proper theology can be erected.

(3) The theologian is not very excited by, nor indeed really concerned with, what the source-critic claims, as a result of his analyses, to be the basic layer (written or oral) or the first-order source of the New Testament message stripped clear of 'later dogmatic accretions' (that would be a kind of 'Q fundamentalism'), for he operates with the whole apostolic tradition in its stratified depth in order to allow himself to be directed from all sides to the objective realities under the creative impact of which all the apostolic tradition incorporated in the New Testament took its rise and shape in the primitive Church. The theologian takes his stance, therefore, within the conjoint semantic focus of the manifold structure of the New Testament witness, where he is concerned with the different layers of tradition only as they are integrated with a bearing on the saving acts of God in Jesus Christ, for that is how he derives the all-important intuitive insights which guide his theological inquiry, but they are insights

[14] See A. Einstein, *The World As I See It*, pp. 134ff.; and for a fuller account of this see my essay, 'The Integration of Form in Natural and in Theological Science', *Science, Medicine and Man* vol. 1, 3, 1973, pp. 152ff.

correlated to and controlled by the intrinsic significance of God's self-revelation. How those insights arise in his mind he is unable to say beyond that it takes place under the generative power of the Word and Spirit of God himself. As a matter of fact, how ideas are related to the realities we experience and apprehend cannot be specified in any area of human knowledge, let alone the knowledge of faith, for this is a relation of an ontological kind which by its very nature eludes, and therefore vanishes in the face of, analytical explicitation and formalization; yet it is in and through that very relation alone that we can attain genuine knowledge of the realities concerned.[15] Hence, what the theologian does, and must do, is to make himself dwell in the semantic focus of the many-layered memory or tradition embodied in the New Testament. In this way his mind gradually becomes assimilated to the *integration* of the different strata in their bearing upon the objective events and realities they intend, and as it falls under the intelligible power of those events and realities there arises a structural kinship between his knowing and what he seeks to know.[16] Thus there begins to form in his understanding a coherent grasp of the subject-matter into which he inquires, and he proceeds to develop it by following through the ontological reference of the various biblical reports so that his apprehension may be progressively informed and shaped under the self-evidencing force and intrinsic significance of their objective content, i.e. the self-revelation and self-communication of God through Jesus Christ and in the Holy Spirit. It is in the light of what becomes thus disclosed to him that the theologian is able more fully to consider and interpret the biblical witness to which he is indebted and to form intelligent judgments not only as to its adequacy or inadequacy in fulfilling its semantic function, but as to the integration in depth of the consecutive levels of meaning in the biblical witness upon which its semantic function depends for its fulfilment. This is an integration which operates at a pro-

[15] Cf. A. Einstein, *The World As I See It*, pp. 128, 133ff., 173ff.; *Out of My Later Years*, p. 6of.

[16] I have borrowed here Polanyi's illuminating way of explaining this epistemic process, which I have discussed fully in ch. 3 of *Integration and Interpretation in Natural and Theological Science*.

founder level than any formal deduction from analytical particulars and which cannot be reproduced or replaced by any explicit processes of a logical or inferential kind which are necessarily empty of ontological content.[17] This is why the theologian knows that he cannot get very far *theologically* with historico-critical and historico-analytical methods, which can be of help to him only at comparatively superficial and formal levels of thought. Important and essential as they are at those levels, they are unable to cope with the all-important integrative process which is of an onto-relational and empirico-theoretical kind, but tend rather to dismantle the in-depth structure upon which the semantic focus finally depends. Moreover, the way in which the theologian handles the Scriptures, by directing his attention along the line of their witnessing to the self-revealing and reconciling God, inevitably has the effect of allotting to the Scriptures a subsidiary status in the face of what he apprehends *through* them, for what really concerns him, to use Pauline language, is the heavenly treasure and not the earthen vessels (2 Cor. 4: 7). In so far as Scripture, to change the metaphor, may prove to be an opaque medium, historico-critical and theologico-critical elucidation may help, as it were, to cleanse the lens, but what really makes Scripture a transparent medium is the divine light that shines through it from the face of Jesus Christ into our hearts. It is only as we allow this light to shine through to us that we may discern any alien material in the lens, but it is of essential importance that that divine light be allowed to burn up the chaff in our own presuppositions and thoughts about God if we are to use the Scriptures in a theologically significant and constructive way. Although the Scriptures have a subsidiary role in the human and earthly coefficient of divine revelation, that is nevertheless essential to the reciprocity which the revealing and reconciling God creates between us and himself, for without all that the Scriptures in the saving purpose of God have come to embody, we would not be able to know God or to have intelligible communion with him within our con-

---

[17] Analytical thinkers are apt to forget that a whole is rather more than the sum of its parts; that a comprehensive entity has an intrinsic significance as a whole which cannot be broken down and specified in terms of the constituent particulars upon which the whole nevertheless depends.

tinuing human and historical existence. Hence Christian theology makes room for a distinctive doctrine of Holy Scripture, among the other doctrines of the faith, which it serves in this subsidiary role.

(4) It should now be evident that the theologian interprets the New Testament Scriptures within the framework of objective meaning which gave rise to the layered character of the apostolic tradition embodied in the New Testament, for example in the profound integration between the self-proclamation of Christ and the apostolic proclamation of Christ which had such a creative impact on the sacred historical memory of the primitive Church and on the whole of the New Testament, without seeking to disentangle them from one another. That would have the effect of disintegrating the distinctively *Christian* understanding of God in Jesus Christ (that is, an understanding of God mediated through Jesus Christ)[18] which it was the purpose of the incarnate and reconciling activity of God to realize within the apostolic mind and within the apostolic foundation of the primitive Church. The framework of objective meaning which concerns the theologian here is bound up with the incarnation of the Son of God to be one with us in our physical human existence within the world of space and time in such a way that through his vicarious life and passion he might redeem human being and creatively reground it in the very life of God himself, and therefore it is also bound up with the resurrection of Jesus Christ in body, or the physical reality of his human existence among us, for it is in the resurrection that God's incarnate and redeeming purpose for us is brought to its triumphant fulfilment. Thus the incarnation and the resurrection, bracketing within them

---

[18] It is to be remembered that Jesus himself was not a Christian, for a Christian is one saved by Christ. Theology is not concerned, therefore, with Jesus' own private religious understanding of God, but with that which he means us to have through his vicarious life and activity, i.e. the understanding which redeemed sinners have of the God and Father of Jesus Christ. This is the kind of understanding of God which took shape in the apostolic mind and which became embodied in the New Testament reports. This is why, evidently, so little attempt is made by St. Paul to ground his teaching about God, mediated through Christ and in the Spirit, upon the *ipsissima verba* or private religion of Jesus, although he does claim to be operating within, and continuing, the authentic tradition.

the whole life and activity of Jesus Christ, constitute together the basic framework within which the New Testament writings, for all their rich diversity, are set, and which gives them their deep underlying unity in which Jesus Christ the incarnate and risen Lord is himself the dynamic centre and the objective focus of their creative integration.

It is when the various writings of the New Testament are abstracted from that underlying framework and are subjected in isolation from one another to formal analysis at the linguistic and phenomenal level (which certainly yields significant results), that their conceptual coherence with one another disintegrates, for the all-important semantic clues deriving from their coordination with the deeper level are erased, so that scholars find it difficult to perceive any basic unity in the New Testament.[19] It is rather similar to what happens when two stereo-pictures are removed from the frame of the instrument which enables us to coordinate our viewing of them. The clues to their integration are effaced, so that their joint meaning, a three-dimensional picture, vanishes.[20] Thus if some scholars are unable (if a change of metaphor may be permitted) to see the wood for the trees, the reasons may lie in the disintegrating methods they adopt, although it seems evident that the fragmentation of the New Testament in their interpretation is also due in part to the cultural pluralism in the presuppositions they bring with them to the understanding of the New Testament Scriptures.[21]

Now it may be objected, quite understandably, that by claiming to interpret the resurrection within a framework of thought, of which the resurrection, along with the incarnation, is itself a

[19] This is what happens when all supernaturalism is cut out of the New Testament – see William Manson's presidential address to the New Testament Society in 1952, reprinted in *Jesus and the Christian*, 1967, pp. 77–88. But cf. also R. R. Niebuhr, *op. cit.*, p. 14: 'The paradox is that the excision of the resurrection tradition from the fabric of the gospel history is followed by the disintegration of the entire historical sequence of the New Testament'.

[20] Cf. M. Polanyi, *Knowing and Being*, pp. 185, 213, 218.

[21] Is is because of these pluralist presuppositions that the powerful argument advanced by Hoskyns and Davey for the *Christological unity* of the New Testament is apparently ignored, far less answered, by many scholars today. See *The Riddle of the New Testament*, especially chs. VII–X.

constitutive determinant, I am operating with an essentially circular procedure. I agree, but reject the implication that this is a vicious circularity artificially intruded into the ground of knowledge. What we are concerned with here is the proper circularity inherent in any coherent system operating with ultimate axioms or beliefs which cannot be derived or justified from any other ground than that which they themselves constitute. It is the case, of course, that the primary axioms of any deductive system are held to be justified if they are included within the consistency of all the axioms and propositions of the system, but, as Kurt Gödel has demonstrated, any such consistent formal system must have one or more propositions that are not provable within it but may be proved with reference to a wider and higher system.[22] However, when we are concerned with a conceptual system or a framework of thought which includes among its constitutive axioms one or more *ultimates*, for which, in the nature of the case, there is no higher and wider system with reference to which they can be proved, then we cannot but operate with a complete circularity of the conceptual system.[23] This must be a proper form of circularity, however, for the system must be one which is internally consistent and which rests upon the grounds posited by the constitutive axioms, without any alien additions, so that the conclusions we reach are found to be anticipated in the basic presuppositions. Such a system, of course, even if entirely consistent within itself, could conceivably be false, and must therefore be open to reasonable doubt: but that means that the system stands or falls with respect to its power as a whole to command our acceptance. And here another important factor must also be taken into account, the capacity of the system to function as a heuristic instrument in opening up new avenues of knowledge which could not otherwise be anticipated, and as an interpretative frame of thought to cope with a wider range of elements not originally in view. Nevertheless, in the last analysis we are thrown back upon the question whether we are prepared to commit ourselves to belief in the ultimates which are constitutive of the system.

[22] K. Gödel, *On Formally Undecidable Propositions of* Principia Mathematica *and Related Systems*, Eng. tr., by B. Meltzer, 1962, pp. 36ff., 60ff., 69ff.
[23] See Michael Polanyi, *Personal Knowledge*, pp. 288f., 292f., 299f.

As examples of such a conceptual system we may point to a formal science like logic and an empirical science like physics. No possible proof of 'the laws of logic' can be offered which does not presuppose those laws, and which does not assume commitments to the belief in the validity of logical reasoning. Similarly in physics we have to presuppose that there is order in the universe if we are to have a science of physics at all, but we are unable to offer any proof that there is order in the universe without assuming it all the time.[24] In both cases we are committed to certain *ultimate beliefs* for which we can offer no independent demonstration, but without which the scientific system would not be possible at all. It is certainly necessary to test our commitment to these beliefs through responsible self-criticism, in order to distinguish them from any subjective constructions or objectifying projections on our part, for we can accept as ultimate only what is objectively forced upon us by the intrinsic intelligibility, truth and authority of the subject-matter (or of the reality in the field of our inquiry) as belonging to the regulative ground of knowledge and therefore as making for the stability and durability of the conceptual system to which it gives rise.

There are occasions, of course, usually great and highly significant occasions, when some ultimate of this kind forces itself upon us which cannot be fitted into the formal framework of hitherto acquired knowledge, for the set of concepts to which it gives rise in being apprehended is found to conflict with the conceptual system within which our present knowledge is expressed: then we are faced with a serious dilemma, of rejecting what has thus become disclosed as absurd, or committing ourselves to a radical reconstruction of that conceptual system, indeed a logical reconstruction of the axiomatic premises of that system. When human thought comes up against such an ultimate conflict between rival frameworks of thought or conceptual systems and the fundamental outlooks that lie behind them, it is poised on the threshold of a far-reaching change of mind or conversion. The conflict cannot be solved by formal argument between two alternative frameworks or systems of thought, but only through radical commitment to

[24] See Alastair McKinnon, *Falsification and Belief*, 1970, pp. 18, 28–46, 72ff.

the intrinsic claims of the subject-matter, through a movement of the mind in which we allow it to fall under the power of the intrinsic intelligibility of things in the conviction that we can do no other in sheer fidelity to the truth. That is the kind of conversion that came over modern physics, for example, in the transition from Newtonian principles to those of relativity and quantum theory – in the latter particularly, the scientific reason had to cope with 'paradoxes' and 'contradictions' and 'absurdities', which forced it to reconstruct the logical basis of classical physics, in such a way that while it became all the more firmly established on a limited basis it could only be treated as a limiting case of relativistic and quantum physics, and therefore as basically incomplete but open toward the disclosure of new knowledge which could not be inferred from the old or be verified in terms of it. It was new knowledge that could only be grasped, affirmed and assimilated within a new outlook of which it constituted the intelligible basis.

It is essentially in this way that the *incarnation* and the *resurrection* of Jesus Christ came to be accepted by the early Church and classical Christian theology: they forced themselves upon the minds of Christians from their own empirical and theoretical ground *in sharp antithesis* to what they had believed about God and *in genuine conflict* with the framework of secular thought or the world view of their age. That God himself had become man was an offence to the Jew and folly to the Greek; that Jesus Christ rose from the dead was deemed to be utterly incredible. Yet the incarnation and the resurrection forced themselves upon the mind of the Church against the grain of people's convictions, as ultimate events bearing their own intrinsic but shattering claims in the self-evidencing reality and transcendent rationality of God himself, and they took root within the Church only through a seismic restructuring of religious and intellectual belief.[25] In the life of Jesus

[25] It just will not do to claim, as Bultmann does, that 'the objective form' in which the New Testament and early Christian presentation of Christ, with respect to the incarnation, atonement, resurrection and ascension, was cast, was the result of mythological objectifying shaped by a primitive and unscientific world-view, as if the early Christians were not deeply aware of the profound conflict between the Gospel and the prevailing world-view! On the contrary, it is apparently his own world-view, with its dualist, obsolete, scientific preconceptions, which make him

Christ an objective self-disclosure of God in Word and Act had taken place within the structure of the world which was discerned to be of a final and decisive nature, commanding commitment in the response of faith, in which Jesus Christ himself constituted the central point of focus in an exclusive relation with God the Father. It involved an extremely difficult Christology, a radically new conception of God himself, and a complete transformation of man's outlook in terms of a new divine order which could not be derived or inferred from anything conceived by man before. But it was that Christology and theology grounded upon the incarnation and the resurrection that did take root within the religious, philosophical and scientific culture of the ancient world and transformed it, in the process of which classical Christian theology developed. And it is upon that basis that the whole of historic Christianity has ever since taken its stand.

It is still in that way that the incarnation and the resurrection force themselves upon our minds, within the vastly changed cultural and scientific outlook of our own times. In the life and work of Jesus Christ we are confronted with an ultimate self-revelation of God into the truth of which there is no way of penetrating from what we already know or believe we know, far less of establishing or verifying it on grounds that are outside of it. It confronts us as an objective reality which must be accepted or rejected on its own ground, but it confronts us by a self-communication of God which lays claim to our commitment with the unreserved fidelity of our minds. It is no blind act of faith that is required, divorced from any recognition of credibility, for the reality of the incarnation or

---

'mythologize' the New Testament in this way, and then 'demythologize' it in terms of his own mistaken exaltation of self-understanding, which transfers the centre of reference away from the action of God in the historical Jesus to some spiritual event of 'resurrection' in man's experience. See the essays 'The problem of Hermeneutics' (*Essays Philosophical and Theological*, Eng. tr. 1955, pp. 234–61); 'Revelation in the New Testament' (*Existence and Faith*, Eng. tr. 1960, pp. 58–91); *History and Eschatology*, 1957, pp. 110–22. Bultmann clearly takes his views of the relation of the Gospel to an antiquated view of the world and history from A. von Harnack, *What is Christianity?* (*Das Wesen des Christentums*, 1900), Eng. tr. (of 5th edit. reprinted 1958), p. 111f.

of the resurrection is the kind of objectivity which makes itself accessible to our apprehension, creating the condition for its recognition and acceptance, that is, in such a way that belief on our part is the subjective pole of commitment to objective reality, but intelligent commitment to an objectively intelligible reality which is to be grasped only through a repentant rethinking and structural recasting of all our preconceptions. That is why the New Testament speaks of the ultimate *Word* and *Truth* of God himself as meeting us in the incarnation, passion and resurrection of Christ, and why the resurrection no less than the incarnation and crucifixion is apprehended only by faith, for it is only on the ground of faith, in which we allow our minds to yield to the intrinsic claims of God's cognitive self-revelation in Jesus Christ, that we are able to think of the incarnation and the resurrection as what they really are, and think of them in terms of the disclosure which they themselves open up for our understanding.[26] It is this interlocking correlation of faith with the intelligible, objective reality of God's self-revelation in the incarnation and resurrection, that does not allow us to make 'faith' itself the ground of our 'belief' in the incarnation and/or the resurrection. The only proper ground of faith is the reality to which it is correlated as its objective pole.[27]

That is certainly the way in which the early theology of the Church regarded the incarnation and the resurrection of Jesus Christ, as intelligible ultimates bearing their own proof in the self-evidencing reality of God's own Word and Truth. This is very clear, for example, in the preamble to Justin Martyr's work *On the Resurrection* in the middle of the

[26] Much the same point is argued by Oscar Cullmann in respect of the interconnection between event and interpretation in salvation history, including the resurrection. *Salvation in History*, Eng. tr. 1965, pp. 97ff.

[27] For an extreme example of this reduction of the resurrection to 'faith' (the so-called 'Easter faith'), see again R. Bultmann, *Kerygma and Myth*, vol. 1, Eng. tr. 1953, pp. 38–43. Against Bultmann it must be argued that such an 'Easter faith' is not at all intelligible or reasonable apart from the actual event of the resurrection of Jesus himself; nor can it be consistently interpreted in association with the crucifixion, as Bultmann rightly wants, if the resurrection is denied the same kind of mundane palpability as is conceded to the crucifixion. Cf. Bultmann, *The Gospel of John*, Eng. tr. by G. R. Beasley-Murray, 1971, pp. 688, 691, 696.

second century,[28] or, a little later in the same century, in the argument with which Irenaeus prefaced his *Demonstration of the Apostolic Kerygma*.[29] They showed that the incarnation and the resurrection belong to the intelligible constitutive ground of the Christian Faith, for in and through them the Word of truth from God himself is communicated to us in its own freedom and authority in such a way that it cannot be grasped through being subjected to any extraneous authority or proof: such is Jesus Christ our Saviour and Lord, incarnate and risen, who constitutes in himself the ground of faith and demonstration in respect of him. As the early theologians of the Christian Church saw so clearly, without the incarnation and the resurrection Christianity would be something entirely different, but, as they anticipated, with the incarnation and resurrection Christianity has been able to stand up to all the forces arraigned against it. Not only has it vigorously stood the test of history ever since, but it has continuously reinforced itself by the way in which on these foundations it has been able to cope with a welter of different cultures and philosophies throughout the centuries, while remaining ever the same – thereby also revealing the inexhaustible reserves it draws from its ultimate beliefs.

As such, then, the incarnation and the resurrection together form the basic framework in the interaction of God and mankind in space and time, within which the whole Gospel is to be interpreted and understood. But they are *ultimates*, carrying their own authority and calling for the intelligent commitment of belief, and providing the irreducible ground upon which continuing rational inquiry and theological formulation take place. It is a case of *fides quaerens intellectum*, or *credo ut intelligam*, as St. Anselm variously formulated the scientific principle operative here.[30]

---

[28] Justin Martyr, *De resurrectione*, 1. Only fragments of this work are extant (preserved in the *Sacra Parallela* of John of Damascus). While their authorship is disputed, this does not affect the force of the argument they bear.

[29] Irenaeus, *Epideixis*, 3, appealing to Isaiah 7: 9, 'If you do not believe, neither will you understand': 'And faith is produced by the truth; for faith rests on things that really are. For we believe in things that are, as they are; and believing in things that are, as they ever are, we keep our confidence in them'.

[30] Anselm, *Proslogion, prooemium* and ch. 1 (edit. by F. S. Schmitt, vol. 1, pp. 94, 100).

There is no point in playing down the staggering significance of the incarnation and resurrection. God the Creator of
the universe, transcendent over all time and space, has himself
become a creature within time and space, the man Jesus
Christ, and precisely as such, 'within the measures and limits'[31]
of our human historical existence, he is at work in immeasurable
love defeating the forces of darkness, irrationality and evil
within creaturely being where they are despotically entrenched. The eternal Word-and-Reason of God has become
human flesh, personally penetrating into and participating in
the contingent intelligibilities of our existence, in such a way
as to bring God himself to bear directly and intimately upon
us within the subject–subject and subject–object relations in
which we live our daily life, so that our personal contact with
God and our personal knowledge of him may be objectively
and durably grounded on the internal being and reality of God.
The fact that Jesus Christ is risen from the dead, that he did
not succumb to decay and corruption in the grave but rose
again in the integrity of his human and somatic existence,
having stripped away the despotic forces of darkness and evil
that had entrenched themselves in our mortal being, means
that the movement of God's love in the reconciling and revealing activity of the incarnate Son, has been brought to a
triumphant fulfilment; it means that the atoning sacrifice of
Christ for the sins of the world, that the vicarious passion of the
love of God, that the bond of union and communion between
man and God established in the incarnate life of the Son,
are finally actualized and remain valid beyond death, as
eternally prevailing reality for man as well as for God. That
God the transcendent Creator of the universe and the infinite
Source of all its structure and order should thus become one
of us and one with us in the birth, life, passion and resurrection of Jesus Christ in such a way as to effect a renewing
of the creation and the setting of it on a new basis in which it is
eternally bound up with the life of God himself, makes our
minds reel with its immeasurable significance; but what is
particularly staggering is the fact that it gives Jesus Christ a

[31] The expression is taken from Cyril of Alexandria – see *Theology in
Reconciliation. Essays towards Evangelical and Catholic Unity in East and West*,
1975, pp. 163ff.

place of cosmic significance, making him, man of earth as he the incarnate Son of God is, the point of supreme focus for the whole universe of space and time, by reference to which all its meaning and destiny are finally to be discerned.[32]

These implications of the incarnation and resurrection will have to be tested to see if they really are forced upon us from their constitutive grounds, but I have spelt out the implications a little to make it clear that the incarnation and the resurrection really are *ultimates* which must be accepted, or rejected, as such, for they cannot be verified or validated on any other grounds than those which they themselves provide. Thus regarded, the incarnation and the resurrection are the basic and all-embracing miracles upon which the Christian Gospel rests, miracles which, by their nature, are not verifiable in terms of the kind of evidence and argument which obtain within the natural sciences where we are concerned only with natural processes and the natural order of things. If they were verifiable in that way, they would not be miracles, far less ultimates. It is illogical, as Michael Polanyi shows, to attempt to prove the supernatural by natural tests, but it is no less illogical to justify ultimates in terms of what is not ultimate.[33] Of course, in so far as the incarnation and the resurrection are acts of God within the contingent intelligibilities and natural structures of space and time, they are open to rational examination and testing in terms of those intelligibilities and structures, and therefore are and must be open to the kind of questions raised within the natural sciences as well as the human sciences.[34] As acts of God, however, they are finally explicable only from grounds in God, and are therefore ultimates which are not open to complete formalization, or therefore verification, within the natural order of things in which they nevertheless share. Within that order they constitute the 'boundary conditions', to borrow a term from Einstein and Polanyi, where the natural order is open to control and explication from a higher and wider level of reality, in a way similar to that in which the various levels

[32] See the sustained discussion by Karl Barth of 'Jesus, Lord of Time', in the heart of his doctrine of *creation*, *Church Dogmatics*, III/1, pp. 437–511.

[33] M. Polanyi, *Personal Knowledge*, p. 284.

[34] See *Space, Time and Incarnation*, pp. 52ff.

with which we operate in any rigorous science are each open to the meta-level above it.[35] This participation of the incarnation and resurrection in the natural order of things, however, must not be understood as an interruption of the natural order or an infringement of its laws, but rather the contrary. As acts of God who is the creative Source of all order in space and time, they are essentially ordering events within the natural order, restoring and creating order where it is damaged or lacking, and it is in terms of that *giving of order* that they constitute the relevant boundary conditions within the natural order where it is open to the transcendent and creative reality of God.

This means, on the one hand, that theological formulations which are concerned with the creative and redeeming acts of God in space and time cannot be without their empirical correlates, in respect of which they are open to critical questioning and testing from the natural (including the human) sciences. And it means, on the other hand, that theological formulations are not explicable, or specifiable, in terms of the laws and operational principles that obtain in the natural sciences, for that would involve a thoroughly unscientific reductionism which, to say the least, would destroy the inter-relations between the sciences themselves and rule out of court the ultimate beliefs with which they have to operate even as natural sciences.

It is because theological science and natural science both operate within the same space-time structures of the created universe, which are the bearers of all our intelligible order, that theological interpretation and explanation cannot properly take place without constant dialogue with the natural sciences, if we are to remain faithful to God as the creative Source of all rational structure and order.[36] It is when theologians and biblical scholars keep their work apart from natural science, and thereby shield themselves from the searching questions,

[35] These are questions to which I have given detailed discussion in *Integration and Interpretation in Natural and Theological Science*, to which I have referred above.

[36] It is in this kind of dialogue that a modern natural theology finds its proper place, in the overlap between a philosophy of theological science and a philosophy of natural science.

not least epistemological and methodological questions, that are directed at them from that quarter, that they tend to develop ways of establishing evidence, determining probability, and developing argument which often would not stand up in any scientifically respectable discipline. What I have in mind here is the acceptance of the fatal cultural split between the arts and the sciences with its devastating effect upon the concept of history, and in that context the kind of exegesis which detaches the phenomenal surface of the biblical narratives from the natural coherences in which they are rooted, so that the ontological import of the narratives and of their evidential grounds is destroyed; and then when this method yields only fragmented results, artificial frameworks of thought from some alien culture are imposed upon them in order to give them some coherent meaning, but since they are bound to fail, they are always being replaced by some newly thought-up framework of reference dictated by a prevailing fashion in popular philosophy. It is German scholarship that has long led the way down this disastrous path, but wherever it is found, biblical and theological scholarship could not but be greatly benefited if it opened itself to the critical questions of modern science, for that would have the effect of exposing its hidden presuppositions and mechanisms, purging it of pseudo-concepts and substitute symbolisms, and throwing it back upon its own proper ontological ground. There it would have to engage in the same kind of basic, rigorous rethinking of its epistemological foundations in the face of ultimate beliefs as, for example, modern physics has had to do in view of the demands of relativity and quantum theory for a profound revolution in the first principles of knowledge. If biblical scholars and theologians imagine that this has nothing to do with them, then that would only indicate to me that they are so deeply trapped in the obsolete dualist and phenomenalist approach to the interpretation of historical texts and events that they are not even aware of the problem!

Let us return to the fact that the resurrection, by its very nature, posits the ground on which it is to be interpreted and discussed. Although, as we have seen, this does not allow us to isolate the resurrection from critical questioning and testing in the context of our scientific inquiry into all that goes on in the space-time universe, it does mean that interpretation and discussion of it must face from the start, or at least very near the start, the question whether we accept it or not as an intrinsic part of divine revelation, i.e. on the ground of God's own self-evidencing activity in the resurrection in coherence with the whole of his revelation. If we are not prepared to accept it like that, as an ultimate belief, then we must try to account for it in terms of ordinary observable experience, subjecting it to the same criteria which we use in testing other phenomena, when – and there is no point in glossing over this fact – it inevitably appears self-contradictory and meaningless. We cannot stop there, but are forced to draw out the consequences of this for our interpretation of the rest of the New Testament message. However, the fact that this line of thinking is found regularly to engage in a 'double think' about the resurrection by 'half-Sadducees', as Tertullian called such people,[37] would seem to indicate that it cannot bring itself finally to get rid of the resurrection, that, even at the end of this road, it remains baffled by it.

If, on the other hand, we are prepared to accept the resurrection as an ultimate belief, while fulfilling the rigorous requirements of self-criticism, we must go on to think it out in coherent relation to other ultimates, such as the creation of the world, the love of God and the incarnation of his Son, which together provide the basic frame within which the resurrection is to be understood and interpreted. But more is required: we must try to draw out the consequences of the resurrection of Jesus in the integrity and fullness of his humanity for the understanding of the Gospel and its message of salvation to be proclaimed to all the world and to the end of time. Here we must give our attention to the relation of the resurrection to the ascension, and to the promise that this same Jesus will come again in the same way as he was seen to go away, but come, the New Testament teaches, to take up his power and reign, to judge the quick and the dead and to make all things new, for all that reflects back on the resurrection and our understanding of it. The way we interpret the ascended and advent *humanity* of Christ and its cosmic and eschatological import for human and physical existence in space and time, will deter-

[37] Tertullian, *De resurrectione carnis*, 2.

mine more precisely how we regard the resurrection of Jesus Christ in body. A concept of the ascension in which the humanity of Jesus somehow is swallowed up in the Spirit or Light of the eternal God, or a concept of the eschatological future which has little more material content to it than that somehow the future is more real than the past or the present, and in which the humanity of the advent Christ is replaced by 'hope', would appear to reflect in the last analysis a rather docetic understanding of the resurrection, and that in its turn would surely reflect a similar docetic understanding of the incarnation. Hence the 'human realism' with which we interpret the ascension and the final advent of 'this same Jesus' is likely to prove a real test for the 'human realism' in our understanding of both the historical and the risen Jesus Christ.

That, at any rate, is the kind of procedure we must adopt in seeking to interpret the resurrection on the ground which, along with the incarnation, it posits for itself, and such are the questions which we must surely put to ourselves in testing our account of the resurrection to see whether it really is matched to the constitutive ground upon which it rests.

CHAPTER 1

THE BIBLICAL CONCEPT OF
THE RESURRECTION

Resurrection as understood in the Bible appears to be without
any parallel in the other religions. An idea of resurrection is
certainly found very widely in Semitic and Hellenic thought,
as is the notion of a dying and rising god, or the divinity
immanent in the processes of nature who is reborn with every
seasonal change from winter to spring and whose divine life
becomes manifest in the resurrection of nature. Against all this
the Scriptures, and not least the Old Testament, are sharply
opposed. Resurrection has nothing at all to do with any
dying or rising god and his cosmic rebirth. It must be admitted,
however, that this heathen notion has invaded the Christian
Church, probably through the syncretistic ideas that developed
in early Mediterranean Christianity, and is still constantly
reflected in hymns and sermons about the springing up of new
life, as well as in Easter eggs and similar symbols of the dying
and rising gods of nature religions.[1]

> 'Earth with joy confesses, clothing her for spring,
> All good gifts return with her returning King;
> Bloom in every meadow, leaves on every bough,
> Speak his sorrows ended, hail his triumph now.'

It is hardly less reflected in the romantic and phenomenalist
notions of history lurking in the presuppositions of those
biblical scholars who attempt to reduce everything to 'history',
and interpret the saving acts of God, including the resurrection,
only within the framework of the historical processes of decay

---

[1] See for example, The *First Epistle of Clement*, 24. 3–5; Theophilus, *Ad
Autolycum*, 13; Minucius Felix, *Octavius*, 34; The cyclic concept of the
resurrection, however, is expressly rejected by Tatian, *Oratio ad Graecos*, 6.

and renaissance in the natural order of things.[2] In view of all this, the teaching of the Old Testament is peculiarly relevant today, not only in cleansing the worship and thought of the people of God from naturalistic ideas, but in laying such strong emphasis upon the transcendence of God, the Creator of heaven and earth, within the world and upon the consummation of his redeeming and renewing purpose for his people within the actuality of their physical and historical existence, for that has the effect of sweeping aside pseudo-concepts of the resurrection or pseudo-substitutes for the resurrection. If people today, including some Old Testament scholars, find so little in the Old Testament relating to the resurrection as it is presented in the New Testament, the reason may simply be that they are operating with a notion of the resurrection already corrupted through alien presuppositions.

1. *The Teaching of the Old Testament*

It is only by looking back at the teaching of the Old Testament Scriptures from the perspective created by the resurrection of Christ that we are able to discern the positive things they had to contribute to our understanding of the resurrection. They may be set out in the following series.

(*a*) Quite basic to everything is the conception of the Covenant which embraces the whole of creation but which is peculiarly related to the people of God. God has bound up his people with himself in the same bundle of life, so that his covenant faithfulness undergirds and supports them beyond anything they are capable of in themselves in life or death. The life and existence of Israel, for example, are so tied to the covenant purpose of God in mercy and judgment that they are restored again and again and are given miraculous continuity throughout the changes, chances and disasters of their history.

(*b*) Hence what is dominant in the Old Testament thought

---

[2] Professor J. S. Stewart remarks, in a comment upon my text, 'I sometimes think that when Paul said, "If righteousness came by the law, Christ need never have died" (Gal. 2: 21), he might have added – "If the Kingdom came by the processes of history, Christ need never have been resurrected".'

is the stress upon the corporate judgment, vindication and restoration of God's people. Any notion of individual resurrection or survival could only be subordinate to that, and in fact largely disappears behind the corporate picture of God and his covenant community. But here it is apparently the concept of restoration through judgment that is a predominating motif, as we can see in passages such as Hos. 2: 16f.; Jer. 3: 19ff.; 29: 10ff.; 31: 1ff.; Ezek. 37: 1ff. (cf. also Deut. 32: 39; 1 Sam. 2: 6; 2 Kings 5: 7).

(c) Along with this corporate restoration there is found the promise of a Saviour who will be raised up out of the people, such as the Prophet whom God will raise up, like Moses, to lead a new Exodus (Deut. 18: 15), or the Shepherd who is to be raised up like David (Ezek. 34: 23ff.; 37: 24f.), or even the Servant of the Lord (Isa. 53: 10–12), upon which Mowinckel has laid such stress.[3] This line of thought in the Old Testamen seems to be bound up with the promised Messiah who will spring from the seed of David and from the seed of Abraham, for all through the covenanted relation of Israel to God, there persists an inner organic continuity in the promised seed which cannot be destroyed but which will be raised up like a root out of the dry ground for the salvation of God's people.

(d) We have to add to this the notion of the *Goel* applied to God in his relations with Israel – i.e. the notion of a Redeemer acting out of a community bond or property tie, out of real or assumed kinship. As the Holy One of Israel God himself stands in as the Advocate who makes Israel's cause his own and redeems Israel out of all its troubles. This applies, apparently, not only to Israel as a whole but to all God's people within the Covenant, as is particularly evident in the Psalms such as 16: 10f.; 49: 16; 73: 26; and 17: 15.[4] It is in dispute

[3] S. Mowinckel, *He that Cometh. The Messiah Concept in the Old Testament and Later Judasim* (tr. by G. W. Anderson, 1956), pp. 163, 204ff., 211ff., 222ff., 234ff., 248f.

[4] Rabbinic Judaism developed the idea that all Israel's experiences, bondage, exodus, lawgiving, and redemption above all, are to be recapitulated in the experience of the individual Israelite. *Pesahim*, 9. 5–6 (*Mishnah*, ed. H. Danby, p. 151). This was given special prominence in the Passover *Haggadah* (cf. edit. by C. Roth, 1934, pp. 34ff.). See also Gregory Nazianzen, *Theol. Oration*, I. 1f., where this is applied in turn to the Christian interpretation of the Easter Festival.

whether these passages have any bearing upon the development of the thought of the resurrection of God's people, but this dubiety may reflect a 'wrong' concept of the resurrection, as well as a failure in understanding 'sheol' (the biblical 'pit' or 'hell', Amos 9: 2; 1 Sam. 2: 6; Ps. 139: 8; Job 26: 6 etc.) as the Hellenic 'hades' rather than as the state of existence after death, characterized by the suspension of God's final judgment. Then we have to note the remarkable passage in Job 19: 25, where the received text is certainly corrupt, but which nevertheless appears to contain powerfully the idea that God remains the *Goel* even in death to those who trust him. On the other hand Job 14: 10–12, 14 appears to reject the notion of a resurrection.

(*e*) In later strata of the Old Testament the conception of a resurrection of the righteous, and even of the unrighteous, appears to emerge, a resurrection to judgment as well as to life, Isa. 25: 8; 26: 19, 21, Dan. 12: 1f., 13. But it is with the Apocryphal literature, such as 2nd Esdras, 2nd Maccabees, the Syriac Apocalypse of Baruch, 1st Enoch, etc., that the apocalyptic aspect of resurrection begins to rise clearly. It is to this that the Epistle to the Hebrews appears to refer in its reference to 'the better hope' (Heb. 7: 19).

(*f*) In spite of all this it is a fact, as Jeremias has pointed out, that 'Judasim did not know of any anticipated resurrection as an event in history. There is nothing comparable to the resurrection of Jesus anywhere in Jewish literature'.[5] It should not surprise us, therefore, that here not least, while the New Testament message is presented in deep continuity with that of the Old Testament, that can be done only with a profound revolution in the tradition of Judaism in which basic categories of thought have to be creatively reconstructed.

2. *The Teaching of the New Testament*

In the New Testament the resurrection is altogether a dominant concept. Basically it is the resurrection of the Shepherd Son of David and therefore of his people for whom he stands in as Redeemer and Advocate (Acts 13: 22f.; Rom. 15: 12). Here resurrection is not associated with the cyclic processes of be-

[5] J. Jeremias, *New Testament Theology*, Eng. tr. 1971, vol. 1, p. 308f.

coming, but is the mighty act of God within our humanity and its sin, corruption and death, shattering the powers of evil in an utterly decisive way. It is the work of the Creator, now himself incarnate and at work in the midst of the fallen creation and its estangement from God the Father. The resurrection takes place in space and time, in physical and historical existence; yet the teaching of the New Testament indicates that it is 'not merely a great event upon the plane of history, but an act that breaks into history with the powers of another world. It is akin to the creation in the beginning; and the Gospel is the good news that God is creating a new world'.[6] It is a creative event within the creation, an abruptly divine act within history, a decisive deed completely setting at nought all cyclic processes, putting an end to the futility to which they are shut up but opening and straightening them out in a movement toward consummation. Such a resurrection of the incarnate Word of God within the creation of time and space which came into being through him is inevitably an event of cosmic and unbelievable magnitude. So far as the temporal dimension of creation is concerned, it means that the transformation of all things at the end of time is already impinging upon history, and indeed that the consummation of history has already been inaugurated. And so far as the spatial dimension of creation is concerned, it means that the new creation has already set in, so that all things visible and invisible are even now in the grip of the final recreation of the universe. The resurrection of Jesus heralds an entirely new age in which a universal resurrection or transformation of heaven and earth will take place, or rather has already begun to take place, for with the resurrection of Jesus that new world has already broken into the midst of the old.

The fact of the resurrection altered the whole situation so drastically that quite new modes of thought and speech had to arise to cope with it, so that it is especially important to examine the *language* which the New Testament employs in order to speak of the resurrection, if we are to go on to interpret it in an appropriate way. Here we have the familiar problems with which scholars have to wrestle: while the forms of thought in the New Testament derive largely from the Hebraic world, the

[6] A. M. Ramsey, *The Resurrection of Christ*, 1945, p. 31.

forms of speech derive largely from the Hellenic world, although as in the Septuagint translation of the Old Testament so here in the expression of the Gospel message in Greek, the Hebraic and Hellenic forms of thought and speech are well-nigh inextricably intermingled. But what is of decisive importance is the intrinsic significance of the resurrection, for it is the reality of the risen Lord that really gives the forms of thought and speech their significant shape, so that we must keep in mind the two-way relationship, the impact of the reality of the resurrection upon the language, and the bearing of the language and its use in the biblical witness upon that reality.

Two main terms are employed by the New Testament writers to speak of the resurrection, built up from the verbs *anistēmi* and *egeiro* (frequently compounded with the prefix *ex*). Both words mean to lift or raise up, which is the common meaning they have in profane Greek. *Anistēmi* is generally used of lifting up from a seat, or rousing from sleep, but also of waking from the dead or coming to life again. *Egeiro* is not used in profane Greek of raising from the dead or of raising the sick, as in the New Testament. Hence this use of *egeiro* is peculiar to the New Testament which would appear, in fact, to prefer *egeiro* to *anistēmi*, and then in the passive rather than in the active sense (although it does not exclude the latter).[7] This preference for *egeiro* appears to lay the major stress on the mighty act of God in raising Jesus from the dead. The resurrection is a supernatural or miraculous event, quite inexplicable from the side of human agency or natural process. It is comparable only to the act of God in the creation itself or in the incarnation. The use of *egeiro* in the New Testament to speak of the raising up of the sick is an indication that the miraculous acts of healing are regarded as falling within the orbit of the

[7] Cf. J. S. Stewart, *A Man in Christ*, 1935, p. 134. See also Karl Barth, *Church Dogmatics*, IV/1, pp. 303ff., who lays the emphasis upon the fact that in the resurrection the relation of the Son to the Father is that of pure obedience, subordination and subjection. In his anxiety not to obscure and weaken the character of the resurrection as 'free pure act of divine grace', he plays down the idea that Jesus actively rose from the dead, but as Cyril of Alexandria once showed, the activity of Christ in the resurrection is essential to the unity of his person as Mediator, *Quod unus sit Christus*, (tr. by E. B. Pusey), *Library of the Fathers*, pp. 303ff.

resurrection, and as belonging to the creative and recreative activity of God in incarnation and resurrection. In these miracles the resurrection is already evidencing itself beforehand in signs and wonders.

Egeiro and *anistēmi* are also used in the New Testament in the middle voice, particularly *anistēmi*, that is, of Christ rising from the dead. Here the emphasis is upon his own victorious activity, his standing up out of the dead, his rising above corruption and mortality, all seen within the orbit of his own sinless life and the regenerating effect of his holiness upon other human life.

It is especially important, however, to consider the way in which these terms are used in the New Testament, within the context of the relation between the Old Testament and the New Testament revelation, for it is this that gives peculiar specification to their meaning. Certain Old Testament nuances are allowed to shine through the New Testament message in a very enlightening manner.

(*a*) We note first the Old Testament custom of speaking of the raising up of a prophet, or a king, or judge, or priest, where the ideas of provision and appointment are blended together. The New Testament uses both *egeiro* and *anistēmi* in this connection. Thus when the New Testament speaks of Jesus being raised up, it evidently refers not only to the resurrection of his body from the grave but to his being raised up as the appointed Messiah, the anointed Prophet, Priest and King. The resurrection implies the installation or enthronement of Jesus in his office as *Christos*.

(*b*) The peculiar semitism, *raising up seed*, is also involved in the New Testament accounts of the resurrection of Jesus. He is raised up as a root out of the dry ground, the shoot of the vine, after it had been cut down to the ground. It is a miraculous act, in line with the raising up of seed out of the barren womb, in the cases of Sarah, Hannah and Elizabeth, etc. This idea also plays its part in the accounts of the virgin birth of Jesus, but here we see already how the birth and resurrection of Jesus are linked, for together they constitute, in the understanding of the New Testament, the raising up of the new seed in whom all nations will be blessed, the First-born of the new creation. This means that the whole life of Jesus is to be

regarded as downright miracle, the raising up of the Saviour
and Servant out of the dry ground, which could not have
produced him spontaneously out of itself, the incredible act of
God inaugurating a new creation where, from our human side,
it was quite unexpected. With the birth and resurrection of
Jesus, with Jesus himself, the relation of the world to God
has been drastically altered, for everything has been placed on
an entirely new basis, the unconditional grace of God.

(c) So far as Christ himself is concerned, therefore, the notion
of the resurrection involves a powerful combination of the
ideas of appointment and the raising up of Messianic seed,
and bears an inner relation to his birth, baptism and triumphant life over sin and evil: all this adds up to the full installation
of the Messiah with power and his declaration as God's Son.[8]
As such, however, the resurrection of Christ carries within it
the notion of a corporate resurrection. The seed that is raised
up is not only Jesus the Messiah as an individual but the body
of all those who are involved with him in his anointed humanity. In Christ the whole resurrection is already included
in a decisive way. The New Humanity is already raised up
in Christ. He is the corn of wheat which falling into the ground
does not come up alone, but with a whole harvest of grain.
This concept of a corporate resurrection, of our being raised
together with Christ and being begotten anew in him, is
found with particular force in the Epistles to the Colossians
and Ephesians (Col. 2: 12, 13; Eph. 2: 5, 6), but it is clearly
implied elsewhere in the New Testament, for example, in 1
Peter or the Epistle to the Hebrews.[9]

(d) There follows from this the universal aspect of resurrection.[10] The resurrection of Jesus as act of God is a decisive

[8] See Matthew Black, *Romans* (*New Century Bible*, 1973), comment on
Rom. 1: 4, p. 36f.

[9] For the rooting of this in the Synoptic pattern of the Christian life, see
William Manson, *Jesus and the Christian*, pp. 91ff., 102–13.

[10] The interconnection between the particular event of the resurrection
of Jesus and the concept of a universal or general resurrection has been
stressed by Wolfhart Pannenberg in a very illuminating and important
discussion (*Jesus–God and Man*, Eng. tr. 1968, pp. 74–88). However, by
making the expectation of a resurrection from the dead within the context
of Jewish apocalyptic expectation a *presupposition* for the recognition of
Jesus' resurrection, and for an understanding of its intrinsic meaning (within

event, a final judgment, which affects the entire state of human existence, the whole situation in which we have our being, and as such affects every human being. It is this concentration of universal significance in the resurrection of Jesus that is so very important for the whole of the Christian message. The New Testament does not teach a doctrine of individual resurrection *first*, in the sense that each man is to rise again because he is made of a body and an immortal soul, a resurrection mainly because of some interior principle in his creation. It is the fulfilment of God's covenant mercies in the incarnation and resurrection that confers immortality. Christ only has immortality and we receive out of his fullness. The general resurrection is absolutely dependent on the resurrection of Jesus Christ himself, for it is in his death and resurrection that God has dealt with death and guilt and hell once and for all. He was put to death for our trespasses and was raised for our justification. In the resurrection of Jesus an objective and vicarious act has been carried out in our human nature in which we are already implicated. The saving power of the resurrection is applied to us through the preaching of the Gospel. He who responds to that message by faith discovers that he has already been involved in the resurrection, and is already included in the objective reality of Jesus Christ risen from the dead. It is also implied that the unbeliever is affected as well, for he will be judged precisely by this man whom God has raised from the dead, and who confronts each man as the decisive embodiment of the saving judgment of God, the justification of the ungodly, proclaimed to every man. Yet the fruit of the resurrection is enjoyed only by believers, and enjoyed even now in Christ in anticipation of the final resurrection of the dead.[11]

(*e*) While the language which the New Testament uses to

---

its sphere in the history of traditions), Pannenberg seems to run together rather confusingly, historical, logical and epistemological priorities. He does not take adequate account of the fact that Judaism did not anticipate resurrection as a *decisive event* in history, nor of the fact that in its happening the resurrection of Jesus radically transformed the whole concept of the resurrection. It is surely in this light that St. Paul's circular argument of 1 Cor. 15: 12ff. is to be understood.

[11] Cf. Gregory of Nyssa, *Catechetical Oration*, 35.

speak of the resurrection of Jesus from the dead is also used in connection with others, not only in cases of healing but, for example, of the rising of the bodies of the saints (Matt. 27: 52) or even of the raising of Lazarus (John 11: 23), there is no suggestion in the New Testament that Jesus himself rose to his old condition which would in due course be followed by death, as with Lazarus.[12] He died and rose again in such a way as never to die again, for his resurrection involved a radical change, not only in a triumph over death and corruption but in a transforming recreation of the humanity which he had assumed from Mary in his incarnation. The risen Jesus was the same as he who was born of Mary and crucified under Pontius Pilate, yet he was not the same, for with his resurrection from the grave something had taken place akin to the original creation, and indeed transcending it. It was not just a miracle within the creation, but a deed so decisively new that it affected the whole of creation and the whole of the future. The resurrection of Jesus Christ has creative and constitutive character, and as such cannot but transform our understanding of the whole relation of God to the universe of things visible and invisible, present and future. If the distinctive language used of the resurrection of Jesus is also used to speak of other incidents or events, it is only because the resurrection has so transformed the whole picture that they have to be seen as falling within the field of its impact.

There is a further point to be noted about the New Testament teaching: the relation between the resurrection of Christ and that of the believer, such as we find it in Colossians 2 or Ephesians 2, where it is declared that as Christ was raised from the dead so we also will be raised, for we were already raised together with him. The parallelism between Christ and the believer is not simply one of similarity. It is that, but more than that. The resurrection of the believer is regarded primarily as the transforming *effect* of the resurrection of Christ, yet not effect in the sense of some new and subsequent event,

---

[12] This is evident, as James Denney has pointed out, in the force of the perfect tense of *egeiro* which St. Paul used to speak of Jesus, *egēgertai* (1 Cor. 15: 4): 'Christ rose, it signifies, and remains in the risen state. Death has no more dominion over him ... Jesus does not come back to the old life at all'. *Jesus and the Gospel*, p. 114.

but effect as something that is already implicated in the resurrection of Christ. Our resurrection has already taken place and is fully tied up with the resurrection of Christ, and therefore proceeds from it more by way of manifestation of what has already taken place, than as new effect resulting from it. That is why the New Testament speaks so astonishingly of our having already tasted the powers of the age to come (Hebrews 6: 5), for in Christ we are already living 'in the end time'. Through Christ the very fullness (*plērōma*) of God, which resides in him, already overflows to us (Col. 2: 9–10).

Before we go on to discuss the inner connection between the person of Christ and the actual event of his resurrection, it will be worthwhile pausing to consider some of the epistemological and indeed methodological consequences that follow from the teaching of the New Testament about the resurrection so far as it has already come before us.

The unique nature of the resurrection, together with the fact that it did not take place as a limited isolated event but only in such a way that it already includes us within its happening, necessarily affects the way in which it is to be appreciated and understood. It means that the risen Jesus Christ cannot be discerned within the frame of the old conditions of life which by his resurrection he has transcended, and cannot be understood except within the context of the transformation which it has brought about. If it could be discerned and understood within the old frame and context, then, as William Milligan has shown, that would imply the subjection of Jesus once again to his passion.[13] But if we really are to understand the resurrection as a genuine resurrection in the sense of the New Testament witnesses, we shall have to recognize that the evidence for the resurrection can be handled and tested, appropriately, only within the orbit of its impact. That is why the evidence for the resurrection presented by the New Testament is and had to be that of believers. There is certainly a problem here, which was appreciated in early times, as is evident from the question of Judas, not Iscariot, 'Lord, how is it that thou wilt manifest thyself unto us, and not unto the world?' (John 14: 22), to the sceptical questioning of

[13] William Milligan, *The Resurrection of Our Lord*, p. 33; see the whole passage, pp. 31–8.

Celsus.[14] The answer that Jesus gave to the question how he would manifest himself to the disciples and not to the world was, as the Evangelist reports, in terms of a circle of love and abiding in the Word of God (John 14: 23f.). It is not something that can be disclosed through extraneous means, or be apprehended except by participating in it and dwelling in it, i.e. from within its reality. This is rather like what Michael Polanyi, in very different contexts, speaks of as 'indwelling', that is 'a utilization of a framework for unfolding our understanding in accordance with the indications and standards imposed by the framework'.[15] This means that the evidence for the resurrection of Jesus will look very different for those who make themselves dwell in it and learn to understand what it is by participating within the circle of knowing which it sets up, and can only appear in a distorted and mutilated way to those who are not prepared to listen in to its message or to allow themselves to fall under its transforming impact. That does not mean, of course, that the evidence for the resurrection is only the evidence of 'belief', but that it is only the believer who is in a position properly to weigh up the evidence and exercise his critical capacities in a way appropriate to that into which he inquires.[16]

We are not concerned here simply with what is often called 'the hermeneutical circle', but with the kind of circle which is posited by an ultimate fact which in the nature of the case cannot be brought within the same circle as other facts, but which stakes out the very grounds upon which experience and knowledge of it are possible. But here, as we have seen, is an objective reality which includes as part of its own comprehensiveness those for whom and in whose existence it has taken place, for it has been built into the structure of the world to which they belong and affects the very ground of their being and knowing. As St. Paul understood it, for example, the resurrection of Jesus Christ did not take place for himself alone, but for us whom he had assumed into a unity of nature with himself, so that in a profound sense we have already been raised up before God in him: to what has objectively

---

[14] Origen, *Contra Celsum*, II, 63ff.; V, 18ff.

[15] Michael Polanyi, *Knowing and Being*, 1969, p. 134, 136, etc.

[16] Cf. here O. C. Quick, *op. cit.*, pp. 146ff.

taken place in him there is a corresponding subjective counter-part in us which as such belongs to the whole integrated reality of the resurrection event.

That is an aspect of the resurrection into which we must inquire further, but meantime, it must be said that this re-lationship which obtains between the objective event of the resurrection in Christ and its subjective counterpart in us, which is part of the whole truth of the resurrection, does not mean that the resurrection of Christ can simply be identified with or resolved into that counterpart.[17] That is the false step which is still being taken today by some New Testament scholars when they identify the resurrection with the Easter faith of the first disciples. It is precisely because the resur-rection has intelligible content as Word of God that its truth requires believing discernment and understanding of it; so the New Testament writers often follow a statement about the fact that Christ rose from the dead by another to the effect that he appeared to or was seen by a disciple. By the very same token, however, a clear distinction is drawn between the event of Christ's rising and its counterpart or coefficient in the be-lieving community. Thus, for example, St. Paul in speaking about the *kerygma* and its believing response, distinguishes the objective events from the 'appearances': 'I delivered to you as of first importance what I also received, that Christ died for our sins in accordance with the Scriptures, that he was buried, that he was raised on the third day in accordance with the Scriptures, and that he appeared to [or, let himself be seen by] Peter, then the twelve. . .' (1 Cor. 15: 3ff.). The 'appearance' is also regarded as objective in its own way, but distinguished from the actual event of the resurrection in the same way as it is distinguished from the events of the cruci-fixion and burial of Christ.[18] The resurrection is truth that

[17] Consult here the valuable discussion by James Denney, *Jesus and the Gospel*, 4th edit. 1913, pp. 107ff. He has in mind here, evidently, the view of A. von Harnack, *op. cit.*, p. 119: 'The New Testament itself distinguishes between the Easter message of the empty grave and the appearances of Jesus on the one side, and the Easter faith on the other' – a passage which was later to influence R. Bultmann.

[18] 'The appearances are not the primal miracle of the resurrection itself but the revealing of it'. W. Künneth, *The Theology of the Resurrection*, 1965, p. 86.

presses for objective realization in the recognition and joy of faith, but there is nothing in the New Testament which allows us to resolve the reality of the resurrection itself into appearances to the believing community, as if the only real historical event here were what is called 'the Easter faith'. That would be a flagrant example of an imposition upon the New Testament text of a subjective way of thinking deriving from a radical dichotomy between things in themselves (which are by definition unknowable) and their appearances to people. To insist on interpreting the New Testament message of the resurrection in that phenomenalist way is to clamp down upon it an alien framework of dogmatic epistemological assumptions which inevitably distorts it. That is surely the very reverse of objective scientific method, for it precludes from the very start any possibility of penetrating into the New Testament and listening to its message from within it.

Yet that is apparently the problem that lies behind so much current biblical interpretation. It still operates within the obsolete Cartesian–Kantian dualism which splits the world into two disparate realms; a physical realm of external reality which is open to investigation and explanation in terms of hard causal connections, for which the appropriate procedures are developed in the mathematical and instrumentalist sciences, and a mental realm of internal reality which is open to investigation and understanding in terms of meaning, for which the appropriate procedures are developed in the historical and human sciences. That is the dualism that gave rise to the dichotomy between the theoretical and empirical components in knowledge which pure science has had to reject but which still lives on in the cultural split between the sciences and the humanities. It was when trapped within that cultural split that German New Testament scholarship threw up the fatal distinction between two kinds of history, one concerned with the kind of event which is rooted in objective empirical reality, and the other concerned with the kind of event rooted in the inner life and experience of men, which is so spaceless and timeless that it has at best only a sort of tangential relation to the world of concrete historical events. When these two kinds of 'events' are entirely detached from one another, the latter can be interpreted only in terms of symbols and metaphors;

but they can be brought into some sort of juxtaposition in which the basic concept is that of occurrence *plus* meaning. Here an attempt is made to integrate interpretation and fact which will do justice to the historical character of the Gospel.[19] But if the interpretation is only put upon the fact by way of valuation and bears no intrinsic relation to it, if the meaning is only a 'plus' to the occurrence by way of the interest it has for the persons involved in it and is not inherent in the occurrence, then in the last resort the interpretation or meaning is detachable from the occurrence or fact and can have an independent life apart from it as some sort of spaceless and timeless 'event'. That, alas, is what so often happens to the 'resurrection' in contemporary thought where it does not appear to fulfil the dominant role which it does in the New Testament, in serving the revelation of Jesus Christ in his objective and personal reality as incarnate Son of God, the Lord of history and of creation.[20]

It is one of the basic canons of hermeneutics, which surely all scholars accept, that the interpreter must seek to penetrate into the conceptual forms and patterns at work in the actual stream of tradition in which the text being interpreted is found, but to do so he must be highly critical of himself and the theoretical and methodological notions he brings with him from his own cultural environments. That is why it will not do to interpret the New Testament accounts of the resurrection by abstracting them from their native setting in Israel and interpreting them on the foreign soil of Graeco-oriental mysticism, gnostic cults and philosophies or later Hellenistic literature, which has been the habit of recent scholars (with some notable exceptions like William Manson, J. Jeremias, Oscar Cullmann, C. E. B. Cranfield and Matthew Black), rather than out of the prophetic religion of the Old Testament and on the background of Palestinian Judaism. The enormous distortion that this involves will be immediately apparent when we recall that Israel has come down to us from history

---

[19] C. H. Dodd, *History and Gospel*, 1938, edit. 1947, pp. 25ff., 103ff.

[20] I find the place given by C. H. Dodd to the resurrection in *History and Gospel*, pp. 107, 138, 145, and in *The Founder of Christianity*, 1970, p. 163f., rather disappointing, in spite of his earlier finding in *The Apostolic Preaching and Its Developments*, 1936.

as (what John Macmurray has called) the only developed civilization that is religious and the only great culture that is basically non-dualist, whereas the culture and thought of the great Hellenistic as well as the Oriental traditions are radically dualist.[21] It was precisely with that dualist culture that the Christian Church had to struggle so hard, as it moved out from its Hebraeo-Christian base in Palestine into the wider world, in order to remain faithful to the fundamental character and content of the New Testament message. That is why it laid such enormous emphasis upon the resurrection of Jesus in body and even in flesh in order to maintain the integrity and wholeness of the humanity of the Incarnate Son, which disintegrated when it was bound down on the procrustean bed of practical and theoretical dualism, as is evident in the twin heresies of 'docetism' and 'adoptionism' (as they came to be called). If, however, the message of the resurrection is interpreted within the non-dualist frame of reference deriving from Israel, then it has seismic repercussions. That is what happened in the primitive Church, as Christian and non-Christian Jews equally realized: for it meant a radical revision of the concept of God himself. The resurrection of Jesus Christ in the full non-dualist sense, in which it was proclaimed by the apostles from the very start, meant that he who was of the seed of David was declared to be the Son of God with power (Rom. 1: 3f.); it meant not only the justification and acknowledgement of Jesus by God the Father and his installation on the throne of divine Power (Acts 2: 32f.; 5: 30f.), but that God himself was directly present and personally active in the resurrection of Jesus, and that implied that he was equally present and personally active in the passion of Jesus, as St. Peter made very clear in his early preaching, reported in the Acts of the Apostles (2: 14ff.; 3: 12ff.; 4: 8ff.; 5: 29ff.), and St. Stephen as well (Acts 7: 1ff.). That Jesus the crucified, now proclaimed to be risen from the dead, should grant forgiveness of sins and judge the quick and the dead, and thus share the ultimate prerogatives of God Almighty, that he the Son of Man should be standing on the right hand of God

---

[21] John Macmurray, *The Clue to History*, 1938, pp. 16ff.; cf. also *The Self as Agent*, 1956, pp. 73ff., etc.; *Persons in Relation*, 1961, pp. 19ff., etc. See also *Theology in Reconciliation*, 8ff., 27ff. etc.

(Acts 7: 55f.), was the great stone of stumbling, which gave such offence to recalcitrant Judaism, for it was unwilling to go forward with the Christian Church in accepting the full implication of the resurrection of Christ. This meant that the fundamental understanding of God, which had more and more assumed a fixed pattern in later Judaism, had to undergo change: far from being namelessly and transcendentally remote or detached, operating only through intermediaries, God himself must be thought of as having visited his people, to take upon himself their nature and their destiny, so that the whole doctrine of God, his relation to the creation, to history, to the guilt and pain of humanity, to all mankind, and therefore even the ancient covenant of God with Israel, had to be reconstructed in face of the crucifixion and resurrection of Jesus. Hence, far from countenancing any form of dualism in the relation between God and the world, the resurrection destroyed the very possibility of such a way of thinking for Christians: the non-dualist mode of thought here came to its complete fulfilment in the resurrection of Jesus Christ in Body, and with it a new understanding of the living God whose very being and life are accessible to human knowing and participating.[22] If that is the case – and certainly early Christian theology was convinced it was – then we do the message of the resurrection the gravest injustice in transposing it into a very different frame of reference in which dualist structures of thought determine how we regard the evidence and how we make intelligible sense of it, for that would not be to interpret it out of its own appropriate frame of reference or even to listen properly to what it has to say.

But if we do try to understand the resurrection of Jesus Christ on its own native ground, in the tradition of Old Testament and Palestinian Judaism, and in terms of the appropriate frame of reference which it created for itself in the

[22] Here we are at the very root of the doctrine of the Trinity, for through Christ we have access by one Spirit to the Father (Eph. 2: 18). The implication especially of the crucifixion for a dynamic understanding of the Being of God and of his Triunity is finely brought out by E. Jüngel, *Gottes Sein ist im Werden*, 1965, Eng. tr. by Horton Harris, 1976, *The Doctrine of the Trinity. God's Being is in Becoming, Scottish Journal of Theology Monographs*, No. 4, pp. 83ff.

apostolic foundation of the Church, and thus in the realist understanding of the New Testament witnesses and writers, how are we to interpret it *for ourselves* in such a way as to remain faithful to its basic character and content? Quite clearly, if it was an objective act of God within the structures of space and time, within the concrete occurrences of history, then we must try to interpret it as such, within the structures of space and time as we understand them. We shall have to wrestle with the problems that are involved here, with the difference between ancient notions of space and time and those which we find ourselves having to develop in a modern understanding of the universe, but must nevertheless be careful, out of rigorous scientific fidelity to the nature of that into which we are inquiring, not to force upon it an alien framework of conceptual connections, but to allow the resurrection in its own integrity to come to view and understanding within modern forms of thought and speech. That is not easy to do, but at least we have been preceded in this by classical Christian theology, which found it could interpret the incarnation and resurrection of Christ within the thought forms of classical Graeco-Roman culture only in such a way as to reconstruct the foundations of that culture, developing radically fresh notions of space and time accordingly. And that is the task of modern theology, and indeed of theology in any and every age. But today, we have an enormous advantage over every other age in the history of western civilization, for now at last out of pure science itself there has come a profound revolution in the foundations of physical knowledge in which the dualist modes of thought, epistemological, anthropological and cosmological (which in different ways have prevailed in one way in classical 'essentialist' science and in another way in modern 'instrumentalist' science) have been overthrown, and we are in the process of developing a non-dualist outlook upon the universe, and basic to all that is the non-dualist understanding of space and time resulting from relativity theory. This does not mean that we must try to understand the resurrection of Jesus Christ by fitting it into such a modern 'relativistic' world-view, but it does mean that we are emancipated in a remarkable way from the tyranny of dualist modes of thought which have throughout the history of biblical interpretation done such damage, for example, in the allegorizing of the ancient and mediaeval Church and in the demythologizing of modern scholars from Strauss to Bultmann. But it also means that here we have being developed new, relational notions of space and time which are astonishingly similar to those which classical Christian theology found itself forced to develop, as it allowed the message of the incarnation and the resurrection, indeed the whole relation of God to history and nature implied in that message, to call for a reconstruction of the cultural foundations of the ancient world. It will be through dialogue at the deepest level between Christian theology and natural science, in which each remains faithful to the nature and character of its own field of inquiry, and in recognition that both operate within the same field-structures of space and time as the bearers of all rational order in the universe, that interpretation and intelligible appropriation of the message of the resurrection may take place. This is what is intended here, but the first prerequisite of such a procedure is to listen into the message of the resurrection on its own native ground and in terms of its own intrinsic postulates, as far as possible unfettered and undistorted by alien presuppositions from a different cultural provenance ancient or modern.

CHAPTER 2

THE RESURRECTION AND
THE PERSON OF JESUS CHRIST

The teaching of the New Testament makes it clear that we cannot isolate the resurrection from the whole redeeming purpose of God or from the decisive deed of God in the incarnation of his Son which ran its full course from the birth of Jesus to his crucifixion and triumph over the powers of evil. The resurrection cannot be detached from Christ himself, and considered as a phenomenon on its own to be compared and judged in the light of other phenomena. Rather it must be considered in the light of who Jesus Christ is in his own Person, in his own intrinsic *logos*, and indeed in the light of his divine and human natures. It was that Christ who rose again from the dead and no other.[1] Nor must it be considered in abstraction from his saving work fulfilled in and through the incarnation when he, the eternal Word and creative Source of all life and being outside of God, entered into our mortal and corrupt existence, that was wasting away under the threat of death and judgment, in order to effect the salvation and recreation of the world. Hence a double duality must be kept in view: (i) the duality formed by the union of divine and human natures in the one Person of Christ, and (ii) the duality formed by the entry of his life into our mortality, his light into our darkness, his holiness into our corruption. It is because he who lives and acts in this situation is divine and human *in one Person*, that all he does in our fallen existence has a dark side and a light side, a side of humiliation and a side of exaltation – the one is the

[1] This is why, as O. C. Quick pointed out, if we find the evidence for the resurrection sufficient, we accept it 'precisely not on the ground that such evidence would establish the resurrection of *anyone*, but on the ground that it is the uniqueness of Jesus which makes it credible'. *Doctrines of the Creed*, 1947 edit., p. 150. Thus also James Denney, *Jesus and the Gospel*, 1913, pp. 122ff., 129ff., 158f.

obverse of the other, but as the Mediator he has come to overcome our darkness and baseness and to build a bridge in and through himself over which we may pass into the light and glory of God.

We must think of the Son of God as engaging with the forces of darkness immediately he became incarnate, for the whole of his life was a redemptive operation in our human nature where the forces of evil have entrenched themselves and seek to enslave us. He was made one of us in order to submit himself to those forces of evil, both to bear and vanquish them in his own human existence and vicariously to provide for us a way of saving obedience and communion with the Father. The incarnation of the Son must be regarded as the entry of the Mediator into a situation where the communion between God and man is broken and distorted, where the divisiveness of sin and guilt has affected the very fabric of human existence. Hence the union effected in the incarnate Person of the Son inevitably came under attack and strain. The forces of evil thrust against that union, seeking to break it, to divide the human life of the Son on earth from the life of the Father above, to divide the divine and human natures in Christ himself. However, by living the life which Jesus Christ lived in our midst, the life of complete obedience to the Father and of perfect communion with him, the life of absolute holiness in the midst of our sin and corruption, and by living it through the whole course of our human existence from birth to death, he achieved within our creaturely being the very union between God and man that constitutes the heart of atonement, effecting man's salvation and restoration to communion with God the Father.

Thus we are not to think of the humiliation and exaltation of Christ simply as two events following one after the other, but as both involved in appropriate measure at the same time all through the incarnate life of Christ. The immersion of Christ the eternal Word into our mortal existence is itself also the exaltation of our lowly existence into union and communion with God. The coming of the Son of God into our lost and alienated being constitutes *Immanuel*, God with us, but if God is with us in Christ then in him we are with God. *We with God* is thus the obverse of *God with us*. The exaltation of man is the obverse of the humiliation of the Son of God. It is in this light that we must think of the mutual involution of mortality and immortality, death and life, the crucifixion and the resurrection of Christ. Seen in this way the resurrection is not to be understood merely as something that follows upon the crucifixion but as the other side of it – that is why we really discern the act of God in the crucifixion of Christ when we penetrate through to the other side of it, and see it not only in its dark and terrible side, but also in its light and glorious side. As a matter of fact the New Testament nowhere presents us with a bare crucifixion, but only with the crucifixion as seen and reported from the perspective of the resurrection where its real secret or significance was disclosed.[2] As Hilary pointed out in the fourth century, it was only in the light of the resurrection that the whole mystery of the faith became visible.[3]

Nowhere does the New Testament present us with a naked Christ, but only with the Christ who is clothed with his message and robed in his promises. There is no Christ apart from his teaching or his saving acts but only the Christ who confronts us in and through his teaching and healing. Even on the purely human level he confronts us as one who is characterized by an absolutely sincere relation between his person and his word, his word and his deed – for he nowhere meets us as a man who ought to have been other than he was or whose actions fell short of his words. But as incarnate Son of God he confronts us as he in whom person and work and word are indissolubly one. It is his own person that he communicates in his words and deeds, while his words and deeds do not only derive from his person but inhere in it. This is why the New Testament nowhere seeks to present Christ to us apart from his *kerygma* or *didache*, or apart from the mighty acts of healing and forgiving that were wrought by him, but always and only with the Christ who is in himself the secret of his *kerygma* and whose

[2] Cf. A. M. Ramsey: 'The Crucifixion is not a defeat needing Resurrection to reverse it, but a victory which the Resurrection quickly follows and seals. . . . So it is that the centre of Apostolic Christianity is *Crucifixion-Resurrection*; not Crucifixion alone nor Resurrection alone, nor even Crucifixion and Resurrection as the finale, but the blending of the two in a way that is as real to the Gospel as it is defiant to the world'. *The Resurrection of Christ*, 1945, p. 19.

[3] Hilary, *De Trinitate*, VII, 12.

kerygma is what it is because of its profound inner relation to his personal Being. The Christ who is proclaimed to us in the New Testament, therefore, is the Christ who is clothed with the *kerygma* of his death and resurrection, for they are ontologically and structurally bound up with who he is in himself and in his relation to the Father.

Similarly the New Testament does not present us with a message of Good Friday and then with a message of Easter, but always and only with the Easter message of Christ the crucified risen again, the Lamb who has been slain but who is alive for evermore. Think of the way in which this is presented to us in the preaching of Peter in the Acts and even more clearly in the First Epistle of Peter. The whole course of events in the last weeks of Jesus' life, the passion period, to which the Gospels devote such a high proportion of their account, is regarded as a continuous and structural unity. The early Christians called it the *Pascha* in view of the *Passover* which was celebrated in Israel at that time and which Christ fulfilled in his own *Passion* as the *Paschal Lamb*. Jesus Christ was regarded as constituting in himself the great Passover from death to life, from man-in-death to man-in-the-life-of-God, from damnation to salvation, from destruction to new creation. But that *Pascha* which he accomplished in himself for our sakes is proclaimed as the great *Pascha* which he has accomplished for the Church and the world. It is, then, in that profound unity and continuity, ontologically structured in and through the Person of Christ as Mediator, that the resurrection was understood as forming with the crucifixion the great *Paschal Mystery* of our salvation.

We return to the fact that the resurrection is inseparable from the Person of the incarnate Son of God who constituted in himself as the Mediator the bridge between man and God and between death and life. He condescended in great humiliation to unite himself with us in our weakness, corruption and damned existence, living within it all the life of unsullied purity, truth and holiness in such a way as to atone in life and death for our sin and guilt, overcoming all the estrangement and separation that it involved between man and God, and in such a way therefore as to resurrect in himself our human nature in union and communion with the Father. The resurrection is to be regarded not only as the completion of that saving work but as belonging to the ontological structure of the Mediator himself who stood in the gap of the *Eli, Eli, lama sabachthani* and bridged it in his own personal existence and supplied for all men the living way from death to life. As such, of course, the resurrection is also the manifestation of the Beloved Son and his installation with power into Messianic and Mediatorial Office. It is the seal that the Father set upon his vicarious life and mission, crowning in a final declaration of power all that he had come to do as incarnate Son of God. The resurrection is the revelation of the Father's acceptance of the life and death of Jesus as full and sufficient sacrifice for the sin of the world and at the same time its finalization as eternally prevailing mediation between God and mankind.

It is worth recalling at this point the *Goel* aspect of redemption which is grounded in the inseparable relation between the redemptive act and the person of the Redeemer, i.e. the incarnational and ontological aspect of atonement. This is the aspect that comes so clearly and powerfully into the light with the resurrection of Christ as the pledge and surety of our redemption. In him our human life is carried across the chasm of death and judgment into union with the divine life, so that it is through our sharing in his humanity in death and resurrection that we participate in all the fruits of his atoning work.

Fuller consideration may now be given to two questions: the relation of the resurrection to the *active and passive obedience* of Christ, and the relation of the resurrection to the *Virgin Birth* of Christ.

1. *The Resurrection of Jesus Christ as Passive and Active*

In line with his *passive obedience* and submission to the Father's judgment, the resurrection of Christ is to be regarded as that act whereby he was raised from the dead by the Father. Here the emphasis undoubtedly falls upon the fact that in death Jesus submitted completely to our condition in utter weakness and powerlessness. It was real and complete death – *our* death into which he entered, and where he was so powerless that he had to be raised up by God himself. That was in line with his whole mission, revealed so clearly in his temptations that followed upon his Baptism. Son of God though he was he declined to use his divine power in order to help himself in the hunger to which he had been reduced in vicarious fasting and penitence, for he had come to appropriate our weakness and meet and overcome all the assaults of evil in our abject condition. The same temptation came with all its force as he hung on the Cross: 'If you are the Son of God, come down from the Cross' (Matt. 27: 40); but he resisted the temptation to use divine power to escape from his vicarious mission and remained still and passive as death overtook him, submitting to the ultimate lot of mankind in the disintegration and finality of death. *Passive* resurrection is the counterpart to that abject passion, and corresponds to the 'anhypostatic' aspect of the Incarnation and the dramatic aspect of redemption in which we are saved by the sheer act of Almighty God. Since this passive obedience of Jesus was essentially a voluntary and deliberately vicarious act in accepting the Father's will, it was also a *positive* and indeed a *creative* act, and as such is the counterpart to the 'enhypostatic' aspect of the Incarnation and the priestly aspect of redemption in which we are saved through the human mediation of the incarnate Son.[4]

If the death of Jesus on the Cross is to be regarded as the sentence of divine judgment inflicted on him for our sakes, and on us in him, the resurrection is to be regarded as the obverse of that, itself the sentence and judgment of God. Both these aspects are involved in the New Testament notion of *justification*. We recall that the Greek word *dikaioun* means to justify in both senses, to condemn and to vindicate. The resurrection of Christ is thus to be understood in terms of justification, the justification of Christ following his condemnation in our place, and therefore as carrying the sentence of divine forgiveness and emancipation from the guilt and bondage of sin. Hence, on the one hand, the resurrection of Christ attests God's own approbation of what he had done and was in his obedient life and death: it is the Father's justification of the Son (Rom. 1: 4; Phil. 2: 6–11; 1 Tim. 3: 16); and, on the

---

[4] While the 'anhypostatic' aspect of the Incarnation and redemption emphasizes that all is due to the grace of *God alone* – there would have been no 'Jesus' apart from the Incarnation of the Son – the 'enhypostatic' aspect emphasizes the fullness and integrity of Jesus' *human* life and agency in the incarnate life and work of the Son.

other hand, the resurrection attests the fact that through the sacrifice of Christ sin has been blotted out and man's life has been placed on a new basis (Rom. 4: 25).[5]

It is of course the positive side of that justifying act that is ascendant here. The resurrection is God's great act of *Amen* to the Cross. In the crucifixion of Christ we have on the one hand God's judgment on sin and on the other hand Jesus' submission to that judgment in obedience unto death. From God's side the crucifixion is his righteous condemnation of our sin, but from man's side it is Christ's high priestly *Amen* to the Father's judgment. But in the resurrection we have the same whole event, not only as God's judgment but as his positive satisfaction in the obedient self-sacrifice of his Son. And here the resurrection is the Father's *Amen* to Christ's high priestly self-offering in obedience and sacrifice for sin. If the Cross is God's *No* against us in judgment on our sin which Christ endured for our sakes – 'My God, my God, why hast thou forsaken me?' – the resurrection is God's *Yes* to us in his affirmation of Jesus as Son of Man and all that he has done for us in our nature and on our behalf. Hence in the resurrection of Jesus the passion is seen as the same event from God's side.

This is the point in which a proper doctrine of *satisfaction* has its right place in the atonement. Historically, satisfaction has been understood mainly as the fulfilment of a legal requirement in making amendment for wrong and meeting the demands of justice. In the New Testament, however, satisfaction is the 'good pleasure' of God in the obedient self-offering of the incarnate Son, manifested and expressed in the raising of the Son from the dead and in a refusal to allow him to see corruption. When Jesus submitted to baptism at the hands of John in order to fulfil righteousness he was greeted with the words of the Father, 'Thou art my beloved Son in whom I am well pleased'. So here in the resurrection, 'Thou art my beloved Son, this day have I begotten thee' is translated into fact, for in him God has made us accepted according to the good pleasure of his will. The atoning sacrifice offered in the life and death of Christ is here acknowledged and affirmed by God; the act of the Son is manifested to be the act of God himself. In Pauline language, Christ was raised for our justi-

[5] William Milligan, *The Resurrection of our Lord*, 1913, pp. 153–9.

fication. Satisfaction is not the divine satisfaction in death, as compensation for violated law, nor only the satisfaction in the fulfilment of divine righteousness, but satisfaction of the Father in the Son who has fulfilled the Father's good pleasure in making righteous atonement. Thus in the resurrection the Father owns Christ as his Son, which has the effect not only of confirming all that Jesus had taught and done, and indeed had claimed, up to the crucifixion, but of acknowledging that his activity in life and death was his very own.

In line with his *active obedience* as Son on earth offering to his Father in heaven a life of holiness and filial love, the resurrection of Christ is to be regarded as his own act in taking again the life that he had laid down.[6] Here the emphasis falls upon the fact that in death and in resurrection Christ acted in entire consistence with the way in which he lived his life in unbroken fellowship with the Father and in the perfection of union with him. Although he assumed our fallen and corrupt humanity when he became flesh, in assuming it he sanctified it in himself, and all through his earthly life he overcame our sin through his righteousness, our impurity through his purity, condemning sin in our flesh by the sheer holiness of his life within it. That is why death could not hold him even when he entered into and submitted to it, for there was no sin in him which allowed it to subject him to corruption. Death had nothing in him, for he had already passed through its clutches by the perfection of his holiness. Thus by entering into our death as the Holy One of God he robbed it of its sting, and stripped away its power as he accepted the divine judgment in the expiatory sacrifice of his own life, and thus triumphed over the forces of guilt and evil which had made death the last stronghold of their grip over man.[7] He triumphed over the grave

[6] Among the Fathers it is Hilary of Poitiers who integrates most fully the active and passive obedience of Christ, both in *kenōsis* and in *resurrection*, with strong emphasis upon the *enhypostasis*, *De Trinitate*, IX. 9–14, 38ff. Among modern theologians see especially Heinrich Vogel, *Gott im Christo*, 1951, pp. 739ff, who distinguishes between the passive and active aspects of the resurrection in terms of *Auferweckung* and *Auferstehung*.

[7] The Evangelical reports clearly relate the *active* resurrection of Jesus (expressed by *anistemi*) to his designation as Son of Man, thereby connecting his resurrection with his triumphant judgment of the forces of darkness and evil. Cf. Mark 8: 31; 9: 9, 31; 10: 34; Luke 18: 33; John 5: 27f.

through his sheer sinlessness, 'according to the spirit of holiness' (Rom. 1:4). Thereby Jesus also denied to death any natural right over man – rather is death 'the wages of sin' (Rom. 6: 23). Death is no more proper to human nature than sin is. Man is made for God, and God is life: therefore death is unnatural.

We may also speak of this in terms of the hypostatic union of the divine and human natures in the one Person of Christ. That was a living and dynamic union which ran throughout the whole of his life, in which he maintained union and communion with the Father in the steadfastness of the Father toward the Son and in the steadfastness of the Son toward the Father. The resurrection means that this union did not give way but held under the strain imposed not only by the forces that sought to divide Jesus from God, but the strain imposed through the infliction of the righteous judgment of the Father upon our rebellious humanity which Christ had made his own – and it held under the strain imposed by both in the crucifixion: the hypostatic union survived the descent into hell and Christ arose still in unbroken communion with the Father. The resurrection is thus the resurrection of the union forged between man and God in Jesus out of the damned and lost condition of men into which Christ entered in order to share their lot and redeem them from doom. Here we are thinking of the resurrection in line with the enhypostatic aspect of the incarnation, that is, in the fullness and integrity of his human life and agency in the saving work of God.

Jesus Christ rose again in virtue of his holiness as the Second Man, the Last Man, the new Adam who heads the race in the new creation opened up in the resurrection from the dead.[8] As such he rose clothed with the power of the resurrection and is spoken of as life-giving Spirit (1 Cor. 15: 45). He was not only an Adam into whom God breathed the breath of life and made a quickened soul, but the Adam with such fullness of life in himself that even as Man he breathed quickening

---

[8] There can be little doubt that St. Paul's Christ–Adam theology (cf. here Karl Barth, *Christ and Adam, Man and Humanity in Romans 5, Scottish Journal of Theology Occasional Papers*, No. 5, 1956) takes up and corresponds to the Synoptic doctrine of the Son of Man, especially when the latter is recognized to include the idea of representation – cf. Oscar Cullmann, *The Christology of the New Testament*, pp. 158f., 163.

spirit into others. He is the resurrected Man who has life in himself, and is become in himself the Source and Fountain of eternal life for others. By living in utter holiness as Son on earth he appropriated for and into our human nature the eternal Life of God, and it was by virtue of that power of an endless life that he broke through the bonds of death and the grave, but it is this same power of an endless life that now overflows from him to all who are members of his body. It is therefore out of his fullness that we may all receive. As St. Paul says, the identical power God exerted in taking Christ out of the grave is available now to help Christians live (Eph. 1: 19–20). It is thus out of the fullness of Christ that we may all live.

Since Jesus Christ is himself the resurrection and the Life, he is himself also the reconciliation and salvation of men. The risen Jesus Christ is the living Atonement, atonement in its glorious achievement not only in overcoming the separation of sin, guilt and death, but in consummating union and communion with God in such a way that the divine life overflows freely through him into mankind. Of course, if Christ had not risen from the dead, that would have indicated that the atonement had not been achieved, that he had not actually been able to stand in for us and take our place; and then his sacrifice on the Cross could have been seen only as a terrible act of final injustice: the atonement would have been a fiasco. However, now that he has risen from the dead, the atonement is shown to have been carried through to its final end. In this accomplishment it is evident that the atonement wrought by Christ, and Christ himself its Agent, cannot be separated from one another – he emerges as the living Atonement eternally prevailing in its advocacy before God and eternally availing in its propitiation for man with God.

As passive and active, then, the resurrection corresponds to *anhypostasia* and *enhypostasia*.[9] It is at once the mighty act of God's pure grace which raises man from the dead where he is

---

[9] Cf. Nels Ferré, *Christ and the Christian*, 1958, who rightly relates the active resurrection of Christ to the hypostatic union, and discerns in the *enhypostasia* not only a safeguarding of the humanity of the historical Jesus Christ but of the continuance of his human nature 'after death and to all eternity', pp. 115ff., 136ff., 216ff.

utterly hopeless and unable to save himself, but it is that mighty act of God translated into the perfection of a human act which is made to issue freely and fully out of man's nature, in which man is made to stand up before God as his beloved son in whom he is well pleased. Resurrection is atonement in its creative and positive result and achievement, in the recreation and final affirmation of man and the assuming of him by grace into union and communion with the life and love of God himself.

2. *The Relation of the Resurrection to the Virgin Birth of Christ*

It is in the resurrection that we have the unveiling of the mystery of the incarnation: the birth and resurrection of Jesus belong inseparably together and have to be understood in the light of each other.[10] The creation of the world out of nothing means that created existence is made contingent upon the Word and Will of God while utterly distinct from him. Therein lies its creaturely contingence and freedom which must be respected. That is why the processes of created existence can be known only by exploring them out of themselves, not by looking at God. It is by looking at God that we understand what the creation really is, but from looking at God and his creative relation to the world we are sent back to the world he made and loves to explore it out of itself. When the eternal Word, by whom all things were made, himself became incarnate, he entered within the contingence and freedom of the creaturely reality, sharing in it to the full, and so may be known only *a posteriori* out of that created order, in Jesus. Such an incarnation of the Son is inevitably a concealing of the divine power, for that power now enters within creaturely reality without abrogating it, in order to operate within it in the fulfilment of the divine will for its healing and recreation. Yet the world into which the Son entered is not merely creaturely – it is the world that has fallen from God and has entered upon a

---

[10] Hence, as with the resurrection, 'the really strong argument in favour of the virgin birth is the difficulty of accounting for the story otherwise than on the assumption of its truth'. H. R. Mackintosh, *The Person of Jesus Christ*, 1912, p. 529. No one wishing to commend the Gospel within the prevailing world-view would have invented the ideas of the virgin birth or the resurrection from the tomb: they forced themselves upon the primitive Church against the grain of current belief.

downward, detached and estranged course in which evil and irrationality and enmity to divine grace have embedded themselves in its existence and are at work destroying it. Hence the incarnation of the Son of God means that he is concealed by what is contrary, the very flesh of sin and the body of death, fallen existence, which he made his own on order to heal and sanctify it. It is not surprising, then, if we are to think of the line from the birth of Jesus to his crucifixion as the line of the hiddenness of God, the line of his activity in penetrating into our estranged existence, in order to get beneath our burden of sin and judgment, to get inside our death and to strip away from us the despotic forces of evil. But there is also a line from his birth to his resurrection which is the unveiling of God, a line that becomes fleetingly manifest in the transfiguration as also in the healing miracles and the other manifestations of Jesus' creative power. If the crucifixion represents the nadir of the hiddenness, the resurrection represents the high point of the revelation of Jesus as the Son of God become man.[11] Just as humiliation and exaltation were involved in one another and were the obverse of each other, so also these two lines of veiling and unveiling mutually involve one another. That is why Jesus revealed himself only slowly and in such a way that his self-disclosure kept pace with the development of his life and the steady march of events to their climax in the Cross: one was not allowed to outstrip the other. Following the utter darkness of the *Eli, Eli, lama sabachthani* and burial in the finality of death came the rending of the tomb and the unveiling of Jesus Christ as the Son of God sent to be our Saviour. He had come deliberately to share with us our life and death in order to make us share with him his eternal life in God. Since the resurrection is the final unveiling of the secret of Christ, the glorification of God incarnate, it is in the resurrection that the passion becomes lit up and is made

[11] This applies, as we have seen, and shall see again, only within the framework of faith, for the miraculous act of God in the resurrection of Jesus is not something that can be demonstrated merely within the framework of the natural order. Cf. Lesslie Newbigin, 'It has never at any time been possible to fit the resurrection of Jesus into any world view except the world view of which it is the basis'. *Honest Religion for Secular Man*, p. 53. Cf. Likewise W. Künneth on the independence of the resurrection from any world picture, primitive or scientific, *The Theology of the Resurrection*, Eng. tr. pp. 67ff.

articulate; it is transformed into luminous Word – the Word of the Cross as Power of God to all who believe.[12]

It is in this context of the relation of the resurrection to the Cross and the whole life of Jesus that we discern the secret of him *who was born of Mary*: that he was in fact none other than the *Creator Word* of God come as a creature within the world he had made. In the resurrection of Jesus we see that the saving act of God in the expiation of sin and guilt, in the vanquishing of death and all that destroys the creation, is joined to God's act of creation. Redemption and creation come together in the resurrection. Indeed God's *No* to all evil and its privation of being falls together with his *Yes* in the final affirming of the creation as that which God has made and declared to be good – for that declaration of God about what he had made is now made good through Jesus Christ. Atonement is unveiled to be the positive reaffirmation and recreation of man. Apart from the resurrection the *No* of God against our sins and the whole world of evil in which we had become entangled, even his rejection of our guilt, would be in vain – that is why St. Paul argues so insistently that if Christ is not risen we are yet in our sins (1 Cor. 15: 17–20).[13] But it is also true that apart from that No, the resurrection is no real Yes. Apart from God's No, in judgment and crucifixion, the resurrection would be only an empty show of wonderful power – it would not have any saving content to it, it would contain no forgiveness. By itself the expiatory death of Christ would mean only judgment, not life, only rejection of guilt – and yet even that could not be carried through apart from the resurrection – but now in the resurrection that act of atonement is seen to be God's great positive work of new creation. Thus the No and the Yes imply one another, and each is empty without the other. The vast significance of the crucifixion and resurrection emerges only as we see that here *redemption and creation come completely together*, in such a way that they gather up all the past and proleptically include the consummation of all things at the end.

When God created the world, all things were made through

---

[12] See the discussion of J. S. Stewart, *A Man in Christ*, 1935, pp. 135f., 138ff., 226ff.

[13] Cf. the kerygmatic exposition of this by J. S. Stewart, *The Gates of New Life*, 1937, pp. 160–9.

his Word. He spoke and it was done. In the resurrection it becomes revealed that Jesus Christ is none other than that almighty Creator-Word of God, but with that disclosure the crucifixion is quite transformed in our understanding, as the way that God's creative activity has taken in the restoration of creation. It is this conjunction of atoning death and recreation in the resurrection which means that out of the Cross there goes forth into the world the creative, saving Word of God Almighty, so that all things, visible and invisible, fall under its purpose and sway and are directed to the consummation of all things in the new heaven and new earth. This is the dynamic meaning of the New Testament *kerygma*, for then the word of the Cross is not just a word about the Cross but the Creator Word and Power of God encountering men in and through the crucifixion of Christ in such a way as to confront them with the last things and to bring upon them the final great acts of the world's renewal and salvation. The resurrection of Jesus Christ from the dead is now in the very forefront of the Church's *kerygma*, for it is a stupendous deed, comparable only to the original creation of the universe, and indeed transcends it in significance, like the incarnation when God himself entered the creation as one of the creatures he had made in order to operate within it.[14]

This brings us back to the birth of Jesus – the resurrection discloses that the Virgin Birth was the act and mode of the Creator's entry into his own creation as Man among men.[15] Abstracted from the whole field of God's operations in creation and redemption, and considered merely in its individual aspect it can be given meaning only in a relation to other human births where they are all comparable, but seen in the con-

---

[14] 'It is indeed the relation of the creation to God that is illuminated by this awful mystery. We cannot see the relation, either of history or of nature, to the Father, except across the mystery of the Resurrection of Christ. Our thought of creation is rescued from abstraction when we see its fulfilment in the tomb of Christ, the birthplace of his glory, and the glory of his own'. D. M. MacKinnon, *The Resurrection* (ed. W. E. Purcell, 1966), p. 68. That is the context in which the Virgin Birth has such convincing meaning.

[15] Hence we have the same problem with the 'facticity' of the Virgin Birth, i.e. its relation to history, as we have with the 'facticity' of the resurrection. See Heinrich Vogel, *Gott im Christo*, 1951, pp. 642ff.; and also Karl Barth, *Church Dogmatics*, I/2, pp. 172ff.

tinuum of God's creative-redemptive work it is quite different.[16] Yet it is only when we see that the Creator Word is God, here at work creatively within the midst of the old creation, breaking its continuity in estrangement and beginning a new creation headed by the incarnate Son, that we really penetrate into its inner happening and understand it out of itself as *grace alone* in our midst. It is then seen to be proleptic to the resurrection of the dead, and building with it the birth of the new creation, which cannot be understood merely through tracing its connecting lines with the old creation but only through discerning the transformation of the old order into the new.

Before we can understand more fully the relation of the resurrection to the Person of Christ we shall have to examine the specific nature of the resurrection event, but meantime we may gather up the discussion so far by saying that *what Jesus Christ is in his resurrection, he is in himself.* The resurrection was not just an event that happened to Christ, for it corresponded to the kind of Person he was in his own Being. With the recognition of this complete consistency between the resurrection event and the essence of the resurrected One, comes the full realization that the whole life of Jesus Christ, together with his resurrection, was the manifestation among men in time and history of the ultimate and original and final creative activity of God. Although we may approach Christ by meeting him and seeking to understand him in his humanity, as soon as we confront him in the power of his resurrection our understanding of his humanity must be set within the fact of *the whole Christ*, as God manifest in the flesh, the Creator in our midst as human creature, come to effect the recreation of human nature from within its existence in space and time. Thus the relation of the resurrection to the Person of Christ discloses to us that it is *the whole Jesus Christ who is the content of the resurrection*, for all of his life from birth to resurrection forms an indissoluble unity.

[16] See the article by Dr. John Wilkinson, 'Apologetic Aspects of the Virgin Birth of Jesus Christ', *Scottish Journal of Theology*, 17. 2, 1964, pp. 159–81. It is probably the case that many of the difficulties that arise in connection with the Virgin Birth are basically due to a confusion in questions: biological questions will not yield theological answers, but only biological answers, but biological answers cannot as such be set against theological answers. While there are two levels of thought here, the biological and the theological, they must be coordinated, not confounded.

CHAPTER 3

THE RESURRECTION AND THE ATONING WORK OF CHRIST

Here we must bear in mind the full content of the doctrine of atonement and shall be concerned only with the place of the resurrection of Christ within it. We may consider this in relation to justification, reconciliation and redemption, leaving to the next chapter our examination of the nature of the resurrection as an event in space and time.

1. *The Resurrection and Justification*

Again and again the New Testament relates the resurrection to the divine act of forgiveness which is not just the non-imputation of our sins but a positive act of the divine mercy in which we are reinstated before God as though we had not sinned: forgiveness is a stupendous act which only God can do, blotting out what is past, and recreating what has been wasted by sin. As such forgiveness has two sides to it. From the side of God who forgives it is an act in which the Forgiver bears the cost and burden of forgiveness. The resurrection reveals that God himself was at work directly in Jesus Christ making himself responsible for our condition, and fulfilling it by bearing the cost of forgiveness in himself. Forgiveness is not just a word of pardon but a word translated into our existence by crucifixion and resurrection, by judgment and recreation. From the side of those who are forgiven, forgiveness means emancipation from the thraldom of guilt and reaffirmation as God's dear children in Jesus Christ. It means that the sinner's status *qua* sinner is rejected, and he is given freely the status of one who is pure and holy before God.

The relation between forgiveness and the resurrection may be seen in the evangelical account of the healing of the paralysed man who was let down through the roof into the house in order to be put in touch with Jesus (Mark 2: 1–12; Luke 5: 17–26). St. Mark, for example, tells us that Jesus at once said to the sick man, 'Son, your sins are forgiven', but, anticipating the objection that only God can forgive sins, he asked whether it was easier to say to the paralysed man 'Your sins are forgiven', or to say, 'Rise, take up your bed, and walk'. Then, after saying to the objectors 'in order that you may know that the Son of Man has power on earth to forgive sins', he turned to the paralysed man with the words, 'I say to you, Rise, take up your bed and go home'. And immediately the man was healed. It is highly significant that the resurrection term *egeiro* is used here, which reveals that the Early Church not only understood this incident as falling within the sphere of the power of the resurrection, but understood the relation of the resurrection to the forgiveness of sins after the pattern of these two words of Jesus – the word of miraculous healing demonstrating the divine power in the word of forgiveness, but disclosing at the same time that forgiveness reached its full reality in the healing and creative work of God upon the whole man. In other words, it is in the resurrection of Jesus Christ that all that God had to say about our forgiveness, and all that Jesus had said about forgiveness, became actualized in the same sphere of reality as that to which we belong. The word of pardon was fully enacted in our existence – that is why, once more, St. Paul could say that if Jesus Christ is not risen from the dead, then we are still in our sins, unforgiven and unshriven.

This is another way of saying that in justification God's No and God's Yes come together, for the resurrection is the fulfilment of the decisive deed of justification, in rejecting sin and the status of the sinner and in establishing the sinner once more as God's child. Justification is not only a declaratory act, but an actualization of what is declared. When Christ said to the paralysed man that his sins were forgiven, they *were forgiven* – as the word of healing made clear. It was not that the subsequent word of healing added something to the first word to make it complete, but rather that the full reality of the healing and recreating word spoken in forgiveness was manifested in the physical event of healing which followed the second word.

The resurrection tells us that when God declares a man just, that man *is* just. Resurrection means that the Word which God sent on his mission does not return to God void but accomplishes that for which he was sent.

When, therefore, the Protestant doctrine of justification is formulated only in terms of forensic imputation of righteousness or the non-imputation of sins in such a way as to avoid saying that to justify is to make righteous, it is the resurrection that is being by-passed. If we think of justification only in the light of the crucifixion as non-imputation of sins because of what Christ has borne for our sakes, then we have mutilated it severely. No doubt we can fill it out with more positive content by relating it to the incarnate life of Christ and to his active obedience, that is, fill it out with his positive divine-human righteousness – and that would be right, for then justification becomes not only the non-imputation of sins but the clothing of the sinner with the righteousness of Christ. Nevertheless, that would still be empty and unreal, merely a judicial transaction, unless the doctrine of justification bears in its heart a relation of real union with Christ. Apart from such a union with him through the power of his Spirit, as Calvin puts it, Christ would remain, as it were, inert or idle.[1] We require an active relation to Christ as our righteousness, an active and an actual sharing in his righteousness. This is possible only through the resurrection – when we approach justification in this light we see that it is a creative event in which our regeneration or renewal is already included within it.[2]

This is a point that must be taken much more seriously today. If justification is only a forensic or judicial act of imputation or non-imputation, then the resurrection is correspondingly an 'event' of the same kind. But if the resurrection is an actual event in the raising of Jesus Christ in the fullness of his humanity from corruption and death, then justification must correspondingly be a creative, regenerating event. A proper doctrine of justification and a proper doctrine of the

[1] John Calvin, *Institute*, 3. I. 1–4.
[2] See William Manson, *Jesus and the Christian*, pp. 144ff. And also Calvin, *op. cit.*, 3. 3. 9; 3. 11. 6ff.; cf. *Kingdom and Church. A Study in the Theology of the Reformation*, pp. 100ff.

resurrection hang together – when one is mutilated the other becomes attenuated. Regarded in this way, justification is a continuing act in Christ, in whom we are continuously being cleansed, forgiven, sanctified, renewed, and made righteous.[3]

Two questions have to be asked here, particularly about the Protestant account of justification. (i) Does there not lurk somewhere in the insistence that justification does not mean a making righteous, a Marcionite dichotomy between redemption and creation? But if we take seriously the fact that in Jesus Christ God's No to sin and evil and his Yes to creation come together, then how can we but expound justification in the unity of redemption and creation? No doubt we must also see this in the eschatological perspective, for there is certainly a time-lag, so far as duration in our space-time is concerned, between the resurrection of Christ the Head of the Body and of us who are members of his Body, yet we cannot without infidelity to the teaching of the New Testament push the fulfilment of the last things wholly into the future. Through the power of the Spirit we have union with the risen Christ here and now and in that union taste already the powers of the age to come. Certainly the New Testament frequently speaks of our resurrection in Christ in the aorist and perfect tenses, and not simply in the future tense, which must alter the perspective in which we tend to speak of justification.

(ii) Does the Protestant rejection of justification as meaning making righteous not imply some form of deistic dualism between God and the world – that is, a situation in which God is thought of as not interacting in any real way with nature or human existence? No doubt there is a kind of suspension between the Word of forgiveness and the actualization of forgiveness in the resurrection of the body, an eschatological suspension which the ascension of Christ makes us take seriously, yet once again we cannot forget the fact of Pentecost when the power of the risen Christ was poured out upon the Church and indeed upon 'all flesh'. This means that we are not left in history with only a dialectical relation between a 'Word of divine pardon' now and 'a Word of divine power' that is held over till the Last Day, but that here and now between the times through the power of the Spirit, who is

[3] See J. S. Stewart, *A Man in Christ*, pp. 133ff.

God himself present in the immediate energy of his divine Being, we are made to participate in the power of the resurrection, and God himself is at work creatively in our midst, regenerating, sanctifying and healing. It is this aspect of *realized justification* through the power of the resurrection that we have mediated to us in the Sacraments – Baptism being here the Sacrament of our once and for all justification, but Holy Communion being the Sacrament of our continuous partaking of the power of the risen Lord in anticipation of the new creation and the final resurrection of the body. Every kind of deistic dualism between God and our world is rejected by the resurrection of Christ.

This raises the question as to how far we are to think of the resurrection as an objective event in the physical and spiritual existence of human being in space and time. The old-fashioned deism which one still finds among positivists and humanists rejected the resurrection of Christ in body on the ground that it was not consonant with the way they regarded the whole relation between God and nature. But one must ask whether there are not other more concealed forms of deism which appear in reinterpretations of the resurrection which detach the dynamic acts of God from any objective and causal (i.e. in God's unique creative way) relation to physical worldly reality. Is it such a deism, for example, that lies behind G. W. H. Lampe's strange, ambivalent attitude to the resurrection of Jesus somehow as an event in the external world but one that has no objective content or empirical correlate?[4]

Quite evidently, the resurrection has become once again, as in the New Testament and early Church, an issue of supreme importance, for what is at stake in it all is the fundamental doctrine of God and the rationality of the Christian universe. As St. Paul expressed it, 'If Christ is not risen then our *kerygma* is empty (*kenon*) and your faith is vain (*mataia*). We are even found to be misrepresenting God' (1 Cor. 15: 14–15). As A. M.

---

[4] G. W. H. Lampe and D. M. MacKinnon, *The Resurrection. A Dialogue between two Cambridge Professors in a secular age* (ed. W. Purcell, 1966), pp. 8ff., 19ff., 30f., etc. St. Paul would not have been mocked in Athens (Acts 17: 32), nor have been thought mad by Festus (Acts 26: 25) when he spoke about the resurrection of Jesus, had he not meant the resurrection of the whole man leaving behind an empty grave.

Hunter has expressed it, 'If the story of Jesus ends there (at the Cross), then it is an unmitigated tragedy and – what is more – the supreme proof of the irrationality of the universe in which we live'.[5] It looks as if belief in the resurrection as real happening in our human existence, as objective act of God, within the space and time of our world, is once again the great dividing line between Christians in our own day.[6] The wholeness and integrity of the Gospel are surely at stake here, for our redemption stands or falls with the reality of the risen body of Jesus Christ. That is why acceptance or rejection of 'the empty tomb' is rightly felt to be so crucial, for it implies, as C. E. B. Cranfield has shown, the *wholeness* of our redemption in a *whole* Christ.[7]

2. *The Resurrection and Reconciliation*

Reconciliation between man and God through the initiative of God's grace is finally achieved and consummated in the resurrection where a bond of unity and love is forged in our actual existence which is everlasting and incorruptible. We may think of this in the light of what St. Paul has to say in Romans 8: 32ff. The union of God and man begun in the birth of Immanuel reaches throughout the incarnate life and work of Christ and is fully and finally achieved on man's side and on God's side in the crucifixion and resurrection of Jesus Christ. That union of divine love has been inserted into our existence in Christ, and now that it has survived death and judgment in the resurrection, it remains final and complete, which nothing in heaven or earth can or will undo. Two primary aspects of that fall to be considered.

[5] A. M. Hunter, *The Work and Words of Jesus*, 1950, p. 123.

[6] Cf. in this respect the powerful work of W. Künneth, *The Theology of the Resurrection*, and his attack upon 'existentialist interpretation' and 'mythifying' of the resurrection; and the incisive questions put by Karl Barth to Rudolf Bultmann's reduction of the resurrection to 'the Easter faith of the first disciples', *Church Dogmatics*, III/1, pp. 445ff.

[7] 'The Empty Tomb certainly implies that it was a whole Christ who died for us and that it is the whole Christ who lives for evermore; that He came to redeem us as whole men, not just a part of us; that the body is part of the human personality; and that contempt for the body and the physical is also contempt for the Creator.' *Scottish Journal of Theology*, vol. 5, 1952, p. 404.

(i) The resurrection brings the contradiction between God and man to an end. The resurrection is the fulfilment of the divine judgment enacted in the crucifixion, and as such is the completed act of God's righteousness.[8] Here we are back again in the relation between the resurrection and justification, but the aspect of that which concerns us here, and which overlaps with reconciliation, is the fact that all enmity between man and God has been brought to an end. The relations of Holy God with sinful man have run their course in such a way that man, judged and condemned by God on the Cross because of his sins, is by the same God justified and raised up, made to stand before God in complete righteousness and peace as his dear son. That took place in Jesus Christ himself in the whole course of his life from birth to death, but in his resurrection Jesus Christ has carried through to its completion the relations of God and man in such a way that there is now no longer any barrier between God and man – enmity is utterly abolished. Communion with God in the resurrection is restored in the fullest and most positive reconciliation. Atonement without resurrection would not be reconciliation and without reconciliation atonement had not reached its proper end in union with the Father, in peace. It is thus the resurrection of our human nature in Christ into communion with the life of God that is the end and goal of atonement.

We may state this in another way. Resurrection means that the steadfastness of the love of God in giving himself to man in spite of judgment and condemnation is a steadfastness that has achieved its end. The resurrection means that God's covenant mercies have triumphed over all the contradiction and separation of evil and their judgment by the holy love of God. God's will of love to give himself unreservedly to man has persisted through the midst of judgment and death and is fully and finally made good in the resurrection (Rom. 8: 32f., 35f.). But the resurrection also means that the steadfastness of the Son of Man is such that it held on its way in utter obedience to the Father in the spirit of holiness in the midst of judgment, death and hell, and in spite of them, so that he raised himself up from the dead in perfect Amen to the Father's Will,

[8] This is the theme which Karl Barth expounds under the rubric 'The Verdict of the Father', *Church Dogmatics*, IV/1, pp. 283–357.

acquiescing in his verdict upon our sin but responding in complete trust and love to the Father. The resurrection is the goal of the steadfast obedience of the Son of Man in answer to the steadfast love of the Father.

God would not have been true to himself had he allowed Jesus to see corruption. Jesus would not have been true to God had he not risen above judgment and therefore out of the grave in complete agreement with the Father, for that would have meant that he had failed in his holiness. The Amen of the Cross was not just an act of infinite resignation on Jesus' part to the Father's Will; it was positive and affirmative fulfilment, and the resurrection is the complete Amen of the Son to the Father as of the Father to the Son.[9] Resurrection means, therefore, that the work of Christ in life and death, his sub-stitutionary and representative obedience unto death, is perfectly efficacious and sufficient, both from the side of God and from the side of man. In summary: the resurrection means that the divine act of reconciliation reaches its com-pletion and end and that apart from the resurrection, reconcilia-tion would prove a hollow fiasco, for separation between man and God would have remained in force.

(ii) It is with the resurrection that the *I am* of God is fully actualized among us – the *Ego eimi* of God to man, of God in man, and so of man in Christ to God.[10] As Jesus is reported to have said in the Fourth Gospel, 'I am the resurrection and the life'. In this *I am* of the risen Lord the atonement becomes abiding and enduring fact, and reconciliation becomes eter-nally valid and eternally living reality between God and man. In the *I am* of the resurrection the atonement is not just an act of judgment, but *active truth in the form of personal Being* – Truth

---

[9] Cf. D. M. MacKinnon, *The Resurrection* (with G. W. H. Lampe), 9, 65, who speaks of the resurrection as 'the Father's Amen to the work of Christ. But that Amen is not word; it is deed. For he is raised. And by his Resurrection an eternity is bestowed upon his work. *Tetelestai; Consum-matum est.* According to the Fourth Evangelist this was his last word upon the Cross as he received the vinegar and gave up the ghost. And that, his finished work, abides. By the Resurrection the very stuff of Christ's self-oblation perfected in death is given a universal contemporaneity. More, it becomes the ultimate context of all our lives'.

[10] See William Manson, 'The EGO EIMI of the Messianic Presence in the New Testament', *Jesus and the Christian*, pp. 174–83.

as the Lord Christ, Atonement as identical with his Person in action, Reconciliation as the living and everlasting union of God and man in Christ. This is the great message that keeps bursting through the *Apocalypse*, 'I am he who lives, and was dead, and behold I am alive for evermore'. Reconciliation is identical with the living and personal Being of the Mediator and as such marches through the ages and is present in the midst of all world affairs, meeting us there in its final destinies. Through the Cross all that was wrought out in the incarnation issues into eternal and prevalent reality, for it is anchored in Jesus Christ in the Being of God himself. Thus the resurrection is the final and eternal concretion of all that was done for us in the life and death of Jesus Christ, so that *he is our peace*, and *he is our reconciliation*. He is the living Atonement or Reconciliation in the form of personal Being and Reality in God.

The implications of this are very far-reaching for our understanding of the whole Gospel, but we may note several corollaries which can serve to bring out its significance.

The resurrection of Christ, and of us in Christ, carries with it the doctrine of our *adoption* or *sonship* through Christ. 'Blessed be the God and Father of our Lord Jesus Christ, who according to his abundant mercy has begotten us again unto a lively hope by the resurrection of Jesus Christ from the dead, to an inheritance incorruptible and undefiled, and that does not fade away, reserved in heaven for you, who are kept by the power of God through faith [i.e. God's faithfulness which calls for answering faith from us] unto salvation ready to be revealed in the last time' (1 Peter 1: 3f.). In Pauline language, we have not received the spirit of bondage but of adoption, in which we pray to God as our Father, for we have been constituted joint heirs with Christ, who is the first-born among many brethren (Romans 8: 14–17, 29). Our human nature is now set within the Father-Son relationship of Christ. Through faith in Christ and union with him we share brotherhood with him and so share with him the Fatherhood of God, and in and through him we share in the one Spirit of the living God. It is essentially the same teaching which we find in the Fourth Gospel, in the 'high-priestly' prayer of the Son to the Father for his own, as reported in the 17th chapter, and again in the Epistle to the Hebrews where we hear of the Son who having

been made like unto his brethren ascends to the Father as their
representative and high priest, presenting them to the Father
as sons consecrated through his own self-offering. In both
those writings we are told that through the consecrated bonds
of our union with Christ we are made to share in the union of
the Son with the Father.

It is not surprising that this could be spoken of as the exaltation of man to be a partaker of the life and love that God is, and
and thereby to be a partaker of divine nature. To think clearly
of this we must not divorce our understanding of the resurrection from that of the ascension in which our human nature
in Jesus Christ is exalted to the right hand of God. But even
with the resurrection itself it is made clear that in Jesus Christ
man is assumed into the divine life embodied in him. The
relation of Jesus Christ to God is unique, for he is God the Son
in the unity of the Holy Trinity, but the resurrection of our
human nature in him implies a reconciliation or oneness with
God which is not identity, yet a real sharing in the union of the
incarnate Son with the Father, through a sharing not only in
his human nature but in the life and love of God embodied
in him. In him the Godhead dwells bodily, and it is out of his
incarnate fullness that we receive, but by grace. Let us recall
here the threefold distinction in union and communion of
which Patristic theology used to speak: (a) the *consubstantial
communion* between the Father and the Son *in the Holy Spirit*
who is Love, the Love that God is; (b) the *hypostatic union* between the divine and human natures in the one Person of
Christ which takes place through the operation of the Holy
Spirit who is the Love of God; and (c) the *communion* or
koinonia of the Spirit who is mediated to us from the Father
through the Son, and who is the Love of God poured into our
hearts. It is in virtue of our union with Christ by the power of
the Spirit that in and through him we are made to partake
of the very Love which God himself is, and are thus partakers
of the divine nature. The same statements may be made with
respect to the Life of God which in the Incarnation and Resurrection has come down to us and is imparted to us in Christ.

It is in the resurrection that we are to understand fully the
fact that Jesus Christ is himself the Truth – 'I am the Truth'.
It is as incarnate Son risen that Jesus Christ remains Truth,

uncreated Truth and created truth in one. He is not simply the eternal Logos of God, but that Logos become flesh, full of grace and truth, not simply Word of God addressed to man, but answering word of man addressed to God in the unity of his one Person. We must think likewise of Christ as the Truth of God, but Truth in such a way that there is in him hypostatic union between the Truth of God and the answering truth of man, the Truth of the Creator and created truth together in the form of his incarnate and personal Being. Jesus Christ is the actualization of the Truth of God among us in such a way that it creates its own counterpart in us to itself, Truth from the side of God and truth from the side of man in inseparable union. As such Jesus Christ constitutes the bridge between the reality of God and the realities of our world, the connection between the transcendent Rationality of God and the created rationalities of this world. He is thus the centre in our midst where the Reality and Word of God are translated into human reality and word and where we human beings may know and speak of God without having to transcend our creaturely forms of thought and speech. It is in and through Jesus Christ therefore that we creatures of space and time may know God the Father, in such a way as to think and speak truly and validly of him, even in such a way that the forms of our thought and speech really terminate objectively on God himself in his own ultimate Being and Reality.

Apart from the resurrection we could not say this. If the resurrection did not take place, then not only is there a final disjunction between God's Word and God's Act, e.g. in the forgiveness of our sins, but inevitably a final disjunction between our acts of knowing and the reality of God himself, or between our statements about God and their objective referent in God. God is certainly greater than we can ever conceive, so that we cannot but reckon with an infinite discrepancy between our human forms of thought and speech and God himself in his transcendent and ineffable Majesty, but the resurrection of the incarnate Son means that God has consummated in Christ such a union between our humanity and himself, and therefore between our human forms of thought and speech as they come to articulation in Christ and himself, that in and through Jesus Christ we may yet know God in his reality beyond ourselves. The whole epistemic function of the incarnation thus comes to its complete fruition in the resurrection of Christ in the fullness of his humanity.

It was for this reason that the early Christians were so concerned in their debates with docetic and gnostic thinkers to insist that the Word became *flesh* and that Jesus Christ arose from the dead in the flesh – in the concrete reality of his human and physical existence.[11] Docetic and gnostic thinkers operated with a radical dichotomy between the realm of God and the realm of this world which meant that the forms of thought and speech that we use in this world to speak of God must be treated as merely symbolic, for God in himself is beyond our knowledge. We do not know what he is but only know what he is not, as Basilides expressed it. That is to say, our cognition does not rest upon any objective ground in God and our statements about him do not terminate upon his reality, but are to be regarded as detached expressions in the realm of myth and ritual. In this way of thinking resurrection is merely the same sort of symbol which we find in the Euripidean play about Alcestis but which does not correspond with reality, although it may play a role in man's dramatic self-understanding and self-expression in face of the mysterious world of what is 'Wholly Other'. The resurrection taken as the New Testament and the Early Church understood it, however, means that God has established a real bond between his reality and ours in this world. In Jesus Christ he has made his divine reality to intersect and overlap with ours, so that we in Jesus Christ may actually and truly know God and have communion with him without having to take leave of the realm of our own thisworldly existence. The resurrection is therefore our pledge that statements about God in Jesus Christ have an objective reference in God, and are not just projections out of the human

[11] See Ignatius, *Epist. to the Smyrnaeans*, 3. 1–3, 7. 1, 12. 2; Hermas, *Similitudes*, V. 6, 7; 2 *Clement*, 6, 6, 9. 1–5; Justin Martyr, *De resurrectione*, 8–10; Irenaeus, *Adv. haereses*, II, 44. 1 (Harvey, vol. I, p. 360); IV. 31. 4 (vol. II, p. 204); V. 2. 1 (p. 318); V. 15. 1 (p. 364); V. 31. 1–2 (p. 411f.); *Fragmenta* XII (Harvey, II, p. 481f.). The two works of Tertullian, *De carne Christi*, and *De resurrectione carnis*, together constitute a powerful witness to the fact that the Apostles' Creed and the baptismal creeds which confess belief in the *resurrection of the flesh* represent a considerable force of tradition in the Church.

heart and imagination, objectifying forms of thought in which we fashion a God in terms of the creaturely content of our own ideas.

The discrepancy between the Reality of God and this-worldly reality which is overcome in the resurrection is not to be thought of simply in terms of the Creator-creature relation, for God continually interacts with what he has made, but rather in terms of the sin and estrangement which have infected both man's relation to God and his relation to himself. The creaturely distance of man from the Creator and the separation of man from God due to his sinful rebellion and self-imprisonment in guilt, are fully overcome in the incarnation and the atonement. That is what is revealed in the resurrection of Jesus Christ from the dead which is itself the final establishment of the bridge between God and man on both sides of the chasm that divides them. The resurrection reveals that the disjunction between God and man is that which has been created by sin and guilt, a disjunction so great that it could be overcome only by God himself stepping into the breach and bridging the chasm through his own Being in the staggering act of incarnation and atonement. But as such the resurrection reveals that what divides man from God is not the discrepancy between the finite and the infinite, since God is not limited by man's incapacities and weaknesses, although that discrepancy does become a real disjunction for us when it is infected by sin and guilt and enmity. The resurrection demonstrates not only that all division has been removed in atoning reconciliation, but that atoning reconciliation has achieved its end in the new creation in which God and man are brought into such communion with one another that the relations of man with God in being and knowing are healed and fully established. Thus the resurrection of Jesus Christ from the dead sets us in the situation where knowing the truth about God and doing the truth in human existence can be and are valid, for in Jesus Christ a genuine congruence has been established between created truth and the uncreated Truth of God.

Since that is the case there is very good reason for agreeing with Karl Barth's designation of the resurrection as the starting-point for a scientific theology. It is basically the same point made by Walter Künneth in concluding his work on the reality and meaning of the resurrection. '*The raising of the Christ is the* act of God, whose significance is not to be compared with any event before or after. *It is the primal datum of theology, from which there can be no abstracting,* and the normative presupposition for every valid dogmatic judgment and for the meaningful construction of a Christian theology. Thus *the resurrection of Jesus becomes the Archimedean point for theology* as such, not derivable from empirical reflection, and established beyond any religious *a priori.* All theological statements are oriented in one way or another towards this focal point. There is no Christian knowledge of God which does not acquire its ultimate fullness and depth from a revelation of God in the Risen One.'[12]

3. *The Resurrection and Redemption*

In its connection with redemption resurrection is seen to be the redemption of the *whole man.* Redemption means the emancipation of man from his bondage and corruption under judgment, his restoration from that condition in which his being is menaced and undermined by death and degenerating into nothingness. Man's very being has become forfeit, and it lapses away from him, crumbling down into the dust, so that his experience is a hovering between being and non-being, between being and rejected being. In that condition he becomes the prey of the forces of evil and darkness, but redemption is the deliverance of man out of all darkness, death and destruction, into light, life and being. When redemption is conceived in terms of resurrection, then we are concerned with the restoration of man in the fullness and integrity of his human being, including the emancipation of his body. It is in the resurrection of the Man Jesus Christ, the Man in whom our nature is assumed and healed, that this kind of redemption is achieved and set forth. Or to express it otherwise, resurrection as redemption means the restoration of man in all the fullness of his *humanity,* for it is redemption out of corruption and the lapse toward annihilation into the new being and new life of the new creation. That is why the early Church laid

[12] W. Künneth, *The Theology of the Resurrection,* p. 294.

such emphasis upon the resurrection of the *flesh*, for it meant the redemption of man's *perishable* form of existence.[13]

The source and heart of this is the redemption of Jesus Christ himself – *his* redemption from the grave, from judgment, damnation and perdition into which he entered through his identification with us, thereby staking his own being, as it were, and hazarding his own existence, for us and our salvation. What does the resurrection of Jesus Christ mean? As Athanasius used to insist, the resurrection must be understood in accordance with the nature and work of Christ – *kata physin*, in accordance with the nature of the One who rose from the dead. If Jesus Christ rose from the dead, then the 'rose again' must be understood as determined by the nature of the Subject of that event, Christ himself. Who is he?

He was the Word of God made flesh, the Word by whom and through whom all things are made that are made, the Creator Logos. The whole life of Jesus, the Word made flesh, is creative life within our fallen and corrupt existence – it is recreative. The resurrection of Jesus Christ in body cannot be separated, therefore, from the resurrection of Jesus in his incarnate actuality out of our mortal and corrupt humanity, where we are dead in trespasses and sins. The very existence of Jesus in history is sheer miracle; his human life in its sinlessness and perfection is itself resurrection, and is in itself the passing of the old into the new. The resurrection of Jesus out of the grave after the crucifixion is thus the same event as the human and historical life of Jesus but now taking place out of the depth of our corruption where corruption is finalized and fixed in death. Or to put it in another way, Jesus is in himself the hypostatic union of the Creator and the creature – it is as such that he deliberately allowed himself to be put to death in order to invade the last stronghold of evil, in the finality and ultimateness of its incarceration of us in death, and as

[13] It is in this way, as St. Augustine pointed out (*Enchiridion*, 91) that one must interpret the words of St. Paul 'flesh and blood cannot inherit the kingdom of God; neither does corruption inherit incorruption' (1 Cor. 15: 50). He notes in the same passage that even after the resurrection the body of Christ was called 'flesh' (Luke 24: 39). Similar interpretations of 1 Cor. 15: 50 are given by Irenaeus, *Adv. haereses*, V. 9. 3, and Tertullian, *De resurrectione carnis*, 50. For a modern interpretation on similar lines see J. Jeremias, *New Testament Studies*, 2. 3, 1956, pp. 151-9.

such that he broke out of it, shattering the bands of death.

Is the resurrection to be regarded, then, as an interruption of what is called 'the natural order'? Is it an intrusion into the natural processes of this world that passes away? Does it import some sort of 'infringement of natural law'? The difficulty with a resurrection of that kind is that there is no consistency between it and the nature of the resurrected One, but it is entirely different with the kind of resurrection to which the New Testament bears witness when it speaks of the resurrection of Jesus Christ.

Let us recall how people reacted to his miraculous acts in the Gospel accounts. Who is this man? What kind of person is he? They were utterly astounded at what was going on, and the language that the Evangelists use to describe their reactions is the language normally employed to speak of what happens in an earthquake, for they were amazed, stunned, alarmed, bewildered at the nature of the events that took place wherever Jesus went and taught and acted. Yet they were confronted by the fact that in Jesus the Person and the Deed corresponded perfectly with one another. They were faced with the sheer simplicity and consistency and unity of Jesus, who was transparently in himself the person revealed in his acts, and whose acts were entirely at one with his essential nature as person. Thus the very question they asked, Who is he? was a question prompted by the astounding consistency between person and event. It arose out of consequential thinking, thinking *kat'akolouthian* and *kata physin*, to use again the language of Athanasius. The same thing happened when the astounding events of Easter overtook the world. The actual resurrection of Jesus from the tomb was recognized to be in entire accordance with his nature and person – but that was the stupendous thing about it. This was not just a miracle, not some wonderful event or portent, but something which in all its wonderfullness was not a whit different from the essential nature of the risen one in himself. And what is more, it corresponded to the claim of Jesus, as given in the Johannine literature: '*I am the re-resurrection and the life*'. '*I am the truth*' (John 11: 25; 14:6). He is in himself the reality of the resurrection and the new life that breaks out of death through it. He is the Creator-God among men, at work even in the midst of death and corruption and perdition and nothingness.

With the recognition of this utter consistency between the resurrection event and the essence of resurrected One, came the full realization that the whole life of Jesus, together with his resurrection, was the manifestation among men and on earth and in time of the ultimate and original and final creative activity of God. That is precisely why the resurrection is so baffling to thought and observation.

Let us consider what it means to think of the creation. In natural science we are concerned with the observations of the processes of nature, with the events of the created order, but in the nature of the case we do not and cannot observe the event of creation itself – the process of creating or of being created. Even if creation continuously goes on all the time as some people would have it, on the outer fringes of the universe, millions and millions of light years away, as far as we may receive radio signals, it cannot be detected by any kind of 'observation'. We often speak in natural science of 'observation' metaphorically, of course, when we talk of the kind of detection and discovery we make through the employment of electronic instruments, but that is beside the point. In the nature of the case it is not possible to observe in any way whatsoever those processes through which whatever is created comes into being out of nothing, for then we would have to get behind the creaturely processes in order to observe them – but that is quite impossible and self-contradictory. You can no more observe the very processes by which the observable comes into observation than you can picture how a picture pictures what it pictures, or state in statements how statements are related to what is stated. Yet we make statements about created entities, and we observe created processes, and explore creaturely events. Thus the idea that creation or resurrection would be the interruption of the natural order is an idea that it is only possible to think, on the assumption that the event of creation, or the event of coming into being, is the same sort of event as other events or processes of things that have already come into being. The natural laws by which we bring the connections immanent in nature to expression are all formed *a posteriori*, as *post hoc* features of nature; they cannot be predicted *a priori* or imposed prescriptively upon nature. Natural laws do not apply at all to those processes by which what is

nature came into being, but only to those observable processes
of a nature that already is in being. Creation itself is something quite different from what can be caught in that kind of
formulation. Far from being an interruption of the processes
of nature, creation is the manifestation of the creative source
of created reality and its immanent order. It is creative activity
itself breaking through and manifesting itself within the events
of the created world. That is the kind of creative happening
that we meet in the resurrection. By its very nature it is no
more observable than creation as such, yet it is just as factual
and real as creation. We cannot observe the creative processes but we may observe the created reality. Nor can we
observe the resurrecting processes, but we may (or will be
able to) observe the resurrected actuality of Jesus Christ – for
here too we are concerned with creation, although it is new
creation: not creation out of nothing but new creation out of
the old order. This brings its further problems, for it means
that we cannot apprehend the resurrected reality within the
frame of the old order, as if it were not after all a new creation
but were continuous with the old creation, comparable to it,
and apprehensible entirely within the connections of the old
order.[14] It stands to reason that it must be known in accordance with its own nature, out of itself – but this does mean
that we have to think through its relations with the whole
order of space and time as we have it in our on-going world.
We shall turn to that later.

Meantime let us consider this in relation to the redemptive
content of the resurrection, in the consistency between the act
and the person of the Mediator who rose again from the dead.
We recall that the resurrection brings the contradiction between God and man to a final end: here we have not only the
rejection of the status of the sinner but the affirmation of man
who had sinned as indeed God's own creature, and the making
good of God's Word in creation that the creature is good, in
face of all the sin and evil that have contradicted it. This is
the point we have already discussed in the justification of
Jesus, and of his being raised for our justification, the fact that
in the resurrection God's Yes is finalized in and through the

[14] This is the kind of argument already put forward by Cyril of Alexandria, *Commentary on St. John's Gospel*, bk. 12. 1, on John 20: 19f.

No of his resistance to all corruption, evil and death. It is in the resurrection, then, that the ultimate content and purpose of atonement and reconciliation come to fruition and to view – in the recreation of man in communion with God. This involves the restoration of true creaturehood to man, the affirmation of man in the fullness of his human existence and reality. *This is the ontological side of redemption, the healing and restoring of being in relation to the creative Source of all being.* The resurrection means that as applied to man the term *is* now has new meaning, and has meaning in objective depth for us, in a profounder reality than ever we had or were aware of before. As Athenagoras argued in the second century, apart from the resurrection, and its link with the creation, man could not survive as man.[15] The resurrection is the actualization of human reality, the humanizing in Jesus of dehumanized man, the establishing of the fact that man *is* – the end of all illusion, and all existentialist philosophies of nothingness, the end of all futility and the void, of all *mē on* (negated being) and the *mataiotēs* (vanity) bound up with it.[16] Now on the ground of the resurrection, and its final rejection of all contradiction between God and man, and therefore in its rejection of all negation of being in judgment, we can really believe that *man is*, that man is man. He is the creature God made him to be and may not now cease to be what he is. He is man in living communion with the creative Source of life. The resurrection of Jesus Christ and of human nature in him is therefore the foundation and source of a profound and radically new Christian humanism.

Thus the resurrection means that the Word which God sent forth in creation, and sent forth in a new way in the incarnation, did not return void but accomplished what it was sent to do (Cf. Is. 55: 11; Ps. 33: 9.) In creation and the affirmation of creation, in recreation and the finalizing of creation, the resurrection is the establishing of the creature in a reality that does not crumble away into the dust or degenerate into nothingness or slip into the oblivion of the past. This is a reality that arises

[15] Athenagoras, *De resurrectione*, 13. 2 and 15. 6.

[16] Redemption from dissolution into non-being and irrationality is one of the recurring themes in the twin treatises of Athanasius, *Contra gentes*, and *De incarnatione*, but the primary emphasis is on the incarnation rather than the resurrection.

and endures, for it is positively and faithfully grounded in its own ultimate source of reality in God.

This was the point of Athenagoras' statement which we have just cited. It was the point of the early Church's unrelenting struggle against all forms of Mandaean and Oriental religion, and all forms of Gnosticism, and also of Neoplatonism – against the idea, in whatever form it arose, that man's actuality as man, as creature in a creaturely world, is ephemeral, that he must vanish away with all the changes and chances of fleeting time. And so against the view that man's existence in space and time is ultimately unreal and but a shadowy evanescent phenomenon, the Christian Church asserted with all its strength the resurrection of the body or the resurrection of the flesh, i.e. the resurrection of man in his actuality as man, as creature of God in space and time. And therein it affirmed the reality of God's creation even for God, as well as the reality of God for the creation. The Christian Church is still concerned with this same problem when faced with Buddhism or Hinduism, but also concerned with it, although in a more superficial and less spiritual way, in the teaching of many so-called or would-be 'avant-garde' theologians for whom the resurrection of Jesus in body, and therefore the resurrection of believers in the body, is strangely abhorrent. Behind all this, however, as the early Church saw so clearly in its own day and in its own opponents, is the sheer horror that people of this kind have for *the being and action of God himself in space and time.*[17]

From this point of view the emphasis of the early Church upon *physis* (the real nature of things, or simply 'reality') and upon thinking *kata physin* (in accordance with the real nature of things), or what we might call 'cataphysic thinking', is entirely understandable, for it meant the rejection in the most downright way of all thinking in terms of abstract 'possibilities' in favour of thinking in terms of concrete realities or actualities. That is to say, early Christian theologians applied to God the same principle which the Alexandrian scientists employed when they allowed the real nature (*physis*) of what they were investigating to determine the proper way in which to think about it, for that was, they held, the only true or real way to think scientifically (*epistēmonikōs*). To think properly or

---

[17] See Karl Barth, *Church Dogmatics*, I/2, p. 130f.

worthily of God, we must think of him in accordance with his real nature as God, the Creator of heaven and earth, of all things invisible and visible, and who gave what he had created its own creaturely reality. But to think of God as present and active in our world of space and time we must think concretely in accordance with the real nature of the physical universe as well. Hence they developed appropriate ways of thinking of God in his relation to the world he had made, so as to take seriously his transcendence over the world of space and time, on the one hand, and yet to take seriously on the other hand the concrete realities of our physical existence in space and time in which God is pleased to be present and to act, without in any way abrogating them. And so classical Christian theology was able to remain faithful to the immense emphasis of the Bible upon the concrete, physical reality of man in the world, and to do justice to what the Christian Gospel has to say about *sōma* (body), *sarx* (flesh), *thanatos* (death), *zoē* (life), *anastasis* (resurrection), etc., for they understood well the message of the Gospel in affirming both the reality of God for the creation and the reality of the creation even for God. In all that, the resurrection of the flesh or of the body was both central and essential. 'If there is no resurrection, human nature is no longer genuinely human.'[18] It was thus Christian faith in the resurrection that differentiated Christian thought so sharply from all Hellenic or Oriental dualism which had a horror of bringing God into such a relation with concrete physical reality as the flesh or body of the incarnate and resurrected Son of God.

Quite evidently, behind the difficulty which many modern people seem to have with the resurrection lies the same horror of *physis*, the same horror of thinking of God in relation to the concrete realities of our world of space and time, and the same horror of all corporeality and externality in the biblical message. That helps to explain why they fail to understand what the Christian Gospel has to say when it speaks about *sōma*, *sarx*, *thanatos*, *zoē*, *anastasis*, etc. But to reject this for the thin air of abstract moral judgments or the repetition of existential decisions, or the morbid fascination for self-understanding, or even neurotic fixations on physical and subjective states, is in

[18] Athenagoras, *De resurrectione*, 15. 6.

point of fact to take the road of human suicide, the rejection of the sheer humanness of man and all his down-to-earth existence. If there is no resurrection, human nature is no longer genuinely human. Since man is the concrete reality he is, resurrection of man in the nature of the case can be only *bodily resurrection* – any 'resurrection' that is not bodily is surely a contradiction in terms.[19] Here above all, we must avoid engaging in any kind of 'double-think'.[20]

The New Testament writers are indubitably clear, as William Milligan pointed out long ago, that the resurrection is to be understood only in association with his death, for they constitute a unity of the closest kind; if the former is to be thought of as only 'spiritual', the latter must be equally so.[21] The argument ran: as death came by *man*, so also by *man* came the resurrection of the dead, for while they were convinced that in the resurrection of Jesus there had broken into their world an activity and power of a divine order, they were no less convinced that it took place within their world of flesh and bone, of human and physical being (before the gates of Jerusalem in the days of Tiberius Caesar). Quite evidently, their accounts of that are presented in rather fragmentary and sometimes in incongruous forms, with indications of imaginative embroidery, reflecting the startling and indescribable nature of what had taken place, but they are nevertheless clearly at one in reflecting the basic conviction that the resurrection of Jesus was bodily and historical fact. As Karl Barth has expressed it, 'None of the authors ever even dreamed, for

---

[19] Thus Tertullian, *Against Marcion*, V. 9. Cf. Karl Barth: 'The statement that Christ is risen necessarily implies the assertion that a dead man is alive again and that his grave is empty'. *Church Dogmatics*, IV/2, p. 149

[20] 'Double-thinking' in regard to the resurrection is made easier when the biblical teaching is interpreted within a dualist structure of thought, e.g. St. Augustine's 'two resurrections', that of the mind and that of the 'flesh', *Homily XIX on St. John's Gospel*, Eng. tr. *Library of the Fathers*, vol. 1, pp. 293ff., 305ff. *Homily XXIII*, pp. 354ff.

[21] William Milligan, *The Resurrection of our Lord*, p. 8. Cf. also here James Denney, with reference to 1 Cor. 15: 3ff., 'The mention of the burial is important in this connection as defining what is meant by the rising. . . . The rising is relative to the grave and the burial, and if we cannot speak of a bodily resurrection we should not speak of a resurrection at all'. *Jesus and the Gospel*, p. 113. Contrast R. Bultmann, *The Gospel of John*, pp. 688–97.

example, of reducing the event to "the rise of the Easter faith of the first disciples" '.[22] And latent in the basic witness, as St. Paul discerned, lay embedded the argument that if the resurrection of Jesus is not actual and historical reality, then the powers of sin and death and non-being remain unconquered and unbroken and we are still in the bondage of death. That is not an idea that could have been anticipated, but once the resurrection took place it yielded as part of its intelligible reality a circle of ideas within which the empirical event of the resurrection was understood and appropriated.[23] Everything in the Christian Gospel, now regarded in the light of Easter, was seen to pivot finally upon the *empty tomb* – that Jesus arose in body, arose as very man in the fullness and integrity of his human nature, but human nature which through the Spirit of holiness had been stripped of corroding forces of corruption and clad in the incorruptible garment of deathlessness.[24] And so after Easter there is something like a history of the risen Jesus who came and went among the disciples, who spoke and ate and drank with them as he willed, in such a way that he could be touched and seen to be no apparition, but above all it was the *personal self-identification of the familiar Jesus* that was the paramount factor: that is surely the importance and yet baffling nature of the forty days before Pentecost.[25] Cer-

[22] Karl Barth, *Church Dogmatics*, III/1, p. 452.

[23] Künneth, *op. cit.*, p. 91 points out that all the gospel reports attest the empty tomb, and that this is inseparably bound up with the message of the resurrection and as specific 'Easter Gospel' is rooted in the faith of the primitive Church. The empty tomb cannot be identified with the primal miracle of the resurrection, but is that aspect of it which faces towards history, which is 'the strongest expression of the Easter message's concern with the concrete, bodily resurrection and at the same time the clear safeguard against every spiritualizing tendency to evaporate the central declaration of the resurrection' (p. 97). See further, C. E. B. Cranfield, *St. Mark* 16: 1–8, 'The Empty Tomb', *Scottish Journal of Theology*, vol. 5, 1952, pp. 398ff.; and his *Commentary on the Gospel according to St. Mark*, 3rd edit. 1966, pp. 462ff.

[24] Cf. the remarkable circularity of the argument of 1 Cor. 15: 13–17: 'But if there is no resurrection of the dead, neither has Christ been raised ... and if Christ has not been raised, your faith is in vain; you are yet in your sins'.

[25] Cf. Emil Brunner, *Eternal Hope*, Eng. tr. 1954, p. 144f.; and Karl Barth, *Church Dogmatics*, IV/2, pp. 144ff.

tainly it is of the risen Jesus that the New Testament bears witness, Jesus unveiled in his divine glory, but nevertheless in the midst of all that quite indescribable sublimity and light, 'one like unto the *Son of Man*' (Rev. 1: 13).

Before the resurrection, Jesus, Son of God incarnate, had lived on earth, not 'in the form of God', not snatching at divine power, not calling in 'supernature' to help him out of the weaknesses of our nature which he had made his own, not therefore in the condition of his transcendent glory as eternal Son of God which he had with the Father before the world was, but after the manner of man and in the form and existence of the humble servant he had become in subjection to law. After the resurrection he lived among us on earth in the mode of the exalted Son of God, yet in his nature as man, now victorious and triumphant man, in the midst of history – that is, in the same sphere of reality as that to which we belong, although in this same sphere he lived as New Man, man of the new creation, man therefore who could not be confined or held down under the sin-infected and guilt-laden structures of the old creation any more than new wine could be confined within old wine-skins. As New Man he stands beyond the corrupting processes of this passing age, on the other side of death and perdition, beyond the final judgment, even while he lived amongst men after the resurrection, talked with them, communed with them, and, as the Evangelists report, ate with them, to show that he was no ghost but real, physical human being.[26] How are we to understand all this, the life of the risen Jesus in the fullness of the new Creation, yet in the fullness of time in the context of real human being? How are we to think of the relation between this new order of being and the order of this world which passes away, the new humanity

---

[26] Thus John of Damascus, *De fide orthodoxa*, IV. 1: 'Although he did taste food after the resurrection, yet he did not do so because it was a law of his nature (for he felt no hunger) but in the way of economy, in order that he might convince us of the reality of the resurrection, and that it was one and the same flesh which suffered and rose again'. See also IV. 27. The same point had been made earlier by Cyril of Alexandria, that Christ took food not to nourish his body but the faith of the disciples, *Commentary on St. John's Gospel*, bk. 12. 1, on John 20. 28. Cf. even Bultmann on this, *The Gospel of John*, Eng. tr. 1971, p. 710, with reference to Luke 24: 42f., which is intended to demonstrate 'the real corporeality of the Risen Christ'.

inaugurated by Christ in his resurrection and our humanity that continues within on-going space-time? What is the nature of the resurrection event, and how are we to apprehend it within the conceptualities of which we necessarily partake in a world that still awaits the consummation of all things?

CHAPTER 4

THE NATURE OF THE RESURRECTION EVENT

The resurrection of Jesus is an event that happens within history in continuity with the living event of the whole historical existence of Jesus, yet as an event of fulfilled redemption the resurrection issues in a new creation beyond the corruptible processes of this world, on the other side of decay and death, and on the other side of judgment, in the fullness of a new world and of a new order of things. How can we think these things together?

We recall the Pauline and Patristic teaching that redemption is an act of *anakephalaiōsis* or *recapitulation* with a dual movement (cf. Eph. 1: 10). On the one hand, it involves a penetration backwards in time and existence into the roots of man's involvement in sin and evil, even into death and hell. We can discern something of the profound implications of that when we think of the descent into hell as a descent into the irreversibility of time and memory and guilt, as a movement that threads regressively along the line of man's transgression and fall, undoing the tangled skein of disobedience and rebellion, and breaking the tyranny of guilt-laden existence and time. On the other hand, recapitulation involves a forward movement, in which the unravelled existence and time of man are gathered up and restored in Christ in ontological relation to God. Now the resurrection is that recapitulation in its positive aspect, answering to the descent into death and hell, for it is the healing, lifting up and projection of human being into a new order of things in which its existence before God is finally made good. Think of the Old Testament account of the healing of Naaman the leper as he was baptized in Jordan, when his flesh was restored to him like the flesh of a little child, or of the prophecy of Joel as to the great day of recovery in which God

would restore the years that the locust had devoured – resurrection is like that, the redeeming back of man's life from the
wasting power of the destroyer and its restoring into the fullness of new being.

We repeat: the resurrecting of Jesus is to be thought of as the
recreating and restoring of man into the same sphere of real
being as that to which we human creatures belong, and is, as
such, an historical happening in continuity with the whole
historical happening of Jesus, the incarnate Son.[1] If the resurrection is not an event in history, a happening within the same
order of physical existence to which we belong, then atonement and redemption are empty vanities, for they achieve
nothing for historical men and women in the world.[2] Unless
the atonement through the resurrection breaks into, and is
real in, our historical and physical existence and continues to be
valid as saving power in our earthly and temporal being, it is
ultimately a mockery. That is why all docetic conceptions of
the risen Christ are quite irrelevant to men and women of
flesh and blood, and have no message to offer them in their
actual existence. It is for this reason that eschatology, with the
heart taken out of it in the denial of a genuine resurrection, is
meaningless, and without relevance to the on-going life of the
world. Everything depends on the resurrection of the body,
otherwise all we have is a Ghost for a Saviour.

Is then the resurrection an event in historical time or not?
Certainly it is an event datable in history, if only by reference
to the complex of historical events and agencies within which

---

[1] It is a baffling feature of the resurrection that it is *more than a historical
fact*, but, as Rahner has argued, 'it nevertheless stands in such inseparable
connection with a series of intrinsically historical facts that on the basis of
the latter it is possible to attain what at least is in an analogous sense an
historical certainty regarding the fact of Jesus' resurrection'. *Sacramentum
Mundi*, vol. 5, Eng. tr. 1970 (ed. by K. Rahner, C. Ernst *et al.*), p. 328.
Cf. here also the appeal of Daniel Fuller to 'historical reasoning', *Easter
Faith and History*, 1968, pp. 145ff.

[2] The history of the resurrection in the sense that it actually happened
at a particular time in the past is so vital to the Christian faith that, as
Cranfield has expressed it, the demythologized Gospel in which the his-
toricity of the resurrection, in this sense, is called in question is an example
of 'another Gospel which is not another'. *The Gospel according to St. Mark*
(Cambridge Greek Testament), 3rd edit. 1966, p. 19f.

witness was borne to it;[3] but since the resurrection is a movement of redemption from bondage and subjection to the dark
and tyrannical forces of this world, it is something that bursts
through the structures and limitations of space and time as we
know them where historical, social and human institutions in a
fallen world are hopelessly infected by sin and selfishness. If
those patterns of our existence, conditioned and determined
by sin and guilt, remain rigid and hard, if Christ has not broken
through them and opened a way for new being beyond them,
he cannot be *our* Redeemer, for we cannot be separated from
that space-time existence of ours in this world. But if he is
the Redeemer who does deliver us from the thraldom of sin
and guilt and therefore breaks through the structures determined by them to which we are subjected, then the resurrection event is not something that can be caught within the
framework of those structures or interpreted by the secular
historian who can only work within it. The methods and canons
of credibility with which the secular historian works are
strictly appropriate only to the kind of historical happening in a
world still schematized to the conditions and determinations of
sin and guilt, and therefore are not adequately or properly
applicable to the resurrection event that triumphs over them
in the redemption of time and history.

The kind of time we have in this passing world is the time of
an existence that crumbles away into the dust, time that runs
backward into nothingness.[4] Hence the kind of historical
happening we have in this world is happening that decays and
is so far illusory, running away into the darkness and forget-
fulness of the past. As happening within this kind of time, and
as event within this kind of history, the resurrection, by being
what it is, resists and overcomes corruption and decay, and is
therefore a *new kind of historical happening* which instead of
tumbling down into the grave and oblivion rises out of the

---

[3] Cf. Oscar Cullmann, *Salvation in History*, p. 143, who speaks similarly
of the *occurrence* of Jesus' resurrection; while not itself accessible to historical
control, and not described in the Gospels, it is linked with facts at least
theoretically provable within the historical framework – the resurrection
appearances and the empty tomb.

[4] See here the article by Emil Brunner, 'The Christian Understanding of
Time', *Scottish Journal of Theology*, vol. 4, 1951, pp. 1–12.

death of what is past into continuing being and reality. This is temporal happening that runs not backwards but forwards, and overcomes all illusion and privation or being. This is fully real historical happening, so real that it remains real happening and does not slip away from us, but keeps pace with us and outruns us as we tumble down in decay and lapse into death and the dust of past history and even comes to meet us out of the future. That is how we are to think of the risen Christ Jesus. He is not dead but alive, more real than any of us. Hence he does not need to be made real for us, because he does not decay or become fixed in the past. He lives on in the present as real live continuous happening, encountering us here and now in the present and waiting for us in the future.

Because this is historical event emancipated from decay, redeemed from bondage, liberated from the guilty irreversibility of dead time, the resurrection is rather baffling to the historian who considers it only in the context of ordinary history, even when as a true historian he leaves room for the emergence of unprecedented factors.[5] Here we have historical happening within our historical existence and within the same sphere of actuality and reality to which we human beings belong – that is why it is plotted by relation to other historical agents, such as Mary Magdalene, John, Peter and a host of disciples in the primitive Church, with regard to which the New Testament offers the historian impressive evidence – yet it is historical happening that breaks through the backward movement of time where it becomes fixed in death and decays, and cannot therefore be netted with the frame of the historical as we know it merely in our interaction with nature and other human agents. Here we have the same kind of continuity and discontinuity that is to be found in the Virgin Birth of Jesus and which makes it so difficult to grasp. Here, however, we have that new decisive kind of happening in final form which is the incursion of the new creation into our sphere of existence and which at the point of decisive change breaks through its

---

[5] Serious questions must be put to Bultmann's use of 'historical method' which does not allow for such unprecedented factors, especially when he rules that the resurrection cannot have taken place because it cannot be established in accordance with what he has already defined as an historically acceptable event. See *Kerygma and Myth*, I, pp. 38ff.

hard and rigid forms in unfettered final disclosure. Hence
while the resurrection is an event that happened once for all,
it remains continuous live happening within history, and must
therefore be interpreted against the patterned stream of
history or the secular framework of our space and time. That
is why resurrection by its very nature involves apocalypse, both
in relation to history and in relation to our understanding of
it. By apocalyptic is meant here the way in which we must
look at history in the light of God's decisive interventions,
interpreting it therefore against the observable patterns of
worldly history formed as time flows irreversibly into the past;
but in the continuing life of the Church apocalypse means that
while we live and work on the plane of ongoing world events as
the newspapers and history books write of them, we nevertheless live in the power of the resurrection as those who are
united to the risen Jesus Christ, and who must not be schematized to the form of the secular world but must be transformed through the renewal of our mind in Christ. We are
called constantly to shed the image of the corruptible and put
on the image of the new creation, for we are caught up in a
vectorial movement that runs counter to the regressive flow
of corruption and decay and carries us forward into the future
to the final and full disclosure of our real being in Christ.[6]

So far we have been thinking of the resurrection as an event
in space and time and yet as one that breaks redemptively
through the framework of space and time, as we know it in a
fallen world, but it is necessary to see that the resurrection
means the *redemption of space and time*, for space and time are not
abrogated or transcended. Rather are they healed and restored,
just as our being is healed and restored through the resurrection.[7] Of course we cannot separate our being from space and

[6] As W. Künneth rightly argues we must operate with a Christocentric
concept of time, for 'time is embraced in the new creation, in the reality
of the resurrection', *The Theology of the Resurrection*, p. 188f.

[7] D. M. MacKinnon makes the point that although in one sense the
resurrection is in time, it 'possesses also a relation to the eternal as ultimate
and unique as that of the universe to its creation. Indeed', he adds 'what I
would be prepared to argue is that here for the Christian is focused the very
relation of the temporal to the eternal itself. So that we would not be
wrong if we saw creation itself through this event, which is more than
event'. *Op. cit.*, p. 64.

time for space and time are conditions and functions of created existence and the bearers of its order. The healing and restoring of our being carries with it the healing, restoring, reorganizing and transforming of the space and time in which we now live our lives in relation to one another and to God. Yet immediately we are concerned with space and time and especially with their resurrection we are in the midst of eschatology in which our thinking is stretched out beyond to the ultimate ends of God's purposes in creation and redemption. We cannot think this out adequately apart from consideration of the ascension, and final *parousia* of Christ when he comes to make all things new, and when redemption will be fully actualized in the sphere of the body and the whole of created reality – but there are certain major aspects of the redemption of space and time, of time particularly, that we must consider now.

We have spoken of the kind of time we have on the plane of this fallen world as the time that crumbles away into the dust, time as it is implicated in corruption, yet we have also spoken of it as irreversible – time that flows only one way, backwards and downwards into the dust. While this time is, as it were, alive in the present moment, it decays right away, and suffers from a sort of *rigor mortis*, a fixity from which we cannot escape and within which we are incarcerated in our ageing and dying.

Let us try to understand this from a merely natural point of view. Think of an historical happening: once it takes place, it cannot be undone. In taking place it appears as a free happening. Throw a stone through that window and you are engaging in a free act, but once it has taken place, the act cannot be recalled – we cannot turn it backwards as we can a film of the event. Thus once an event has taken place, it becomes 'necessary' – in the sense that it cannot now be other than it is. At this point, however, we are liable to suffer from a delusion, for we tend to think that, because it is now a necessary fact, it had to happen. This is the kind of optical illusion we suffer from on the golf course when we watch another player putt a ball from the other end of the green and it goes right down into the hole – immediately that happens we somehow think it had to happen from the start, but what we have done is in a flash read the final result back all along the line of the ball's course into the free act behind it. It is through this kind of illusion or indeed delusion that some historians think that they must interpret historical events in the same way they interpret the events of natural processes as concatenated through causal necessity. But it is important to distinguish in historical happening between causal necessity and factual necessity, between causal determination of events and the fact that once they happen they cannot be otherwise. An historical event, once it has taken place, is factually necessary for it cannot now be other than it is, but an historical event comes into being through a free happening, by means of spontaneous human agencies. Certainly all historical events are interactions between human agents and nature as well as interactions between agents and other agents – so that there are elements of causal determination in historical happening that we have to take into account, physical factors relating to the kind of patterns of space and time in which we live and work. However, historical events are not by any means merely natural physical processes, for as happenings initiated and bound up with purposeful agents they embody intention which often conflicts with and triumphs over the course of events that nature would take on its own. It is this interweaving of natural processes and human agencies, of nature and rational intention, that gives history its complicated patterns. The course of events has often quite unforeseen results, for human acts may fail to achieve what would have been expected or may achieve far more than would or could have been anticipated. But in our interpretation of history we must never forget that in the heart of historical events there is free happening which bears the intention in which the true significance of history is to be discerned. Thus while we must appreciate fully the physical factors involved, we must penetrate into the movement of time in the actual happening in order to understand the event in the light of the intentionality and spontaneity embedded in it. The handling of temporal relation has proved very difficult and elusive in the history of thought, for it has so often been assimilated to logical relation and transposed into something very different. The confusion of temporal with logical connection corresponds here to that between spontaneity and causal determinism in natural science. We can see this error recurring, for example, in notions of predestination where the free *prius* of the divine grace is converted by the scholastic mind into logico-causal relation, while the kind of time-relation with which we operate between natural events is imported into the movements of divine love and activity. It is a form of the same mistake that people make in regard to the resurrection, when they think of its happening only within the logico-causal nexus with which they operate in classical physics.

We distinguish, then, in historical happening between logico-causal necessity and factual necessity. This is not to say that the time order of historical events is different from the time order of events in nature, but that the kind of events with which we have to do in history is different, and has a different kind of movement, from that which we have in nature. Nevertheless it remains true that as in nature we can appreciate, for instance, the movement of light only by engaging in a movement along with it, only through a mode of kinetic thinking and by renouncing all thought of it from a centre of absolute rest, so here in historical happening we understand it only through a similar kinetic mode of thinking in which we penetrate into the living happening behind the factual necessity and appreciate it as far as possible from within its own movement. But how far can we do that, when time, so to speak, dies on us as it passes from the present moment into the past, and gets all stiffened up in a sort of *rigor mortis*? That is the problem of the historian which he seeks to overcome by penetrating into the *intentionality* embedded in the happening – and it is a problem we cannot escape in historical interpretation of the Scriptures or of the historical events they record.

There are, at least, two primary factors which we have to take into account theologically.

(*a*) If we interpret historical events not by converting their factual necessity into logico-causal necessity but by penetrating kinetically into their free happening, what is the kind of happening with which we are concerned in the resurrection, for it is the nature of the happening that determines the nature of the historical event once it has happened? The kind of happening of course is determined by the nature of the subject of the happening. We distinguish between the kind of happening we see in natural events, such as the eruption of a volcano, from the kind of happening in history, as, for example, the stabbing of Julius Caesar. The subjects are different. In one case we have to do only with determinate objects and subjects, in the other case with personal agents and a different kind of subject. Here, however, we have to reckon with the nature of the subject in the incarnation and in the resurrection, for, as we have seen, the resurrection is to be understood in consistency with Jesus Christ himself, who is the person who rose from the dead. Here, in fact, we have a divine-human subject, and therefore a unique happening defined by the nature of this unique Agent. Other human agents were involved in the life of Jesus, Mary, and Judas, Caiaphas and Pilate, so that we have to interpret the historical Jesus within the kind of historical happening that we find in all other human history, but because we have here a different Subject, the Son of God incarnate in human existence in space and time, we have to understand the inner movement of his history in a way appropriate to his nature – that applies to his birth, to the whole of his life, and to his resurrection, which is all of the same genus. This is why we can speak of the whole historical Jesus from birth to resurrection as sheer miracle or downright *resurrection* from beginning to end. Now this means that we cannot interpret the historical happening of the resurrection of Jesus, any more than of his birth and life, without doing it from within the free movement of his life and agency, that is, to use older language (if we divest it of its false psychologizing) from within the Messianic secret of Jesus. In other words, we can interpret the resurrection only if we interpret it theologically as well as historically. It will not do, however, to interpret it merely 'theologically' as if it could be done apart from history, for that would mythologize and docetize it, and then we would have nothing to interpret. Nor can we interpret it merely 'historically' in the sense that we interpret other historical events in human history, only by reference to human agency and natural processes, for that would be tantamount to insisting that all we have here is an ordinary historical happening, and so to rejecting from the start the claim that the Agent is the Son of God. To say the least, it would be neither open-minded nor scientific, since it would foreclose the issue completely as to who Jesus Christ is, before we have even considered him in accordance with his nature and self-disclosure.

Since this is one of the false approaches regularly adopted in the quest of the historical Jesus, it is not at all surprising that the quest pursued on these lines breaks down time and time again, and is increasingly baffling and bewildering. It could not be otherwise when approached in this way.

To get back, then, to the point from which we started here, it is incumbent upon us to interpret the resurrection as historical event in accordance with the nature of the Agent or Subject concerned, and therefore through penetration into the free and dynamic happening of his life. We can do this because, as we have seen, this is a historical happening not of the kind that fades away from us and crumbles into the dust, but of the kind that remains real and therefore that resists corruption and moves the other way, forward throughout all history to the end-time and to the consummation of all things in the new creation. Jesus remains live and a real historical happening, more real and more historical than any other historical event, for this is the only historical event that does not suffer from decay and is not threatened by annihilation and illusion. It is historical event in the fullness of time, and not historical event suffering, as all other historical events do, from the privation of time. Here time itself is redeemed and re-created, and as such is carried forward into the future, for it is not allowed to see the corruption of the grave. But we can also penetrate inside this historical happening in Jesus because of Pentecost and our union with Christ through the *koinonia* of the Spirit. It is through the Spirit that we may understand the resurrection of Jesus in accordance with its own inner and free happening, as the sovereign act of its Subject. And that is why, as we saw earlier, the resurrection must be understood enhypostatically as well as anhypostatically. If it is only understood anhypostatically then it can be interpreted merely in terms of some sort of super-history, touching our history only in a tangential manner, and therefore not as really historical. That was the tendency of the early Barth and Brunner, which Barth certainly sloughed off, much as a snake sloughs off its skin, but into which people like Bultmann, Dodd, and Rheinhold Niebuhr have slipped in their eschatology of continual crisis and of timeless events![8]

[8] See *Karl Barth. An Introduction to his Early Theology, 1910–1931*, pp. 74ff.

(b) There is a second factor that we have to take into account, for it is the foil, so to speak, of what we have just been considering, the fact that the time-form of the world as we now have it in fallen existence is characterized by *law* – by what the New Testament calls *nomos*. This assumes one form, of course, in natural events, and that is in accordance with their determinate nature and their kind of rationality, but it assumes another form in historical events, and that too must be in accordance with their nature and their kind of rationality. This is the *nomistic form of human existence* that is thrown into sharp relief by justification, i.e. the time-form of our fallen existence within which we are fixed in our mortality, and through which we are caught in the irreversibility of guilty deeds and lives which have the force of 'necessity' because once lived or performed they cannot be undone.[9] It is what St. Paul called 'the curse of the law' from which we need to be redeemed. Redemption had to take the form of justification 'under the law' yet 'apart from law' (Rom. 7: 8f.). 'When the fullness of time was come God sent forth his Son, made of woman, made under the law, to redeem those who were under the law, that we might have the adoption of sons' (Gal. 4: 4–5).[10] This is precisely the situation with which we are concerned here, as we think of resurrection as the *redemption of time*, for it takes place within the nomistic character of our existence, and yet emancipates us from it into a new relationship with God the Father.

For Karl Barth's early views (later rejected) on the timelessness or tangential character of the resurrection event, see *The Resurrection of the Dead*, 13ff., 143, etc.; *Epistle to the Romans*, 29f.; and even *Christliche Dogmatik*, 1927, pp. 8of., 232ff., 247f., 254, 262f., 273f., 340ff.

[9] See *Royal Priesthood*, ch. 2, 'The Time of the Church', *Scottish Journal of Theology Occasional Papers*, No. 3, 1955, 2nd edit. 1963, pp. 5off.

[10] I have kept to the translation '*made* of woman, *made* under the law', in spite of RV and RSV which have '*born* of woman, *born* under the law', for St. Paul's word is *genomenos* (from *genesthai*) as in LXX Gen. 2. 7 with reference to Adam, which he uses elsewhere of the earthly origin of Jesus, Rom. 1: 3, Gal. 4: 4, Phil. 2: 7, and not *gegennēmenos* (from *gennasthai*, to be born, cf. Gal. 4: 23, 29) which Paul never uses of Jesus. Cf. the patristic distinction between *agenēton* (unmade) and *agennēton* (unbegotten) as in Athanasius, *Con. Arianos*, 1. 30–34, or John of Damascus, *De fide orthodoxa*, 1. 8.

Man was made for fellowship with God, but when that fellowship was broken by sin, he lapsed into a state in which he was no longer the man he ought to be. The moral awareness of man, his inescapable sense of obligation, belongs to that condition. His relation with God became refracted and took the form of ethical or legal relation. In the Old Testament account, a barrier came in between man and God – God made known to man his divine will but withheld himself from him lest he should be consumed by the divine Majesty. The effect of this was to establish man in an ethical or legal order over against God, for the manifestation of the divine will contained lawlessness, restraining chaos from overwhelming man, and at the same time confined man within an order of existence validated by God but within which he was not the man he ought to be. Man was thus the prisoner of an ethical or legal order from which he could not extricate himself, for he could not be the man he ought to be or bridge the gap between himself and God within which the ethical or legal order had its validity. But God in his free grace has come in Jesus Christ to redeem man from his helpless condition under the tyranny and curse of the law, that is, from the 'necessity' or inescapable 'nomistic form' of his existence, and to lift him up into living fellowship and loving communion with God the Father.

Now the kind of time we are concerned with in historical events is the time of human agents, the time of free happening in the interrelations of human beings, and is therefore time that is inescapably involved with moral and legal experience. That is why the New Testament speaks of the *schema* of this present *aeon* as *nomos*, for the kind of time we have in our fallen existence is refracted time, time that has broken loose from God, as it were, and yet not time that has been allowed to slip into sheer chaos and nothingness but time that is contained, upheld and overruled by God, within which he works out his redeeming purpose. The kind of time we have in historical events is the time of creation that has fallen from what it ought to be into disorder, and yet is contained through *nomos* from disappearing or vanishing into illusion, but as such it is time in which we are subjected to law, time within which we are all servants. But when the fullness of time was come the Son of God entered this existence and this time of ours as a servant under law; he partook of life within the nomistic structure of our time, and wrought his redemptive work within it in order to emancipate us from its tyranny. It was in his resurrection that he broke through the nomistic form of our existence, rising again no longer in the form of a servant under the law, but in the form of the life-giving New Man, entirely and fully human, yet man no longer confined to the kind of limits that are imposed on us in our fallen world by the time-form of law or by the nomistic form of time. However, far from violating or abrogating time, he redeemed it. Just as in justification the law was not destroyed but established, so in the resurrection time is not annihilated but recreated, for it is taken up in Christ, sanctified in his human life and transformed in his resurrection as man.[11]

How are we to state this positively? Here we may revert to the doctrine of the *hypostatic union* of the divine and human natures in the one Person of the incarnate Son of God.

In the risen Christ, in whom hypostatic union between God and Man is carried through to its *telos*, there is involved an hypostatic union between eternity and time, eternity and redeemed and sanctified time, and therefore between eternity and new time. The resurrection of the man Jesus, and his exaltation to the right hand of the Father, mean the taking up of *human time* into God. In Christ the life of human being is wedded to eternal life. The ascension also means that this time of the new creation in Christ is hidden from us, and, as it were, held back until in the mercy of God Jesus Christ comes again to judge and renew all his creation. Nevertheless it remains valid that in the risen Christ our human nature in its creaturely and temporal existence is redeemed and renewed and established through being taken up in its affirmed reality into the life of God.

How are we to think of our participation in this new creation and its redeemed time? This is best understood, perhaps, in the perspective of the Church as the Body of Christ, the Body not

[11] Cf. Karl Barth: 'It is as man of his time, and not otherwise that he is Lord of time. We should lose Jesus as Lord of all time if we ignored him as a man in his own time. It is in this history – the history which is inseparable from his temporality – that the man Jesus lives and is the eternal salvation of all men in their different times'. *Church Dogmatics*, III/2, p. 440f.

only of the crucified but of the risen Christ, the Body upon which he has poured out his Spirit as he ascended to fill all things, the Body which, though on earth and within history, is yet made participant in his risen power. The Church thus lives, as it were, in two times: in the time of this passing world, that is in the midst of on-going secular history and world events, the time of decay that flows down into the past and into the ashes of death, but also in the time of the risen Saviour and of the new creation that is already a perfected reality in him. This happens through the *koinōnia* of the Spirit, so that the Church lives and works and fulfils its mission in the overlap of the two times or two ages, this present aeon that passes away and the new aeon that has already overtaken us in Christ Jesus, the end-time that has telescoped itself into the present and penetrated the Church through the coming of the Spirit. Because of its participation in the time of the new creation, the Church can continue to live on earth and in history only through being crucified with Christ to the time-form of this world. On the other hand, because of its union with Christ the Church is sent by him to fulfil its mission within the time and history of this world, and therefore within its temporal and nomistic structures. In other words, though risen with Christ and already a partaker through the Spirit in the new creation, the Church is sent like Christ into the world as the servant of the Lord, humbling itself and containing itself in *kenōsis* within the limits and laws of this world in order to proclaim the Gospel of reconciliation and to live out reconciliation within conditions of fallen human existence. It is the new wine by which the old wineskins will be burst, and the whole framework of the ages will be changed. This is why the New Testament calls the Church and its members to 'redeem the time', not to live as those who are dead and asleep, rigid with the fixities of dead time, but to keep vigil as those who are already risen with Christ and wait his coming for their final release, not like Lazarus freed merely from the shrouds of the grave, but freed from the shackles of the past and all that holds us back from entering into the fullness of our inheritance in the new creation.

In carrying our thinking this far we have already moved into the realm of *apocalyptic*, in which we may speak of the new

world and the new time only by using language culled from the
old world and the old time. That is to say, we are permitted
to speak here of the new age only with a prayer for forgiveness,
for the very language we use is improper and must pass away
with the nomistic forms of this world. We are reminded here
of the apocalyptic theme of 'the new song', in *The Revelation
of St. John the Divine*, which is sung on the other side by those
who have been redeemed, or 'the new name' which no one
knows but which is sealed on the foreheads of the redeemed,
imprinted with the sign of the cross in their baptismal incorporation into Christ. Thus out of the cross of Christ there
breaks in upon the vision of faith something quite indescribable, as indescribable as the Majesty of the risen Son of
Man that confronted the Apostle at the start of his visions. We
can speak about it only in stammering ways, in the fragmented
figures of apocalyptic imagery. Let us merely note several
features or images used by the New Testament as the reality
of the new age is glimpsed shining through the old.

The old man perishes day by day, but in Christ the new man
is renewed day by day. That is the characteristic of the Christian who is dead and hid with Christ in God, for he is already
risen with Christ, and already partakes of the power of his
resurrection through sharing in his Spirit. That is also the life
of the Church which in Christ has so partaken of the powers
of the age to come that it gets younger and younger with the
youth of eternity, or rather with the new time of the new
Man in whom eternity and redeemed time are united for ever.
Think here of the language of Ephesians 5, regarding the
nature of the Church of Christ as she will be presented to
Christ at the end of history, without spot or wrinkle but as a
chaste virgin; or think of the *Vision* of Hermas, II: 10, of the
ecclesia presbytera becoming the *ecclesia neōtera*, for though the
Church as Hermas saw her, was an old lady with white hair,
her flesh was getting younger and younger.[12] 'Now is our
salvation nearer', as St. Paul used to say, 'than when we first
believed' (Rom. 13: 11).

---

[12] Yet even in her most youthful appearance, J. S. Stewart remarks, her
hair was still completely white, to show that she was eternally young, yet
older than the world.

Let us take the image of the millennium.[13] How are we to understand this in the light of the redemption of time? Here we have evidently an apocalyptic figure made up of 'alpha and omega', 1 and 1000, 'the First and the Last', which is Christ, 'he who was and is and shall be for evermore', 'he who is and was dead and behold he is alive and has the keys of death and hell'. It is the apocalyptic figure of *the perfect time of the Kingdom of Christ,* the sanctified time of the new creation which was inaugurated with the resurrection of Christ, the *Protos,* and reaches out to the final advent when he will come again as the *Eschatos* to judge and renew the earth, finally to make all things new. The millennium is the time of Christ the New Man, and therefore the sabbatical time of the new humanity which in Christ is wedded to the perfection of eternity. It is in this time, millennium time, that the Church participates as throughout history it lives in union with the risen Christ through the Spirit. This millennium time is hidden from our sight with the ascension of the risen Lord, but it remains, so to speak, *the other side* of the time of this world, for although it has been redeemed by Christ and involved in his vicarious self-sanctification, it still waits for the full actualization of redemption in its physical existence. On this side we see the time of human failure and sin, the time of dark and tragic history, the time of wrath, the time of crucifixion, but on the other side, seen only by faith, there is the time of the resurrection or the new age which is, as it were, the silver lining behind the time of secular history. Millennium time will be unveiled with the advent of Christ, for then there will take place the *apocalypse* of all that Christ has done throughout history in making the wrath of man to serve him in the eschatological outreach of his Kingdom to its consummation in the new creation. Because the Church is already participant in that new creation, i.e. in the millennium time of the resurrection, the Kingdom of the risen and ascended and advent Christ already knocks at the door of the Church. That happens above all at the Holy Supper, where the risen Lord is present, in *Eucharistic Parousia,* and where we taste already the powers of the age to come and are given an antepast of the great banquet of the

[13] See here ch. 12 of my exposition of Rev. 20, *The Apocalypse Today,* pp. 161ff.

Kingdom that is to come. As often as we communicate in the Sacrament, we participate in the new time of that Kingdom. That is why the New Testament thinks of the sacraments as falling within the overlap between the two ages, this present age that passes away and the age that is to come but which in Christ has already telescoped itself into the present and catches us up into it in the Communion of the Spirit. Thus as often as the Church partakes of Holy Communion in the *real presence* or *parousia* of Christ it becomes ever anew the Body of the risen Lord.

But what about *the individual*, and what about the death of the believer? This is where it is impossible for us to think completely together the two times in which we are involved, yet we may discern something of how the two 'moments' fall together in our being in Christ. When the believer dies, he goes to be with Christ and is in his immediate presence, participant in him and made like him. That is to each believer the *parousia* of Christ to him.[14] Yet when this is regarded on the plane of history and of the on-going processes of the fallen world, the death of each believer means that his body is laid to sleep in the earth, waiting until the redemption of the body and the recreation of all things at the final *Parousia*. Looked at from the perspective of the new creation there is no gap between the death of the believer and the *parousia* of Christ, but looked at from the perspective of time that decays and crumbles away, there is a lapse in time between them. How do we think these together? Only by thinking of them exclusively *in Christ*, in the one Person of Christ in whom human nature and divine nature are hypostatically united, and in whom our human existence and history are taken up into his divine life. We must think Christologically here. But when we relate Christology to the time-form of this world what we do see is that the Church is sent out in the mission of the everlasting Gospel into history, under the sway of earthly authorities and powers, and within the structures of space and time. It cannot be true and faithful to its Lord if it refuses to live the life of the servant within and under all that, even though it is crucified

---

[14] For a similar idea see Emil Brunner, *Eternal Hope*, Eng. tr. 1954, pp. 147ff. But Brunner seems to have a rather docetic conception of the resurrection, p. 149f.

to the world in Christ and is already risen with him and as such shares his triumphant victory over the powers of the world. But if we think Christologically we have to reject the mythologizing of biblical eschatology, that is, reject the objectifying of apocalyptic imagery and the fixation of the Kingdom of Christ within the old structures. When Christ comes again it will be with all his unveiled majesty and power, all the manifest glory of the new creation, but if so, as Calvin warns us, it would be an insult to that advent Christ to think of him as dwelling and ruling 1000 years on earth, once more in the form of a servant, even if his reign will be in the glorified form of the chiliast visionaries. Chiliastic or millenarian thinking of this kind fails to realize the nature of the resurrection and the glory and majesty of the risen Lord, or indeed the finished and accomplished nature of the atonement.[15] When Christ comes again it can only be to make all things new and to reveal what he has already done and is even now working in and under and with all world-events. Then the great unveiling or apocalypse will take place, the judgments of the Cross at work throughout history will be brought to their consummation in unveiled finality, and the salvation of Christ that has been proclaimed throughout all history will be brought to its fruition in the unveiled glory of the new creation. It is by the man Jesus that God will finally judge the earth, and by the man Jesus that resurrection and new creation will finally come upon the old creation. Then at last the vast cosmic significance of the incarnation of the Word, and of the reconciliation through the sacrifice of Christ, and of the resurrection of our human nature in him, will be made clear and manifest to all, and we shall know as we are known.

Until then, the Church and all its members live *between the times*, between the time of the resurrection and Pentecost and the time of the final advent; they participate in the time of this on-going world, yet already participate in the time of the new creation through the Spirit of the risen Christ. If Christ holds back the final unveiling, and keeps us within the overlap of the two ages, still engaged in the humble mission of the servant under the Cross, it is in his compassion and patience,

[15] Thus John Calvin, *Institutio*, 3. 25. 5. For further references see *Kingdom and Church. A Study in the Theology of the Reformation*, 1956, p. 145.

for he waits to be merciful, and wills to rule over history solely by the Word of the Cross. It is as enthroned Lamb, as Mediator and High Priest, that he rules from the right hand of God over Church and State, over faith and world-happening. In that 'patience' of Christ we have 'the time of the Gentiles', the time of the proclamation of the Gospel to all nations, in which the Church must live in patience with its Lord, never seeking to force his hand, or to force upon the world the consummation before its time, for then there will be no time for decision, no time for repentance, and no time for change, but only the time of finality. Yet it is because the time of finality presses hard upon us in history, and impinges now upon the Church from all sides, that the Church finds time running out and knows that at any hour, at such a time as it thinks not, the moment of great reckoning will suddenly come upon mankind.[16] Here we are, as it were, back in the days of Jesus as he pressed to-ward the Cross throughout the three years of his ministry, straightened with the baptism with which he was baptized in the mission of the Cross, yet as crisis after crisis came, he refused to force the issue, waiting for the ripening of God's will in the situation into which he had entered, and only when at last he knew that his 'hour' had come, did he go forward to the passion and the resurrection that transformed everything. The book of *Revelation* clearly looks at the whole course of history from the resurrection of Christ to his final advent in the light of the course of Christ's own earthly life from his birth at Bethlehem to his crucifixion and resurrection, for it is that incarnate Son of God, crucified and risen for all men, who is at work in all history and who reigns over it all. Once again he waits for the 'hour' of final consummation when what took place intensively in Christ himself once and for all in his crucifixion and resur-rection, will be actualized extensively in the broad field of creation and history, where the new heaven and the new

---

[16] This is surely the meaning of Jesus' own insistence on the *imminence* of the *parousia* in those passages which many modern scholars, following Schweitzer, find embarrassing, as though our Lord had been mistaken. Yet all this seems quite consistent with Jesus' teaching from the beginning that with his presence and saving activity among men the Kingdom of God had drawn near and had already come upon them. Cf. here the dis-cussion of J. Jeremias, *New Testament Theology*, Eng. tr. 1971, vol. 1, pp. 96ff., 131ff., 310.

earth will supervene in the unveiled glory of the triumphant Lord.

Meantime in all its waiting and expectation the Church is commanded by its Lord to lift up its head in thanksgiving and joy, for its *redemption draws nigh*. The Church of the risen Lord has no right to be a prophet of gloom or despair, for this world has been redeemed and sanctified by Christ, and he will not let it go. The corruptible clay of our poor earth has been taken up in Jesus, is consecrated through his sacrifice and resurrection, and he will not allow it to sink back into corruption. Hence the whole creation groans and travails waiting for the manifestation of the sons of God, looking forward with eager expectation to the hour of final liberation and renewal in the advent of its risen Saviour.[17] The Church must learn to take into its mouth the Good News of the resurrection and new creation, for that must be its primary note, one of limitless joy and thanksgiving. That is how the Church began its mission at Pentecost where the dominant emphasis in all its preaching was the resurrection of the crucified Christ and the astounding fact that because of Christ the Spirit of God himself was poured out upon men. They knew that the Last Times had overtaken them and that they were caught up in the onward and outward thrust of the resurrection of Christ toward the new creation in which all nations and peoples and all times would be brought to share. The involvement of the Church in the suffering of mankind must never be allowed to stifle that supreme note of resurrection triumph or to smother the eschatological joy at the astounding events that have broken into history and pledged for mankind the final day of regeneration.[18]

[17] As H. R. Mackintosh has pointed out, the transformation of nature which St. Paul has in view (Rom. 8: 19ff.), takes in even the irrational creation which will be redeemed from vanity, bondage and corruption. 'In the Pauline conception of the consummated order, distinctions between earth and heaven seem to fall away.' *Immortality and the Future*, 1915, p. 73.

[18] See Karl Barth's sustained and moving discussion of 'the determination of world reality and human existence by the resurrection of Jesus Christ', in *Church Dogmatics*, IV/3, under the title of 'The Promise of the Spirit', pp. 275–367.

CHAPTER 5

THE ASCENSION OF
JESUS CHRIST

It is with his ascension that Jesus Christ was fully installed in his kingly Ministry.[1] His prophetic ministry began with the incarnation, that is the ministry of the Word made flesh, but even there Jesus was born to be King, and as he entered his public ministry he stepped forth as the King of the Kingdom he proclaimed. His priestly ministry is associated mostly with his passion in which as High Priest he offered himself in sacrifice for our sins and holy oblation to the Father, but even in the midst of this ministry he was King, crowned with thorns, but King because of the Cross and through the Cross. However, it is with his exaltation to the throne of God and his sitting at the right hand of the Father that his kingly ministry properly began. It stretches from the ascension to the final advent, when he will come again as Lord and King of all in open majesty, power and glory. Nevertheless within this kingly ministry we must not lose sight of the *triplex munus* of Christ, his threefold office as Prophet, Priest and King. That is the general order in which it is natural to study Christology, for it would appear to be the order determined by the mighty salvation events in the course of Jesus' life among us, but as we consider the threefold office within the period inaugurated by the ascension, it is evidently with another order that we have to work: King, Priest and Prophet. His kingly ministry is supreme from ascension to *parousia*, but within that his ministry as Priest and

---

[1] Neither St. Matthew nor St. John speaks about the ascension in their Gospels; St. Mark alludes to it, at least in the addendum to his Gospel, 16: 19, but a fuller account is given by St. Luke, 24: 50–53, Acts 1: 9–11. There are, however, references to it elsewhere as in the early *kerygma* reported in the Acts of the Apostles (2. 32f.; 5: 30f.), etc., and in the epistles (Phil. 2: 6–9, 3: 20; Eph. 4: 8–10; 1 Tim. 3: 16; 1 Peter 3: 22; Heb. 2: 9, 12: 2; cf. also Rom. 8: 34; Col. 3: 1; 1 Peter 1: 21).

Prophet is no less evident than before, for it is brought to full-
ness in the consummation of his Kingship; the priesthood of
Christ is a Royal Priesthood, and the proclamation of Christ is a
Royal Proclamation.

1. *The Language of Ascension*

Four main verbs are employed in the New Testament to speak
of the ascension of Christ: *anabainein*, to go up; *kathizein*, to sit
down; *analambanein*, to take up; *hupsoun*, to exalt. These words
are all used in very ordinary ways in Biblical Greek with much
the same meaning that attaches to them in extra-Biblical
literature. But behind the biblical employment of these terms
there lies a theological and cultic significance in certain contexts which lends them deeper meaning. That is the specific
usage and meaning with which we are concerned here in relation
to the ascension or exaltation of Christ to the right hand of the
Father.

(*a*) *Anabaino*. This term often renders the Hebrew *alah*, to go
up, and in its causative form to make to ascend or offer. It is a
word with a powerful cultic significance. It is used regularly
in the Pentateuch of Moses' ascent of Mount Sinai, with the
sense of going up to or ascending to the Lord. It came to be
a regular term for the ascent to Mount Zion, or to Jerusalem,
and for going up to the Temple, while within the Temple it
was used for ascension into the Holy of Holies. At the same
time the word was used for the offering of sacrifice, while the
noun, *olah*, may be used as a technical term for the whole
burnt offering. It is also found in the Enthronement Psalms,
with regard to ascent to royal sovereignty, but beyond that
there lies the thought of the enthronement of Yahweh himself –
cf. Pss. 2, 24, 68 etc. It is sometimes used to speak of the ascent
of the Ark to Jerusalem which appears to carry with it the idea
of the sacral enthronement of the king. It is language taken
from this context of Old Testament thought that we have, for
example, in Ephesians 4. The same language of ascent is used
also more generally in the Old Testament in various contexts.
That is to say, when *anabaino*, meaning to *ascend*, is used *re-
ligiously* or *theologically* it tends to have strong royal or priestly
associations. It is a cultic term.

This is very apparent in the New Testament Scriptures, but it ought to be noted that the cultic nuance of *anabaino* is by no means confined to Biblical Greek, for it is regularly used in profane Greek literature of ascent to a temple or a shrine. Such a statement for example as Luke 18: 10 'and they went up to the holy place' is just ordinary Greek. But it is particularly in the Fourth Gospel that we find the term regularly used in a cultic context, of Jesus going up to Jerusalem, or of his 'anabasis', so to say, to a Feast or the Temple itself. St. Paul uses it in much the same way. In the Acts we find it used of the ascent of prayer, e.g. in regard to the prayer and alms of Cornelius, Acts 10: 4, 'they have ascended for a memorial before God'.

It is in this way, apparently that the term *anabaino* is applied to the ascension of Jesus Christ with distinct theological import – cf. Acts 2: 34; John 3: 13; 6: 62; 20: 17; Eph. 4: 8–10. When it is used in these contexts of the ascension it does not shed its cultic nuance, but of course this depends on the significance of the particular context. The main ideas we are concerned with here, then, are: (a) the ascent of the king, and beyond that, the enthronement of Jahweh, the King of Glory; (b) the ascent to the Temple, to the presence of God, for priestly service; (c) the ascent to God of the whole burnt offering, or more generally of prayer. Used in these ways the term *ascension* is essentially concerned with the Royal Priesthood of the crucified, risen and ascended Christ, exercised from the right hand of divine power.

(*b*) *Kathizo.* A study of this term and its employment confirms the applications of *anabaino* we have been discussing. One need only refer to the 110th Psalm which is cited in Acts 2: 34f., of the ascension of Christ. It is not surprising that this entered into the full stream of the early Christian tradition and crops up in the later strata of the New Testament as well, as in Eph. 1: 20; Heb. 1: 3; 8: 1; 10: 12; 12: 12; cf. Rev. 3: 21. In several of these passages analogical reference to Melchizedek the royal priest is evident.

We recall the fact that in the heart of the Holy of Holies, to which the priest made his ascent, was the mercy seat between the cherubim which came to play a role in the prophetic literature, as we see in Is. 6: 1.[2] Some passages in the *Apocalypse* refer directly or indirectly to this, but there are also passages in the Gospels which bear upon it with reference to the Messianic King. It would appear that when the New Testament uses this term in connection with Christ, it is the concept of Messianic enthronement that seems to be determinative, that is, his installation in the office of the Messianic King in which he dispenses the divine mercy and peace.

(c) *Analambano.* The use of this term is not so straightforward – cf. particularly Mark 16: 19; Acts 1: 2; 11: 22; Tim. 3: 16. Like the other terms this is employed, of course, in quite non-theological senses, and with the usual meanings such as lift up, take up, take on board, putting on armour for battle, e.g. in Paul's similes. But once again the word is given special significance in certain contexts where it acquires a distinctly cultic nuance, as in the lifting up of the heart in prayer to God. We are familiar with this kind of usage in the Scottish liturgical tradition in which we speak of the 'uplifting' of the offering or the 'lifting up' of the Cup at Holy Communion. In the Old Testament the term is also used of the assumption of Elijah into heaven, and this is given greater frequency in the Apocrypha, with respect to Enoch and others. The noun *analēmpsis* is not found in the LXX, but became, apparently, a technical term in the apocryphal literature, e.g. with reference to the 'assumption' of Moses. In profane Greek this term is used in various ways, of receiving back into the family, of acquisition of knowledge, of assumption into office, of various senses of reception, recovery, recuperation, etc. but it is *not used of death* or of assumption in that sense.

The only time *analēmpsis* is found in the New Testament itself is in Luke 9: 51, where it is translated as receiving up, but where the reference is clearly to the death of Christ. The combination of noun and verb thus indicates that the ascension of Christ to heaven began with his lifting up on the Cross. The apocryphal use of assumption has here an evident bearing upon the New Testament use, but the same applies to the cultic use we have noted in the Old Testament.

---

[2] In St. Paul's reference to this in Rom. 3: 25 the ascension or exaltation of Christ does not come into view. For concise comments on the meaning of this passage see Matthew Black, *Romans* (New Century Bible, 1973), pp. 68ff.

(*d*) *Hupsoo.* The consideration of this term confirms the meaning found in connection with *analambano.* *Hupsoun* means to lift up on high, e.g. Luke 1: 52 from Mary's *Magnificat*: 'He hath put down the mighty from their seats and exalted them of low degree'; or in a more general sense, 'Whosoever shall exalt himself shall be abased, and whosoever shall abase himself shall be exalted' (Matt. 23: 12; Luke 14: 11; cf. James 4: 10; 1 Peter 5: 6). But this term also is used technically of the exaltation of Christ from humiliation, e.g. Acts 2: 32; 5: 31. And yet like *analēmpsis* it is used directly of the *death* of Christ, especially in the Fourth Gospel, John 3: 14; 8: 28; 12: 32, 34. It is thus made clear that the glorification of Christ begins not with his actual ascension or resurrection, but with his crucifixion and indeed with his ascent to Jerusalem and Calvary for sacrifice. Theologically, therefore, this tells us that the unity of crucifixion and ascension means that the sacrifice of Christ falls also within the eternal sphere, within the very presence of God himself, or to use Old Testament language, within the veil in the Holy of Holies where God's presence dwells and his mercy-seat is flanked by the cherubim.[3]

The raising up of Christ begins, paradoxically, with his crucifixion, and his ascension begins, paradoxically, with his lifting up on the Cross.[4] Although the beginning is there, the movement of ascension leads straight to his being lifted up on high to be at the right hand of the Father, where he is exalted to be a Prince and a Saviour. At the same time we must not forget here the other meaning of the resurrection, used often together with ascension and exaltation in these contexts, namely, that of installation in the Messianic Office, the exaltation of Christ with power as the Mighty Son of God. Once

---

[3] It should not need to be said that the use of spatial language here, as with the ascension, does not imply some alleged mythical 'three-storied' picture of the world; even in the Old Testament it is clearly recognized that 'the heaven of heavens cannot contain God' (1 Kings 8: 27; 2 Chron. 2: 6, 6: 18; and Acts 7: 48f.); As I have shown (*Space, Time and Incarnation*) the problem lies in the presuppositions of the biblical interpreter in respect of a receptacle view of space, not in biblical or early Christian theology. Cf. Origen's criticism of such a misinterpretation of spatial language, *On Prayer*, 23. 1–5.

[4] This mutual involution of humiliation and exaltation has been very finely expounded by Heinrich Vogel, *Gott im Christo*, 1951, pp. 732ff.

again the term *hupsoun* chimes in here, for it also has the meaning of exaltation, or of being raised to an exalted height, or
hupsos, so that the exalted One is clothed with power from on
high. This is found in several New Testament passages, but
perhaps the meaning comes out most clearly in the language
that is used of Melchizedek who is spoken of as 'the priest of
the Most High God' (Heb. 7: 1), for this is the sense in which it
is applied to Christ.[5]

To sum up, then, the ascension of Christ in this sense is his
exaltation to power and glory but *through the Cross*, certainly
an exaltation from humiliation to royal majesty, but through
crucifixion and sacrifice, for the power and glory of the Royal
Priest are bound up with his self-offering in death and resurrection. It is ultimately in that fusion of resurrection with the
ascension in one indivisible exaltation that we are to understand the continuing ministry of Christ in presenting his
'many brethren' along with himself, amidst the sanctities of the
new creation and in eternal glorification of the Father. It is as
such that he blesses mankind by pouring out upon them his
Spirit and fulfilling in them the work of God's reconciling love.[6]
'This Jesus did God raise up, of whom we are all witnesses',
proclaimed Peter on the day of Pentecost. 'Being therefore at
the right hand of God exalted, and having received of the
Father the promise of the Holy Spirit, he has poured forth this,
which you see and hear' (Acts 2: 32f.). Likewise the apostles
Peter and John declared before the Sanhedrin, 'The God of
our fathers raised up Jesus . . . him did God exalt at his right
hand to be a Prince and a Saviour, to give repentance to Israel
and remission of sins.' (Acts 5: 30f.).

[5] It is from this perspective that William Milligan's two works *The Resurrection of Our Lord* and *The Ascension of Our Lord* were written. For what
follows on the three-fold office of Christ, see *The Resurrection of Our Lord*, pp.
136–52; and *The Ascension of Our Lord*, pp. 61–226. The Ascension is here
regarded as 'a corollary from the resurrection'.

[6] William Manson, *The Epistle to the Hebrews*, p. 116: 'Just as St. Paul
cannot think of faith except as faith in the God of the Resurrection, so for
the writer to the Hebrews Jesus is *Priest of the Resurrection* and the inaugu-
rator of a "better hope" by which we draw near to God'.

2. *The Three-fold Office of Christ in Ascension*

(i) *The Ascension of Christ the King*

The nature of the kingship that is indicated in this context is appropriate to the language of the ascension that is used. Christ ascends as Lamb of God and as Son of Man, he is exalted to royal power in redemption and creation. It is in the conjunction of grace and omnipotence that Christ ascends to the throne of God in order to fulfil his saving work and fill all things with his sovereign presence and power – yet, as we shall see, the ascension involves the veiling of his divine majesty and power, or the holding back, from our visible and physical contact in space and time, of his unveiled majesty and power. In the language of the *Apocalypse*, he who has all power in heaven and earth, who alone is able to break open the sealed books of destiny, is the Lion of the tribe of Judah; but this figure is identified with the Lamb as it had been slain (Rev. 5: 1–14). Even in ascension the power of Christ is exercised through his sacrifice, through his atoning expiation of guilt, through his priestly mediation before God. It is in this very connection that we are to understand the ascension of the Son of Man. It is the ascension of representative Man in whom all humanity is gathered up and made participant in his self-offering, so that in his ascension Christ is installed as Head of the New Humanity, the Prince of the New Creation, the King of the Kingdom which he has won and established through his incarnate life and passion. The ascension is the enthronement of that Christ at the right hand of the Father in the sovereignty of Grace. Henceforth all things are directed from the mercy-seat of God, by the enthoned and exalted Lamb, who reigns not only over the Church, but over all creation.

(ii) *The Ascension of Christ the Royal Priest*

We recall that the priestly ministry of Christ is set forth in the New Testament, notably in the Epistle to the Hebrews and the Johannine literature, in the light of the Old Testament priestly and liturgical tradition. In this the fundamental priesthood was regarded as that of the Word from God to man (which Philo called 'the high-priestly Logos')[7] with respect to

Moses, while the liturgical priesthood was regarded as bearing witness to that divine Word in cultic acts of mediation through oblation and sacrifice, with respect to Aaron. Because the Aaronic priesthood exalted itself beyond the function of witness and obedience to the Word of God, arrogating to itself an independent status and clutching at authority or rule through cultic manipulation of the divine Will, it was fiercely criticized by the prophets whom God raised up to bring the priestly function back to its true relation to the Word of God and in subordination to it.[8] It was in this connection that they called for 'obedience' not 'sacrifice'. This did not mean a rejection of the divine provision in the cult, but a reintegration of it with the primacy of Torah, so that out of the prophetic tradition came the rehabilitation and interpretation of the cultic tradition in the redacted form in which it has been handed down to us in the Pentateuch. But then there developed a tension between a priestly and scribal tradition which can be characterized as that between legalized liturgy and liturgized law. It was in that context and in the tradition of the cultic prophets such as the Isaiahs, Jeremiah, Ezekiel, Zechariah, that Jesus engaged in dialogue with the priestly and scribal authorities of the Jews in order to force them back upon true priestly relation to the Word of God. He criticized the hardened priestly and scribal traditions and confronted them with the Kingdom of God which had 'drawn near' of itself through Word and Spirit in direct acts of forgiveness and healing, calling forth the liturgy of praise and thanksgiving from outcast sinners and little children which shamed the priestly and scribal authorities of Israel.[9]

The New Testament interprets Christ in this situation both as *Apostle from God* and as *our High Priest* (Heb. 3: 1f).[10] In

---

[7] Philo Judaeus, *De gigantibus*, 52; *De migratione Abrahami*, 102; cf. also *De cherubim et flammeo gladio*, 17; *Quod deterius potiori insidiari soleat*, 132.

[8] See *Royal Priesthood*, Scottish Journal of Theology Occasional Papers, No. 3, 1963, pp. 5ff.

[9] Cf. the interesting discussion by Jeremias on 'The quenched spirit', *New Testament Theology*, Eng. tr. 1971, vol. I, pp. 80ff.

[10] William Manson has pointed out that in Judaism the high-priest on the Day of Atonement was recognized as the *Shaliach* (the apostle, commissioner) not of men but of God, *The Epistle to the Hebrews*, p. 54.

Christ both sides of the Old Testament revelation are fulfilled. He himself is the Word of God come down into our midst, and himself the perfect response of man to that Word in his obedient self-offering in life and death. Now it is in the ascension of Jesus to the throne of God, or his entry through the veil into the Holy of Holies, that both aspects come fully and finally together. Here we have Priesthood that is no merely symbolic or institutional priesthood of witness to what God has done, for this Priesthood is the Reality to which the Old Testament priesthood bore witness; it is God's mediatorial action translated into terms of the Son of Man. Here, therefore, the symbolic and liturgical priesthood of the Aaronic tradition is transcended in a final way. Jesus is not Priest in the sense that what he does symbolizes or bears liturgical witness to something else, to what God does. No, he *is* Son of God, God himself come to us as Priest, Priest sent from God, Apostle-Priest, as well as Priest qualified to act for us through his incarnational solidarity with sinners. It is only on that ground that he ascends as Priest. But here we pass from the Aaronic priesthood to priesthood of quite a different order, for he is Priest not on the ground of legal ordinance but in a royal and sovereign way on the ground of his own endless Life. He is Priest in final reality, and his sacrifice actually bears away our sins and cleanses us from guilt, and takes us into the presence of the Father. He makes a true atonement which no Aaronic priesthood could ever make. This is Priesthood that arises out of Christ's Sonship (Priesthood in which Apostleship from God and Priesthood from man are hypostatically united in his own Person), Royal Priesthood – for it is priesthood in which the liturgical witness and the reality witnessed to are one and the same, priesthood in which Word and Act are identical in his Person and therefore priesthood which is sovereign in its own right. Here liturgical act is identical with kingly act, for what Jesus Christ does on our behalf is actually fulfilled with final power, whereas other priesthood at the very best can only symbolize it or bear witness to it.

This is what the ascension of Christ means for his priestly ministry; it is the coincidence of grace and power which makes it Royal or Sovereign Priesthood. The resurrection and ascension, however, do not mean that Christ's priestly sacrifice and oblation of himself are over and done with, but rather that in their once and for all completion they are taken up eternally into the life of God, and remain prevalent, efficacious, valid, or abidingly real. Christ is spoken of in the Epistle to the Hebrews, as the *Prodromos* or the *Archēgos*, the One who has gone ahead and broken a way through into the immediate presence of God, and is *our* Prince and Leader, so that all who are united with him may through the living way which he has prepared in himself enter into the heavenly sanctuary. But Christ is spoken of also as himself the *Leitourgos*, the Leader of the Heavenly Worship and Chief Executive as it were, in the heavenly Kingdom. Through the power of his endless Life he ever lives to exercise his priestly ministry on our behalf and in the worship that surrounds the throne of the Most High.

How then, are we to think of the work of Christ in his heavenly priesthood?

(*a*) *It is his endless self-oblation.*[11] In the humanity of the ascended Christ there remains for ever before the Face of God the Father the one, perfect, sufficient Offering for mankind. He presents himself before the Father as the Redeemer who has united himself to us and has become our Brother. He represents us before the Father as those who are incorporated in him and consecrated and perfected together with him in one for ever. Here we think of the ascension as the act of Christ's self-offering to the Father in which his self-sacrifice on the Cross is backed up by his own resurrection and endless Life, and made an offering to God through Eternal Spirit. The New Testament and patristic understanding of this is evidently an extension of the Old Testament conception of the *minhah*, the thank-offering or tribute which we offer to the King of Kings.[12]

(*b*) *It is his eternal intercession or advocacy for us.* We cannot consider this properly without taking into account the vicarious life of Jesus in obedience and prayer, and the fact that the whole existence of the incarnate Son was both the fulfilled intervention of God among men and the fulfilled response of men toward God, in filial obedience, faith, trust, love, worship, prayer, and praise. The very existence of Christ among us, his life, work, crucifixion, resurrection, are all modes of his

[11] For the following see *Theology in Reconciliation*, pp. 106-38.
[12] See *Didache*, 14. 2 with reference to Malachi 1: 11, 14.

divine-human intervention or intercession – in Greek, the words for 'intervention' and 'intercession' being the same, *entughanein*.[13] In the indissoluble fusion of his human life with his divine activity, his vicarious representation of us was backed up by his divine Life. We recall how in the incarnation the Son of God staked his own divine being for us by entering into the existence of man as it had fallen under the judgment of God and the imminent privation of being, in order to redeem us, and how in the resurrection that *Goel*-redemption is efficacious over death, so that Jesus Christ remains in himself, in his very union with God the Father, the eternal pledge or surety of our redemption. It is with that ontological content of his Advocacy on our behalf that we are concerned here. It is an Advocacy in which his Word and Person and Act are one and indivisible.

Here is an Advocacy in which Christ is the eternal Leader of our prayer and intercession, in which he makes himself the true content and sole reality of the worship and prayer of man.[14] That is the prayer which (as reported by the Evangelist) we overhear at the Last Supper, in John 17, the prayer we overhear in Gethsemane, the prayer we hear from the Cross, the prayer of his whole Life, the prayer that is summed up in the words of his own Prayer, *Our Father*, which he prayed with us in our flesh and which he puts into our mouth. That is the prayer which Jesus Christ *eternally is* before the face of the Father and in God himself where he ever lives in active intercession and prayer for us. We have to think of this in terms of *substitution* as well as *representation*. If he were only our representative before God, he would represent us in *our* prayer and worship and would be, so to speak, their instrument. But as substitute as well as representative he acts in our place and offers worship and prayer which we could not offer, yet offers them in such a vicarious way that while in our stead and on

[13] For the meaning of this term, see William Milligan, *The Ascension of our Lord*, pp. 19ff. 'The Intercession and the Offering cannot be separated from each other. The offering is itself a continuous intercession; the continuous intercession implies the offering as a present thing.' (p. 160).

[14] See *Theology in Reconciliation. Essays towards Evangelical and Catholic Unity in East and West*, ch. 4, 'The Mind of Christ in Worship: The Problem of Apollinarianism in the Liturgy', pp. 139ff.

our behalf they are made to issue out of our human nature to the Father as our own worship and prayer to God. We worship the Father not in our own name, nor in the significance of our own prayer and worship, but solely in Christ's name who has so identified himself with us as to make his prayer and worship ours, so really ours that we appear before God with Christ himself as our one true prayer and our only worship. That identification is so profound that through the Spirit Christ's prayers and intercessions are made to echo in our own, and there is no disentangling of them from our weak and stammering and altogether unworthy acts of devotion. It is in this light that we have to understand Eucharistic worship and prayer, and are to think of the heart of it all in the Lord's Prayer which we take into our mouths at his command. It is Prayer backed up with the pledges of his broken body and shed blood which he puts into our hands, with which to appear before the Father, for it is his one sufficient and once for all offering of himself for us that is our only sacrifice before God. This is neither a Pelagian offering of the immolated Christ by man nor a Pelagian offering of ourselves in addition to the sacrifice of Christ, but the pleading of a sacrifice which by its very nature is offered on our behalf and in our place and in our stead, so that it is not we but Christ himself who here stands in for us as our Mediator and Advocate, while we take refuge in his sole sacrifice, finding shelter in his prayer and intercession and not in our own. 'Nothing in my hands I bring, simply to Thy Cross I cling'.[15]

(c) *It is his eternal benediction.*[16] In his ascension Jesus Christ blessed his people, and fulfilled that blessing in sending down upon us the presence of the Holy Spirit. The language which the New Testament uses to speak of these aspects of Christ's heavenly priesthood is taken from the Old Testament accounts of Melchizedek's blessing of Abraham, and from the Aaronic blessing of God's people after the completion of the sacrificial liturgy on the Day of Atonement. We recall the account given of Christ's ascension, and of the lifting up of his hands in blessing upon the disciples with the promise of the

---

[15] See further, *Conflict and Agreement in the Church*, vol. 2, *The Ministry and the Sacraments of the Gospel*, 1960, pp. 148f., 181ff.

[16] Again see William Milligan, *The Ascension of Our Lord*, pp. 161ff.

power of the Spirit (Acts 1: 1–11). Pentecost is the content and actualization of that high priestly blessing. He ascended in order to fill all things with his presence and to bestow gifts of the Spirit upon men. It is this image of Christ the Royal Priest that occupies such a central place in the *Apocalypse*, not least in the opening chapters but also at the end in the consummation and fulfilment of Christ's blessing, in the New Jerusalem that descends from above.

This is, again, an aspect of Christ's royal priestly ministry which is especially relevant to the Church's Communion in the body and blood of Christ through the Spirit. It is through the Church's *koinōnia* with Christ that various gifts are distributed to members of the Church which in their manifold character and working together in the one Body are made to echo the one Priesthood of Christ. The Church is thus also a 'royal priesthood' on earth through the Spirit, but a royal priesthood in a secondary sense, participating in the one Priesthood of the ascended King through its *service* of him (1 Pet. 2: 9; cf. 2: 5).[17] The New Testament does not speak of 'a priesthood of all believers' for it no more speaks of the *individual* as a 'priest' than it speaks of him as a 'king'. The priesthood of the Church is not constituted through the aggregation of the priestly functions of its individual members but is only a reflection of the one indivisible Priesthood of Christ. Through the Spirit Christ's own priestly ministry is at work in and through the Church which is his Body.

(iii) *The Ascension of Christ the Prophet*

Just as the concepts of king and priest are essentially changed when they are applied to Christ, inasmuch as he makes himself their Subject and Content, so the concept of the prophet is

---

[17] I have translated the Greek word *basileion* as an adjective, which makes 'royal priesthood' mean a priesthood in the service of the King – see Bo Reicke, *The Epistles of James, Peter and Jude*, 1964, pp. 93, 137; and E. Best, *I Peter* (New Century Bible), 1971, p. 107; cf. 102f. Best himself prefers to take *basileion* as a noun (cf. Exod. 19: 6) which in view of 'holy (*hagion*) priesthood' of v. 5 is rather difficult but nevertheless possible, but when he translates *basileion* as 'group of kings' his argument involves a movement from 'a possible meaning' of *basileion* to the conclusion ' "royal" is to be taken as a noun, preferably with the meaning "group of kings" ' (p. 108). As far as I know there is no patristic support for such a translation.

also changed. He is Prophet in a unique sense, for he is in himself the Word he proclaims just as he is himself the King of the Kingdom and the Priest who is identical with the Offering he makes. Christ ascended, then, as the Word made flesh, as he is both Word from God to man and word from man to God. He is God's own Word translated into human form and reality and returning back to the Father as answering Word in perfect fulfilment of his Will. It is in that identity of Word of God and Word of man that Christ's prophetic ministry is fulfilled.

Let us think of this in terms of the longer or additional conclusion of St. Mark's Gospel, 16: 19f., 'So then after the Lord had spoken unto them, he was received into heaven, and sat at the right hand of God. And they went out and preached everywhere, the Lord working with them and confirming their word with signs following'. Here we have a statement about the relation between the Church's proclamation of Christ and the activity of Christ himself in that proclamation where, through their common objective and dynamic content, the proclamation of the Gospel in the name of Christ and Christ's own proclamation are one and the same. That is the New Testament concept of the *kerygma*, in which proclamation is objectively and dynamically controlled by the reality proclaimed. Primarily, it is Christ's own *kerygma*, his self-proclamation, which through the Spirit he allows to be echoed and heard through the preaching of the Church, so that their *kerygma* about Jesus Christ is made one with his own *kerygma*. In an important sense that happened once for all in the fulfilment of the apostolic office, for it was the special function of the Apostles to translate the self-witness of Christ into witness to Christ, the self-proclamation of Christ into proclamation of Christ by the Church, in such a way that this evangelical *kerygma* was made communicable by men and given extension throughout history as the saving Word of God.[18] In and through the preaching and teaching of that Word it is Christ himself the incarnate and risen Word who is mightily at work, confronting men and women with himself and summoning them to believe and follow him.

---

[18] See the extensive discussion of the issues here by Hermann Diem, *Dogmatics*, Eng. tr. 1959, especially chs. IV and XI; and more recently, Oscar Cullmann, *Salvation in History*, pp. 110ff.

Here, then, we have to think of Christ as the ascended Word – that is, the Word from God to man incarnated in our human existence, made articulate in human word and therefore communicable to men and understandable by them; but he is also the word from man to God which in Jesus is directed to the Father. The ascension is not only the bearing of that Word up before the Face of the Father, but that Word accepted and honoured by God, that Word fully installed in the divine Kingdom, sent back to earth through the Spirit and by means of the Church proclaimed to all nations and all ages. Thus the ascended Christ through the Spirit, which he has sent down upon the Church to abide with it, continues to exercise his prophetic ministry throughout all history.

It is perhaps in connection with the notion of the 'Mediator' (in Latin *Mediator* or *Interpres*) that we should seek to understand this prophetic ministry, for it is the ministry of the Word which is not separable from the ministry of Reconciliation. It is Word of forgiveness now finally actualized by Act of God in the Cross and Resurrection, Word that is itself Act of God, but it is Word in which the historical Jesus Christ and the eternal Word of God are in indissoluble union. That is the kind of Word that is mediated to us through the Blessing of Christ and the pouring out of his Spirit, a prophetic ministry in which Christ is himself its living, actual and full content, or in which Christ effectively ministers himself to us.

How are we to think of this ministry as taking place? It takes place in the relation between the Church on earth and Christ himself as the relation between the Body and the Head of the Body. The Church is the bodily and historical form of Christ's existence on earth through which he lets his Word be heard, so that as the Church bears witness to him and proclaims the Gospel of salvation in his Name, he himself through the Spirit is immediately present validating that Word as his own, and communicating himself to men through it.[19] The Church's proclamation of the Gospel becomes thus the *sceptre*, as Clement

---

[19] See Karl Barth, *Church Dogmatics*, IV/1, pp. 643ff., where he expounds the proposition that 'The Holy Spirit is the awakening power in which Jesus Christ has formed and continually renews his body, i.e. his own earthly-historical form of existence, the one holy catholic and apostolic Church'.

of Rome called it,[20] through which the risen and ascended Christ rules over the nations and all history. It is by the Word of the Gospel that he rules over all things until he comes again to judge and renew his creation.

It is within this 'sacramental relation' between the Church as the Body of Christ and Christ the Head of the Body, in which the Church is given '*koinōnia* in the mystery of Christ', that we are to think of the relation between the earthly ministries that arise in the Church under the gifts of the ascended Lord, and the heavenly ministry of Christ himself. As King and Head of the Church Christ has instituted the ministry of Word and Sacrament within history, whereby he continually nourishes, sustains, orders and governs his people on earth. Within the 'royal priesthood' of the whole Church which reflects his own Royal Priesthood, Jesus Christ has called some to be set apart to this special ministry, to be his ambassadors to teach and preach, and administer the sacraments as the seals of their ambassadorial office in his Name. This institutional ministry was given its specific form and shape by the Apostles in obedience to the commands of Christ himself. Not only did they, therefore, mediate to us the New Testament revelation, in which Christ's own self-witness was translated into the form of witness to Christ, and made communicable from men to men in history (which is handed on to us in the Canon of the New Testament) but they instituted a historical ministry at the same time, dependent on their own unique ministry, and going out from theirs with the specific function of handing on the *kerygma* and *didache* of Christ from generation to generation. But Christ himself is at work in this continuing ministry. Not only did he pour out his Spirit upon the Apostles inspiring them for their special task, and not only did he pour out his Spirit in a decisive and once for all way, at Pentecost, constituting the people of God into the New Testament Church which is the Body of Christ, but within that Church and its Communion of the Spirit he continues to pour out special gifts for ministry, with the promise that as the Gospel is proclaimed in his Name he will work with the Church confirming their ministry of Christ to others as his own and making it the ministry of himself to mankind. Those who are called and thus endowed

[20] *1 Clement*, 26. 2.

with gifts of the Spirit to engage in this ministry, fulfil their office by *serving* Christ who is Prophet, Priest and King of the Church. In the Name of Jesus Christ they expound the Holy Scriptures, preach Christ crucified and risen, declare the forgiveness of sins, and call all men to be reconciled to God, but the Lord himself is immediately present with them in his Spirit, making the preaching of the Gospel effectual as Word and Power of God. In the name of Jesus Christ these ministers lead the worship of God's people, declare the forgiveness of sins, and celebrate Baptism and the Lord's Supper, but through the power of his Spirit it is Christ himself who confers forgiveness, builds up his Church on earth, renews it in the power of his resurrection, and presents it as his own Body to the Father. In the name of Jesus Christ they also have charge over the Church on earth, to shepherd it as the flock of Christ, to feed it with the bread of life, to build it up in the unity of the faith, so that by the power of the Holy Spirit, through whom Jesus Christ himself governs the Church, it becomes the instrument for the renewal of the world and the extension of his Kingdom among all nations. Although in this way Jesus Christ calls some to be set apart to special office in his Church and endows them with the appropriate gifts of the Spirit for its fulfilment, every member of the Church which is his body through sacramental incorporation into Christ is engaged in the mission of the Gospel, to bear the reproach of Christ, to witness to him as Saviour and Lord, to participate in his ministry of reconciliation and to live in the world the new life in him. Thus the mission of the whole Church as the Body of Christ on earth and in history is called through the Spirit, as it were, into contrapuntal relation to the heavenly ministry of Christ, King, Priest and Prophet, yet in such a way that the Church cannot draw attention to itself, for the patterns of its life and work on earth have their significance entirely and only in directing the world away to the risen and ascended Lord himself.

CHAPTER 6

THE NATURE OF THE ASCENSION EVENT

We are back again here at the same question that we had to face in regard to the event of the resurrection, and certainly it has the same baffling character, especially when it is taken out of the context of the whole movement of the incarnation and the saving acts of God within it. That we cannot do this is surely one of the lessons to be learned from 'the forty days' between the resurrection and the ascension, for they had nothing to do, as is sometimes alleged, with a progressive spiritualization or immaterialization of the body of Christ, but with the training of the disciples through a manifestation of Christ in which the thoughts of suffering and glory, of humiliation and exaltation, were bound together in his own Person in indissoluble union.[1] Nevertheless, while closely tied up with the crucifixion and resurrection in this way, and indeed as continuous with them, as is assumed in the Epistle to the Hebrews,[2] the ascension must be understood in a correlation with the incarnation, as the *anabasis* (ascent) of the Son of God corresponding to his *katabasis* (descent).[3]

1. *How is the Event of the Ascension Related to Space and Time?*

This is the other pole of the question as to the relation of the incarnation to space and time which gave rise in the sixteenth century to the controversy over the so-called *extra*

[1] Thus William Milligan, *The Ascension of Our Lord*, p. 5.

[2] 'The resurrection and ascension of Jesus Christ are two distinct but inseparable moments in one and the same event. The resurrection is to be understood as the *terminus a quo*, its beginning, and the ascension as its *terminus ad quem*, its end.' Karl Barth, *Church Dogmatics*, IV/2, p. 150.

[3] This was a favourite theme of Irenaeus, *Adv. haereses*, 3. 1. 6, 18. 2, 19. 3; 5. 21. 1, 36. 3, etc.; cf. *Epideixis*, 83f.

Calvinisticum, 'the Calvinist extra'.[4] Did the eternal Son of God, in becoming incarnate, really become man at Bethlehem and so really enter within our existence of space and time? If so, was he incarnate in the Babe of Bethlehem in such a way that he left the bosom of the Father or left the throne of the universe? Or are we to say that while he really did become incarnate, flesh of our flesh and bone of our bone, subjecting himself to the conditions and determinations of our existence in space and time, nevertheless he continued to rule the universe as the Creator Logos by whom all things that are made are made? Patristic and Reformed theology have always claimed that the Eternal Logos did enter space and time, not merely as Creator, but as himself made creature, and therefore within the creaturely limits of space and time, and yet did not cease to be what he eternally was in himself, the Creator Word in whom and through whom all things consist and by whom all things derive and continue to have their being. This view was rejected by Lutherans because like the Mediaevals but unlike the Fathers they operated with a receptacle view of space as the place containing within its limits that which occupies it. Hence when Calvin said of Christ that he became man born of the Virgin's womb without leaving heaven or the government of the world, he was interpreted by Lutherans to imply that in the incarnation only part of the Word was contained in the babe of Bethlehem or wrapped in the swaddling clothes in the cradle, and that something was left 'outside' (extra) – hence the so-called 'Calvinist extra'. It was undoubtedly the Lutheran intention to maintain in the fullest possible way real and full incarnation. And that was certainly right.

Nevertheless, it is clear that a rejection of the 'Calvinist extra' raises very great difficulties, as one can see in a kenotic theory of Christ's *self-emptying*. Quite clearly if one operates with a receptacle view of space, one must think of the *kenosis* as the emptying of the Son of God into a containing vessel, but this way of thinking creates difficulties that need not be there and which once created need to be solved. The same problem arose in the Mediaeval doctrine of the real presence. If a receptacle view of space or place is held, how are we to think of the Body

---

[4] See *Space, Time and Incarnation*, pp. 30f., 49f.

of Christ as contained in the host, in every part of it, and in a multitude of hosts at the same time, and how can we think of it as being contained without any relation between the dimensions of the Body of Christ and the space of the place that contains him? The usual Mediaeval answer was given in the doctrine of transubstantiation in which an artificial distinction was drawn between the substance and the accidents of the elements, their substances being changed into the body and blood of Christ, while the accidents remained as before. It was basically the same problem that faced the Lutherans and indeed the same kind of answer that was given by them in regard to the question as to how we are to conceive the being of the Son of God as contained in the body of the historical Jesus Christ. The kenotic theories answered by drawing a distinction between the immanent and relative properties of the Son and claiming either that he shed those that were incompatible with creaturely existence or that their use was restricted in the incarnate state. But in actual fact this way of relating the 'immensity' of God to the finite receptacle – *finitum capax infiniti* – usually meant the extension of the human receptacle to contain the divine, e.g. in the doctrine of the ubiquity of the body of Christ, which could hardly avoid a form of monophysitism. Another answer which had already been adopted by Luther was to think of the relation between the divine Being and the physical existence of Jesus Christ in space and time as a mathematical point, but that tended to reduce history to a vanishing point. In Lutheran thought it came to imply a radical disjunction between the divine and the human in which there was no interaction between them. This in effect is the same sort of answer now given by the 'demythologizers' who posit such an infinite difference between the divine being and the creaturely realm of space and time that they are related to one another only tangentially at the point called 'Jesus' whose historical existence is then only a sort of springboard for a constant leap in existential decision that leaves history behind. The problem is 'solved' by the reduction of the historical Jesus to a vanishing point.

The original Lutheran position had its extremely important truth in the insistence that a real and genuine incarnation took place, an incarnation which means that the Word of God is nowhere to be found except in inseparable union with Jesus, the Babe of Bethlehem, the real and proper Man. But if we press that to mean that in the incarnation the Word was resolved into this Jesus without remainder, so to speak, then insuperable difficulties arise – and solutions such as a metaphysical *kenōsis* or demythologizing have to be found. Now of course we cannot say that the eternal Logos became flesh in such a way that part of the Logos was excluded – that is what the early Lutherans were afraid of, for the Logos was totally incarnate – nevertheless he remained wholly himself, the Creator and Ruler and Preserver of the universe of all creaturely reality. He became man without ceasing to be God, and so entered space and time without leaving the throne of God. Our difficulty is that we have to think *both* in accordance with the nature of the Logos as eternal Son of God and in accordance with the nature of the human Jesus as creature of space and time. It will not do to think of this in terms of a receptacle view of space and time, nor will it do to cut the knot and think of him only in one way or the other.[5] Hence if we are to be faithful to the nature of Christ as very God and very Man we have to let that determine our thinking of the incarnational event, and say both that he really and fully became man, as we men are in space and time, and yet remained God the Creator who transcends all creaturely being in space and time, and work with a *relational view of space and time* differentially or variationally related to God and to man.[6] Unless we think in this way we cannot really think the incarnation itself without falsifying it. That was the problem of the kenoticists which the demythologizers sought to solve by resolving away the incarnation as an objectifying form of thinking, but at the expense of detaching faith entirely from space and time, from any ground in physical and historical existence.

The question may be easier if we approach it along the line of 'existence'. When we say that God exists, we mean that God

[5] This dilemma was well expressed by William Temple, *Christus Veritas*, 1924, p. 142.

[6] See *Space, Time and Incarnation*, pp. 10–21; and 'The Relation of the Incarnation to Space in Nicene Theology', in *The Ecumenical World of Orthodox Civilization, Russia and Orthodoxy*, vol. III, *Essays in honor of Georges Florovsky*, edit. by A. Blane, and T. E. Bird, 1974, pp. 43–70.

exists as God, in accordance with the nature of God. Hence divine existence is of an utterly unique and transcendent kind. When we say that man exists, the term 'exists' is defined by the subject man, for it is the kind of existence which a man has in space and time. Now when we try to think together the existence of the Son of God and the existence of Jesus, Son of Mary, in one Person, we have to think them in the same way in which we think of the union of divine and human natures in the one Person. Similarly we have to think together the relation of God to space and time and the relation of the man Jesus to space and time.

It is this question that arises again in an acute form when we come to the ascension of Christ, of Jesus who is very Son of God, and who ascends from man's place to God's 'place'. In so far as he is man, truly and perfectly man, we must think of the ascension as related to the space and time of creaturely reality. But this involves a duality in itself. So far as the companions of Jesus were concerned, that is the disciples who were men of this fallen world, living historically on earth, the ascension of Jesus *from* Peter, James and John, etc., must also be related to the kind of space and time with which *we* men and women are involved in the on-going existence of this passing world. But in his own resurrection Jesus had healed and redeemed our creaturely existence from all corruption and privation of being, and every threat of death or nothingness, so that in him space and time were recreated or renewed. We have no adequate language to describe this, and can speak of it only in apocalyptic language, that is in language that breaks down in its very using, but which must break down if it really is to point us to this new reality beyond, which cannot be captured or enclosed in the language of this fallen world. Nevertheless the humanity of Jesus, although risen and triumphant over all decay and corruption, was fully and truly human, and indeed more fully and truly human than any other humanity we know, for it was humanity in which all that attacks and undermines creaturely and human being is vanquished. In the risen Jesus therefore, creaturely space and time, far from being dissolved are confirmed in their reality before God. On the one hand, then, the ascension must be thought out in relation to the actual relations of space and time. On the other hand, however, the ascension must be thought of as an ascension beyond all our notions of space and time (cf. 'higher than the heavens', Heb. 7: 26), and therefore as something that cannot ultimately be expressed in categories of space and time, or at least cannot be enclosed within categories of this kind. That is why Calvin used to insist that while the ascension was an ascension into the heavens, away from us, yet it was also an ascension beyond the heaven of heavens, beyond anything that can be conceived in terms of earth or heaven.[7] We have heavens that are appropriate to human beings, the sky above the earth, the 'space' beyond the sky, but all these are understood anthropocentrically, for they are conceivable to men as created realities. But God in his own nature cannot be conceived in that way – God utterly transcends the boundaries of space and time, and therefore because he is beyond them he is also everywhere, for the limits of space and time which God transcends are all around us. Hence from this aspect the absence or presence of God cannot be spoken of in categories of space and time, but only when categories of space and time break off and point beyond themselves altogether to what is ineffable and inconceivable in modes of our space and time. Calvin was also right when he said that the Biblical writers never thought of the presence of God or of the ascension simply in terms of our space and time or in terms of earth and heaven. What does the ascension to the right hand of God mean? he asked. What else is the right hand of God but the power of God, and 'where' is that but everywhere 'where' God is? What do we mean by 'everywhere where God is', except what is defined by the nature of God himself as the existence of God is defined by this nature?

In order to express this more positively, let us turn back to the incarnation for a moment. Jesus Christ, the man Jesus, is the *place* in this physical world of space and time where God and man meet, and where they have communion with one another. The Temple in the Old Testament was the place where God put his Name, where he kept tryst with his cove-

[7] John Calvin, see especially *Comm. on Ephesians*, 1. 20 (tr. by T. H. L. Parker, p. 136f.), 4. 10 (p. 176f.); *Commen. on Hebrews*, 6. 26 (tr. by W. B. Johnston, p. 102); *Institute*, 2. 16. 14f. Cf. further *Kingdom and Church. A Study in the Theology of the Reformation*, p. 108ff.

nanted people, and where they kept covenant with him. Jesus Christ is that Temple of God as a living reality on earth and among men where God has put his Name, and where he has appointed us to meet him. It is the place where heaven and earth meet, the place of reconciliation within our historical existence in flesh and blood. Jesus Christ is himself among us God's mercy-seat, God's place in the world where he is really present to us in our place.

Now we have to think of this Jesus Christ ascended to God as 'in heaven'.[8] In its way this is the reverse of the incarnation. As in the incarnation we have to think of God the Son becoming man without ceasing to be transcendent God, so in his ascension we have to think of Christ as ascending above all space and time without ceasing to be man or without any diminishment of his physical, historical existence. That is what we normally mean by saying that Christ is 'in heaven'. But we surely mean something more, for the ascension of the incarnate, crucified and risen Jesus Christ inevitably transforms 'heaven': something quite new has been effected in the heavenlies which must alter its material content in our understanding of what heaven is.[9] Whatever else 'heaven' is for us it is the 'place' where Christ is in God. Hence we can speak of Christ as having a 'heavenly place' in God far beyond anything we can understand and far beyond our reach. Nevertheless through his Spirit Jesus Christ bestows his presence upon us in the Church, so that the Church on earth, in the continuing space-time of this world, is the 'place' where God and man are appointed to meet. In the incarnation we have the meeting of man and God in man's place, but in the ascension we have the meeting of man and God in God's place, but through the Spirit these are not separated from one another (they were not

[8] ' "Heaven" in biblical language is the sum of the inaccessible and incomprehensible side of the created world, so that, although it is not God himself, it is the throne of God, the creaturely correspondence to his glory, which is veiled from man, and cannot be disclosed except on his initiative.' Karl Barth, *Church Dogmatics*, III/1, p. 453. See the lengthy discussion of this in III/3, pp. 418–76, and also IV/2, pp. 153f.

[9] Cf. Karl Rahner (*Sacramentum Mundi*, vol. 5, p. 333): 'The occurrence of the resurrection created "heaven" ... and taken together with the ascension (which fundamentally is an element in the resurrection), is not merely an entry into an already existing heaven'.

spatially related in any case), and man's place on earth and in the space-time of this world is not abrogated, even though he meets with God in God's place. 'Our Father who art in heaven, hallowed be thy name. Thy kingdom come, thy will be done *on earth* as it is in heaven'.

There are two points here we have to try to think together: (i) In the ascension Jesus Christ ascends from man's place to God's place; (ii) By his ascension Jesus Christ has established man in man's place in time and space.

(i) Jesus Christ has ascended from man's place to God's place, and yet he is in himself the one place in our human and created reality, and therefore in the immanent order of time and space, where God and man fully meet.[10]

We have great difficulty in speaking about this because of our abstract notions of space, but let us remember that as time is to be understood as *time for* something, the time in which we live our life, time for decision, time for repentance, time for action, and the 'time' of God is the time in which God lives his own life, the time which God has in himself for his own eternal will of love, so we must think of space as *room for* something, as place defined in terms of that which occupies it. This means that we must not abstract the notion of space from that which is located in space – for space concretely considered is place, but place not abstracted from purpose or content, and place not without ends or purposeful limits. Time and space must both be conceived in relational terms, and in accordance with the active principles or forces that move and make room for themselves in such a way that space and time arise in and with them and their movements – they are not receptacles apart from bodies or forces, but are functions of events in the universe and forms of their orderly sequence and structure. Space and time are relational and variational concepts defined in accordance with the nature of the force that gives them their field of determination. In modern thought we cannot separate space and time but think of space-time in a

---

[10] 'What the "Ascension" tells us about heaven is that it is the dimension of divine and human fellowship which is based on the resurrection and exaltation of Jesus. Henceforth it designates the "place" (in the strictly ontological sense) in which man can have eternal life.' Joseph Ratzinger, *Sacramentum Mundi*, vol. 1, p. 110.

four dimensional continuum – although there is a difference between them, for, whereas space is three-dimensional, time is one directional or irreversible. But in the nature of the case we cannot separate space from time, or location from time – temporal relation belongs to location. This is another way of saying that we must think of place as well as time in terms of that *for which* they exist or function. This is why we must speak of man's 'place' and God's 'place', but in the nature of the case 'place' is differently defined in each case. Man's 'place' is defined by the nature and activity of man as the room which he makes for himself in his life and movement, and God's 'place' is defined by the nature and activity of God as the room for the life and activity of God as God. Man's space-time is defined in accordance with the field of change and the sequence of coherent structures in which he lives his life, and this way of speaking is appropriate to man as a creature of this physical world – although we would also have to speak about the space-time of his personal, social or mental life in appropriately differential ways. We do not speak of space-time in relation to God, but we must speak of the 'place' and 'time' of God in terms of his own eternal life and his eternal purpose in the divine love, where he wills his life and love to overflow to us whom he has made to share with him his life and love. 'Time' for God himself can only be defined by the uncreated and creative life of God, and 'place' for God can only be defined by the communion of the Persons in the Divine life – that is why doctrinally we speak of the '*perichorēsis*' (from *chora* meaning space or room) or mutual indwelling of the Father, Son and Holy Spirit in the Triunity of God.

When, therefore, we come to speak of the ascension of Christ from man's place to God's place, we make a statement which is delimited and defined or bounded by the nature of man and his space at one end, but a statement which at the other end is 'bounded' by the boundless nature of God, and 'limited' only by the limitless room which God makes for himself in his eternal life and activity. In the nature of the case, statements regarding that ascension are *closed at man's end* (because bounded within the space-time limits of man's existence on earth) but are *infinitely open at God's end*, open to God's own eternal Being and the infinite room of his divine life. Here we discern the theological significance of the intention in Byzantine art in a deliberate reversal of the natural perspective in depicting the dais on which the figure of Christ is made to stand, lest it should be enclosed within converging lines, which when produced meet at a finite point. When the lines depicting the dais are made to diverge, against the natural perspective, then when produced they never meet but go out into infinity. At one end of the ikon or mosaic the figure of Christ stands in bounded space and time, but at the other end he transcends all such limitations. He became man without ceasing to be God, and lived within our physical and historical existence without leaving the throne of the universe. Epistemologically, this means that statements about God or Christ must not be such as to enclose them within the finite limits of the conceptualities and determinations of creaturely forms of thought and speech, that is, within the 'room' or 'space' of the creaturely comprehension. Here also, then, in respect of the ascension we must say with Calvin that the ascension is an event which we must speak of, on the one hand, through its relation with space and time as we know it on earth and in history, and within creaturely existence, but, on the other hand, we must speak of it as transcending all that, and as an event infinitely beyond the boundaries of our space and time or anything we could conceive in terms of them. It is the event in which Christ ascends to God's place and God's place is wherever God is, the place of the omnipresent God, who is as far removed from us as the Creator is from the creature and yet as intimately and indeed infinitely near us as the Creator is to the creature to whom he ever gives being, sustaining its reality through a relation of himself to himself, since he is so present to the creature as to complete its relation as a creature to himself the Creator. The ascension of Christ is thus an ascension to fill all things with himself, so that in a real sense he comes again in the Ascension. He had to go away in one mode of presence that he might come again in this mode of presence, leaving us in the mode of man's presence to man, and returning to us in the mode of God's presence to man, and thus not leaving man bereft of himself.

There are two things to consider here. (a) The ascension is the revelation of the *gap* between the time of the new man and the time of the old man, the gap between the resurrection reality of our humanity in Jesus Christ and the corruptible existence which we still wear and in which we are fully implicated. (*b*) The ascension is the exaltation of new man, with his fully and truly human nature, and therefore of man with his 'place' as man, with the 'room' which he is given for his human life, to participation in the divine 'place', the 'place' which God makes by his own life, and the 'room' which he has for the fulfilment of his divine love. It is ascension in which our humanity in Christ is taken up into the full Communion of Father, Son and Holy Spirit in life and love.[11]

(ii) By his ascension Jesus Christ establishes man in man's place in space and time.

The withdrawal of Christ from visible and physical contact with us in our space-time existence on earth and in history means that Jesus Christ insists in making contact with us, not first directly and immediately in his risen humanity, but first and foremost through his historical involvement with us in his incarnation and crucifixion. That is to say, by withdrawing himself from our sight, Christ sends us back to the historical Jesus Christ as the *covenanted place* on earth and in time which God has appointed for meeting between man and himself. The ascension means that our relation to the Saviour is only possible through the historical Jesus, for the historical Jesus is the *one locus* within our human and creaturely existence where God and man are hypostatically united, and where man engulfed in sin and immersed in corruption can get across to God on the ground of reconciliation and atonement freely provided by God himself. The ascension thus means that to all eternity God insists on speaking to us through the historical Jesus. Just because it is the historical and risen Jesus who is ascended, what Jesus says to us, the Jesus whom we meet and hear through the witness of the Gospels, is identical with the eternal Word and Being of God himself. *Jesus speaks as God and*

---

[11] Irenaeus includes within a statement of faith held by the whole Church 'the resurrection from the dead and the ascension into heaven in the flesh of the beloved Christ Jesus, our Lord, and his manifestation from heaven in the glory of the Father "to gather together all things in one" (Eph. 1: 10) and to raise up anew all flesh of the whole human race...'. *Adv. Haereses*, I. 10. 1.

God speaks as Jesus. Therefore we are sent back to Jesus, for there and there only may we hear God speaking in person, and there and there only at the foot of the Cross, where God, and man meet over the judgment and expiation of sin and guilt may we meet with God face to face and live, may we be judged and cleansed and have living communion with him in love through the propitiation of Jesus Christ.

Thus the ascension means that we cannot know God by transcending space and time, by leaping beyond the limits of our place on earth, but only by encountering God and his saving work within space and time, within our actual physical existence. Hence the ascension is the opposite of all demythologizing, for demythologizing means that we have to slough off the space-time involvement of the Word and Act of God as merely our own projecting and objectifying mode of thought, and so demythologizing means that we have to try to get to know God in a timeless and spaceless way. The ascension, on the contrary, sends us back to the incarnation, and to the historical Jesus, and so to a Word and Act of God inseparably implicated in our space and time. It sends us back to a Gospel which is really accessible to frail creatures of earth and history, and a Gospel that is relevant to their bodily existence day by day in the structures and coherences of space and time. Thus all true and proper knowledge of God is mediated through the historical Jesus Christ. Now that God has taken this way of revealing himself to us in and through the incarnation of his Word in the space-time existence and structure of Jesus Christ, he has set aside all other possibilities for us, no matter how conceivable they were *a priori*. Jesus Christ as the actualization of the way God has taken towards us thereby becomes the one and only way of approach to God, so that we have to *follow* Jesus exclusively. We derive our knowledge of God *a posteriori* from him who is constituted the Way, the Truth and the Life – there is now no other way to the Father. We cannot and must not try to go behind the back of Jesus Christ, to some kind of *theologia gloriae* reached by direct speculation of the divine majesty. All contact with the majesty of God as of the glorified Lord is in and through the crucified One. But the obverse of this is, that through the historical and crucified Jesus we really meet with the risen and ascended Lord, we really meet with

God in his transcendent glory and majesty, and we really are gathered into the communion of the Son with the Father and of the Father with the Son, and really are taken up through the Spirit to share in the divine life and love that have overflowed to us in Jesus Christ.

How are we to think of these two aspects of the ascension together? Clearly this can be done *only through the Spirit*. As it is the pouring out of the Spirit that links the historical Jesus with the ascended Lord, so it is through the Communion of the Spirit that we can think these things together, that is, think of the ascension both as actual historical event, in which Christ departed from man's place, and as the transcendent event in which he went to God's place. But since God's place is the place where God is, it is through the Spirit that we can think of Christ as historically absent and as actually present. It is through the Spirit that things infinitely disconnected – disconnected by the 'distance' of the ascension – are nevertheless infinitely closely related. Through the Spirit Christ is nearer to us than we are to ourselves, and we who live and dwell on earth are yet made to sit with Christ 'in heavenly places', partaking of the divine nature in him.

2. *The Material Implications of the Doctrine of the Ascension*

We must now try to gather together some of the principal points in the material content of the doctrine of the ascension.

(*a*) The ascension means the exaltation of man into the life of God and on to the throne of God. In the ascension the Son of Man, New Man in Christ, is given to partake of divine nature. There we reach the goal of the incarnation, in our great *Prodomos* or Forerunner at the right hand of God. We are with Jesus beside God, for we are gathered up in him and included in his own self-presentation before the Father.

The staggering thing about this is that the exaltation of human nature into the life of God does not mean the disappearance of man or the swallowing up of human and creaturely being in the infinite ocean of the divine Being, but rather that human nature, remaining creaturely and human, is yet exalted in Christ to share in God's life and glory.[12] This is the

[12] This is why Matt. 22: 30, 'For in the resurrection they neither marry,

ultimate end of creation and redemption revealed in the
Covenant of Grace and fulfilled in Jesus Christ, of which he
himself in his ascension is the pledge and first-fruit of its fulfilment in us. We ourselves are given a down-payment of that, as
it were, in the gift of the Spirit bestowed upon us by the
ascended man from the throne of God, so that through the
Spirit we may already have communion in the consummated
reality which will be fully actualized in us in the resurrection
and redemption of the body.

A warning should be given at this point on the danger of
vertigo that quickly overwhelms some people when they think
of themselves as being exalted in Christ to partake of the
divine nature. One finds a form of this vertigo also in some
mystics and pantheists who tend to identify their own ultimate
being with the divine Being. This would be the exact antithesis of what the Christian Gospel teaches, for the exaltation
of man into sharing the divine life and love, affirms the reality
of his humble creaturely being, by making him live out of the
transcendence of God in and through Jesus alone. The hypostatic union of the divine and human natures in Jesus preserves
the human and creaturely being he took from us, and it is in
and through our sharing in that human and creaturely being,
sanctified and blessed in him, that we share in the life of God
while remaining what we were made to be, men and not gods.

(*b*) The ascension means the establishment of a Church in
history, within space and time on the historical foundation of
the Apostles and Prophets. The ascension finalizes the ground-
ing of the Church on the historical Jesus Christ, and its con-
firmation on that foundation through the Baptism of the Spirit
at Pentecost. By withdrawing himself from continuing visible
and immediate contact as our contemporary in history Jesus
Christ establishes the people of God within the processes and

---

nor are given in marriage, but are as the angels in heaven', cannot be interpreted to imply any denigration of the flesh, on the ground that in the
resurrection we will put off the flesh and take on a bodiless angelic nature,
for the resurrection does not mean a transformation into another nature,
but rather the establishment of human nature in an imperishable state.
The resurrected are to be like angels, Methodios argues against Origen,
'not in respect of having no flesh, but in respect of not marrying and being
married, and of existing henceforth in immortality and light'. *On the
resurrection*, 1. 51.

structured patterns of history as a coherent Body, sends it on an historical mission and determines for it an historical development, since it must live and work in the on-going sequences and this-worldly forms of life as they develop among the nations and peoples and kingdoms of historical existence.

Part of this establishing of the Church as a fact within the space-time structures of history, is the establishing of Holy Scripture on the apostolic tradition, in its distinction from all other traditions. Another part of it is to be discerned in the development of the Church's worship and prayer within space and time out of the basic forms found in the apostolic Community, when the self-witness of Christ was translated into witness to Christ, and a foundation was laid for continuing patterns of life, worship and prayer in Christ's Name. The Church's life, worship and prayer can no more be spaceless and timeless than its historical existence can be detached from historical relation to its historical roots in Jesus Christ. The same applies to the coherent structures of the Church's life and mission within space and time, for the Church is sent to live as the 'servant of the Lord' within the nomistic structures and patterns of creaturely and historical being, yet in such a way that these are made to serve the Gospel and must not be allowed to restrict or obstruct it. Because of the resurrection and ascension, the coherent and ordered sequences of the Church's life and mission are essentially *open structures*, and more like the scaffolding which is necessary for the erection of a building but which is cast away when the building stands complete. Hence we can never identify the patterns of the Church's life in worship or ministry with the real inner forms of its being in the love of God but may regard them only as temporary forms which will fall away when with the advent of Christ the full reality of the new humanity of the Church as the Body of Christ will be unveiled.

(c) The ascension of Jesus Christ and his session at the right hand of God the Father is the mystery of world history. Our history has been gathered up in Jesus Christ and is taken up with him into the life and rule of God, but in his ascension, it is, as it were, anchored within the veil, by an anchor that will not drag, no matter how fierce and terrible and devastating may be the storms that sweep over the earth and its history.

Here we are back again in the theme of the *Apocalypse* which must not be interpreted in the old manner of idealistic Christianity as a flight from history, but precisely the reverse, as the invasion of history by the Kingdom of Christ through the everlasting Gospel. It is because the Kingdom of Christ is operative in and throughout all nations and peoples and all ages that such apocalyptic strife is generated among men. Hence to the eyes of faith the great movements of history, even the darkest and most terrible of them, appear as reactions to the real movement within history that takes its cue from the initative of God's grace deriving from the mighty acts of God in Jesus Christ and perpetuated in the proclamation of the Gospel. The obverse of the invasion of the Kingdom of Christ and its struggle with the kingdoms of this world is the *millennium-time* of the Kingdom of Christ stretching from resurrection to final advent, which is history seen from the point of the triumph of the risen Lamb of God who subornes all world events to serve God's saving purpose. He who made the terrible Cross to be the supreme instrument for the salvation of mankind, is by the same Cross able to make all history serve the ends of God in the new creation. The ascension of Christ is here to be seen as the transcendent act whereby Jesus Christ who is and remains the culminating point of all history is taken up into the consummation of God's Kingdom so that he remains the ultimate secret of the history of mankind. Because of the ascension the course of world history is to be regarded in the light of the heavenly session and ministry of the heavenly Mediator, for it is what he has done and is that will prevail until all history is subdued and brought into conformity to his saving Will. So far as the Church in history and on earth is concerned, therefore, the great connecting link between world history and the heavenly session of Christ is to be found in *prayer and intercession*. That is why when the New Testament speaks about the relations of Church and State it regularly directs the Church to prayer as its most important service, for it is in prayer that through the Spirit the heavenly intercessions of the risen and enthroned Lamb are made to echo in the intercessions of mankind and the people of God are locked with Christ in the great apocalyptic struggle with the forces of darkness. But because he who rules from the throne of God is the

Lamb who has been slain, but behold he is alive for evermore and holds the keys of death and hell, the Church's engagement in prayer is already a participation in the final victory of the Kingdom of Christ. Thus the life, mission, and worship of the Church on earth and in history are, as it were, in counterpoint to the victorious paeans of the hosts above who surround the throne of the Lamb and worship and glorify God.

3. *The Resurrection and the Ascension*

It should now be clear that the resurrection and the ascension have to be taken closely together as, for example, they are in the Epistle to the Hebrews. Think of them in the perspective of Christ's victory over the powers of darkness and over the evil that separates the creation from its Creator. Think of the risen and ascended humanity of Christ in the perspective of what the Johannine literature in the New Testament especially has to say about the triumph of light over darkness. Must we not, then, think of the risen and ascended humanity, even in respect of the body, as transfused with light, and as perfectly transparent? This is not to say that the Body of Christ in the resurrection and ascension was transmuted into pure spirit, whatever that may mean, but that the opaqueness and darkness that come from separation from God are utterly overcome and put away. Here redemption makes contact again with the creation in which God turned his back upon the darkness and brought what he had made into the light of life. If the resurrection and ascension bring the work of atoning reconciliation and recreation to their consummation in the humanity of Christ, then here all darkness (our darkness into which Christ descended) is done away, and even the human nature he took from our dark and fallen existence is completely and finally restored to the light of God (2 Cor. 4: 6).

We cannot think out all that this means, for it is something we may only glimpse and on which we dare not speculate. But it does help us to understand the nature of the resurrection – for example, the action of Jesus at Emmaus when he vanished out of the sight of the disciples, and also the event of the ascension when he withdrew himself from the sight of the world in accordance with his evangelical purpose for all nations, but also those fleeting glimpses of him which he allowed the disciples to have and which they could not capture and fix down in the grasp of mere sense, or in the kind of historiography accommodated to this fallen existence. But it does mean, surely, that only when we are redeemed in body ourselves, in the fullness of humanity, when our eyes are truly and finally pure, that we will be able to see Christ in all his risen and transcendent glory. Only, that is, when Christ comes again and transforms us in the whole of our human nature, so that we are resurrected in the wholeness of our humanity, in physical as in spiritual life, will we be able to see him and to know as we are known. When we see him we shall become like him, and when we become like him we shall see him with healed vision and recreated natures.

The idea of the spiritualization and transparency of the risen and ascended humanity of Christ through its complete impregnation with divine light developed in Origenist circles in the early Church.[13] Apparently 'the spiritual body' of the resurrection was regarded as an incorporeal orb of radiant light (this was partly in accordance with the Platonic idea that the essential form of the real was the 'mathematical' sphere) – traces of this idea appear centuries later in Dante, and in the picturesque mythologizing of the drama of salvation that is found in the stained glass of many Mediaeval Cathedrals.[14] But this is to fail to observe the proper theological reserve at the boundary of the eschatological; we inevitably fall into error as soon as we transgress the limits set by the Word.

Two points here deserve our reflection. The resurrection of

[13] How far Origen himself was responsible for this idea is not clear, but certainly his speculations in this respect brought him into some discredit. See *De principiis*, II. 10; *Commentary on St. John's Gospel*, Bk. I. 24f., 42; X. 20f.; *Contra Celsum*, V. 17–19, 22–24; VI, 32; VIII. 49f. Methodius wrote several discourses in the form of a Platonic dialogue attacking Origen's theory that the resurrected put off the fetters of the body and take on a rational form, common to all. See *Aglaophon or on the Resurrection*, especially 25; discourse 3, 15. Cf. also Justinian, *Epist. ad Mennam*, in G. D. Mansi, *Collectio*, IX. 516D, 533C.

[14] There probably lies behind this development also the teaching of St. Augustine who, under the influence of Plato, held that the incorruptible bodies of the saints are like the ethereal bodies of the stars – *Sermones*, 241. 7; *De civitate Dei*, LO. 29, 22. 26; *Retractationes*, 1.4.3; cf. Plato, *Timaeus*, 41A–B. See Eugene TeSelle, *Augustine the Theologian*, 1970, p. 252f.

the body to be a 'spiritual body' no more means that the body is resolved away into spirit than the fact that we are made 'spiritual men' in Christ means that our humanity is dissolved away in him. To be a spiritual man is to be not less than man but more fully and truly man. To be a spiritual body is not to be less body but more truly and completely body, for by the Spirit physical existence is redeemed from all that corrupts and undermines it, and from all or any privation of being. Hence we must take the *empty tomb* in the Gospel reports quite seriously –. the body of Jesus Christ was raised, certainly a spiritual body, but it was no less body because it was a body healed and quickened by the Spirit in which all corruption had been overcome. It is *the empty tomb that constitutes the essential empirical correlate in statements about the resurrection of Christ,* the point where the triumph of Christ over the space-time of our fallen world is nevertheless correlated with the space-time of our on-going existence in this world.[15] We cannot observe or pin down in our grasp the process of resurrecting any more than we can observe or pin down in our grasp the process of creating, but as the created reality is observable, so the resurrected reality was apprehensible to the disciples, apprehensible, of course in a mode appropriate to its nature, i.e. by faith, which is the mode of the human reason adapted to divine revelation.

There is, however, a deep element of truth in the doctrine of the transparency of the new creation in Christ – its utter lack of all opacity and darkness – which is relevant for our understanding of Christ. So long as we ourselves wait for the resurrection of the body we can only see through a glass darkly, as in an enigma; yet so far as through the Spirit the uncreated light of God already shines upon us in Christ, we may discern the reality of God's ways and works in a deeper and more transparent mode. Theologically this belongs to the content of the doctrine of the Holy Spirit who is sent upon us by the

[15] See *Space, Time and Incarnation*, pp. 85f., 89f. As Karl Barth has expressed it, 'The function of the empty tomb, with its backward, downward reference, is to show that Jesus who died and was buried was delivered from death, and therefore from the grave, by the power of God; that he the living, is not to be found among the dead (Luke 24: 5). "He is not here: behold the place where they laid him (Mark 16: 6). "He is not here; for he is risen, even as he said" (Matt. 28: 6; Luke 24: 6).' *Church Dogmatics*, III/1, p. 453.

risen and ascended Lord, and who creates in us the capacity to discern and understand beyond what we are naturalistically capable of in ourselves, and who enables us to know the reality of God himself in Christ in such a way as to distinguish it from our own objective states and conditions. If we say of the risen Jesus Christ that he is spiritually and not carnally discerned, this does not mean that he rose only as Spirit and not as body, but that it is only through the power of the Spirit that we are able to apprehend Christ in his actuality as resurrected in the body and thus as the First-fruits of the new *creation* and the First-born of every *creature*. As the early Fathers used to express it, when a baby is born it is usually born head first, but when the head is born the whole body follows naturally, for it is the birth of the head that is the most difficult part. Now Christ the Head of the Body is already resurrected, the First-born of the New Creation, and as such he is the pledge and guarantee that we who are incorporated with him as his Body will rise with him and be born into the new creation in our physical as well as our spiritual existence.[16] Here we must think of the Sacraments with their physical elements as pledges of our participation in that whole reality of the risen humanity in Christ, given for us in the time of our pilgrimage through history until Christ comes again. As surely as the saving work of God was carried out in the physical existence of Jesus Christ, as surely as his body was broken and his blood was shed for us, and as surely as he rose again from the dead in his human identity and physical existence, so surely will we be saved in our physical and creaturely being. It is of this that the bread and wine consecrated in the Eucharist are pledges. As surely as in Holy Communion we eat the bread and drink the wine which become assimilated into our own physical existence, so surely we who partake of the body and blood of Christ given for us, will rise with him out of the grave into newness of life, attaining at last to the redemption of the body in the new creation. No wonder early Christians could speak of the Eucharist as 'the medicine of immortality'.[17]

[16] Cf. Irenaeus, *Adversus Haereses*, 3. 20. 3 (edit. by W. W. Harvey, vol. ii, p. 105).

[17] Ignatius, *Epistle to the Ephesians*, 20. 2; Serapion, *Euchologion*, 17. 2; cf. Clement of Alexandria, *Protrepticos*, 10.

CHAPTER 7

THE ASCENSION AND THE
PAROUSIA OF CHRIST

Parousia, normally translated as coming or advent, means coming and presence, the *real presence* of him who was, who is, and who is to come. 'All is present, and yet all is future'.[1] It is not applied in the New Testament or in the early Church in a spiritualized sense, as if it meant a presence in Spirit only. Rather does it refer to a coming-and-a-presence in the most realist and effective sense. This is made clear by its application to the coming of the Son of God in the incarnation – it is the special kind of divine presence in which God is present in his own being (*ousia*), but who has come to us not only as Creator but as creature within our creaturely being (*ousia*), for he has entered within the created order to which we belong and is present within its space and time as one of us (*par-ousia*). Moreover, the physicality of the incarnation, in which the Word was made flesh and in which Jesus Christ rose again in body, indicates that here we have to do with a presence in which God has bound up the life and existence of his creation with himself. This is not a *parousia* in the flesh which is merely a temporary episode, so that all it represents is a transient epiphany or manifestation: it has a finality about it, even for God. This is not a *parousia* of God in the flesh which consumes the flesh, but one in which the physical being of the creature is established and confirmed through being included in a covenanted relation with the Creator actualized in the incarnate Son. It is here that the resurrection of the man Jesus is of decisive and determinative significance, for with the crucifixion it constitutes the epitome and consummation of the incarnation: through the resurrection the incarnate *parousia* is established and exalted as the material content of all the

---

[1] H. R. Mackintosh, *Immortality and the Future*, 1915, p. 64.

parousia of Christ from the ascension to his coming again; the presence of the historical Jesus is eternally fused into the presence of the risen Jesus and as such constitutes the one indivisible *parousia* of the ages. 'Behold I am with you all the days until the consummation of time' (Matt. 28: 20). 'I am the first and the last, and the living one; I was dead and behold I am alive unto the ages of the ages' (Rev. 1: 17).

It is significant that the New Testament uses the term *parousia* only in the singular – the plural, *parousiai*, is found only with Justin Martyr and Hippolytus and thereafter, but when a distinction is clearly drawn between the first and the second *parousia* or *advent* of Christ.[2] In the New Testament, however, there is only *one parousia*, which is applied equally to the first advent and the second advent. This indicates the continuity between the first and second advents and the nature of the coming-and-presence which is envisaged when Jesus Christ comes again to make all things new, but also the impact of that *parousia* upon the present all through history – it is a sort of *space-time parousia*, not a *parousia* which we split apart, as we do space and time in our ordinary every day experience, because our eyes cannot keep up with the speed of light in terms of which all motion and structure in the universe are defined. Here we have a *parousia* in which the breach between space and time is healed, which is neither spaceless nor timeless but which determines the whole invisible structure of history and is ultimately regulative of the shape and mission of the Church and indeed of the new creation inaugurated by the resurrection of Jesus Christ from the dead. And yet precisely as *parousia* it reaches out beyond the limitations of our place in time and space and directs us throughout the ages toward that ultimate point when in the saving economy of Christ he will come again, to unveil to us in space and time, the glory and the power, the majesty of God Almighty through himself. But even the *parousia* in that future aspect, at the second or final advent of Christ, will nevertheless be a *parousia* of essentially the same texture as that of the historical Jesus in the incarnation and the risen Jesus of Easter and the ascension. 'This same Jesus will

[2] See for example Justin Martyr, *Apology*, I. 52; *Dialogue with Trypho*, 14, 32, 40, 49, etc.; Hippolytus, *On Christ and Antichrist*, 44; *Commentary on Daniel*, IV. 18, 23, 39, etc.

come again', it was said on the day of ascension, 'in the same way as you have seen him going into heaven' (Acts 1: 11). 'How then, did he go? By what process did he fulfil the mission which was written of him? The New Testament answers by saying: "This is he who came by water and blood; not by water only, but by water and blood", in other words by baptism and crucifixion. If, then, his going and his coming are to be "in like manner", it is plain that *the Parousia*, whatever it may signify in its eternal dimension, is not to be understood in separation from the Incarnation and from Calvary. It is not discontinuous with the latter but is their consummation'.[3]

Although there is one whole indivisible *parousia* including the first and the last advent of Christ, the effect of the ascension is to create a kind of interval 'in the midst of his *parousia*' (*en tō metaxu tēs parousias autou*).[4] The ascension of Christ thus introduces, as it were, *an eschatological pause* in the heart of the *parousia* which makes it possible for us to speak of a first advent and a second or final advent of Christ. By withdrawing his bodily presence from contact and sight, that is from historical contact and observation, the ascended Christ holds apart his first advent from his final advent, distinguishing the first advent as his advent in great humility and abasement, and pointing ahead to his final advent in great glory and power, when the eschatological pause will be brought to an end, and we shall see him as we are seen by him. John Calvin preferred to speak, not so much of the two comings of Christ's kingdom as of the two 'conditions' or 'states' of that kingdom, e.g. with reference to the teaching of Christ himself in 'the little Apo-

---

[3] William Manson, *Jesus and the Christian*, p. 73. Significantly it was as 'Son of Man' that Jesus referred to himself in this eschatological perspective. See Manson, *Jesus and the Messiah*, pp. 101f., 113ff.; and *Jesus and the Christian*, 67ff., 174ff. E. Hoskyns and F. N. Davey have shown that it was under this title that the two comings of Jesus in humiliation and in glory are linked together, *The Riddle of the New Testament*, pp. 151ff.

[4] Justin Martyr, *Dialogue with Trypho*, 52. Cf. Karl Barth: 'The resurrection of Jesus Christ from the dead, with which his first *parousia* begins to be completed in the second, has in fact already happened. It has happened in the same sense as his crucifixion and his death, in the human sphere and human time, as an actual event within the world with an objective content. The same will be true of his return to the extent that as the last moment of time and history it will still belong to time and history'. *Church Dogmatics*, IV/1, p. 433; cf. also IV 3, pp. 290ff.

calypse'.[5] The Kingdom of Christ was fully inaugurated with his crucifixion in its condition of humiliation, and with his resurrection in triumph over the forces of darkness and evil and his ascension as Lamb of God to the throne of the Father. That was in the most intense sense the fulfilment of Christ's Kingdom. In other words, this is the immediacy and the finality of the Kingdom of which Christ spoke as taking place in the life-time of his hearers; but it is that same inaugurated Kingdom which will be openly manifested at the end of time when the veil will be taken away. This is what we traditionally refer to as the 'final advent' or simply the '*parousia*' of Christ. Since it is not different from the first advent but is essentially continuous with it, that final *parousia* constantly impinges upon the Church in the present so that inevitably it feels and must feel that the final advent is about the dawn.[6] It is in fact already there knocking at the door and waits only the eschatological moment of its open manifestation when the veil of sense and time of our world will be torn aside (Rev. 3: 20). This is all the more inevitable because of the Communion of the Spirit, for through the Spirit the Church in every age and place is united to the risen and ascended and advent Lord so that it cannot escape the pressure of the consummation of all things upon it. Nevertheless within that tension in which it is called to keep vigil and be alert waiting for the manifestation of Christ, the Church lives and works in the time that is established by the ascension for the proclamation of the Gospel to all nations and ages. God has established a time in the midst of history in which he waits to be gracious, allowing time and history to run on its course in order that the world may be given time to

[5] John Calvin, *Commentary on the Harmony of the Gospels*, on Matt. 24: 30 (tr. by A. A. Morrison, vol. III, p. 94); See *Kingdom and Church. A Study in the Theology of the Reformation*, pp. 122ff.

[6] What makes this inevitable is the fusion of the life and time of the historical Jesus with the life and time of the risen Lord. Our difficulty is that we can only apprehend that *presence = parousia* through the refraction of our place in on-going history, so that we tend to split up what in Christ is indivisible. 'For us the resurrection and the *parousia* are two separate events. But for him they are a single event. The resurrection is the anticipation of his *parousia* as his *parousia* is the completion and fulfilment of the resurrection'. Karl Barth, *Church Dogmatics*, III/1, p. 490. Cf. also Cranfield, *The Gospel according to St. Mark*, p. 288.

repent and believe. It is in this connection that many of the parables of Jesus are to be understood, those in which he spoke of a king taking a journey into a far country and commanding his servants to occupy until he came back, or the parable of the pounds and talents in which after a season of departure the householder came back for a day of reckoning with his servants. I find it difficult not to accept the fact that Jesus envisaged a considerable lapse in time between his first and final advents – and that, so far as the Church's communion with him was concerned in that long interval, he gave them the Holy Supper that they might eat and drink sacramentally in his presence, proclaiming his death, till he should come again. Thus the ascension must be thought of not only as introducing an eschatological pause in the one *parousia* of Christ but as thereby determining the pattern of mission of the Church in history and the relation of the Church in space and time to himself. The ascension, in fact, constitutes a three-fold relation to Christ.

1. *Historical Relation to the Historical Jesus Christ*

As we have seen, by withdrawing himself from visible and physical contact with us as our contemporary throughout history, Jesus Christ sends us back by his ascension to the Gospels and to their witness to the historical Jesus Christ. That is the appointed place in which nations and ages may meet with God. But with his ascension Jesus Christ also sent upon the Church and indeed upon 'all flesh' his Holy Spirit so that through the Spirit he might be present, really present, although in a different way. In order to think out the relation of the Church in history to Christ we must put both these together – *mediate horizontal relation* through history to the historical Jesus Christ, and *immediate vertical relation* through the Spirit to the risen and ascended Jesus Christ. It is the former that supplies the material content, while it is the latter that supplies the immediacy of actual encounter. A signal instance of this, and of course a unique instance, was the conversion of Saul of Tarsus. His encounter with the risen Lord and his self-witness on the Damascus road threw him into blindness, and he required the testimony of an historical agent or witness sent to him by Christ before what he had received by divine revelation fully came home to him, and his eyes were opened.[7] The vertical and the horizontal, the immediate and the mediate relations, intersect and mutually require one another for their fulfilment.

2. *Sacramental Relation to the Crucified and Risen Jesus Christ*

Communion with Christ through the Spirit gives the Church participation here and now in the mystery of Christ, which takes concrete form in the Word and Sacrament. The New Testament regards the pouring out of the Spirit upon the Church as one of the mighty acts of God in 'the last days', and as signalizing that the end-time had precipitated itself upon the world. As we have seen, this means that the Church that lives and serves Christ within the time-form of this age, also lives in the new age through being made to participate in him the Head of the new creation. The Church in history exists in that overlap of the two ages, the overlap that is constituted by the ascension to belong to the whole of the Church's world-mission. The Sacraments also belong to that overlap, spanning at once, the two ages, the old and the new in which the Church lives, i.e. in the time between the first and second advents. On one side the Sacraments belong very much to earth and its on-going space and time, as is made clear in the visible, tangible and corruptible elements of this world, water, bread and wine, that are used. But on the other side they are signs of the new order which has once and for all broken into our world in Jesus Christ and in which we have constant participation through the Spirit even though since the ascension that new order is veiled from our sight.[7a]

[7] Prof. J. S. Stewart has shown that the revelation of the risen Jesus must be understood as being 'real and objective', with some measure of directness and immediacy. *A Man in Christ*, 1935, pp. 125ff., 133ff. This is consistent with the fact that it was only with the word of Christ through Ananias that the revelation 'not through man' (Gal. 1:1) came 'home' to Paul.

[7a] While the resurrection power of the Holy Spirit is already at work, it is at the final appearing of Christ that he will take hold of the creation, including our mortal bodies. Meantime, we continue to live in salvation history. See Oscar Cullmann, *Salvation in History*, p. 267.

With the immediate presence of the Son of God in the In-carnation the authoritative signs of that new order were his acts of healing and of forgiveness taken together, signs that pointed ahead to the crucifixion and the resurrection, as the mighty acts of cosmic significance that constituted the ground for all acts of forgiveness and healing in the Name of Christ. But with the ascension the unique revelatory signs associated with the Incarnation, and therefore with the apostolic Com-munity immediately surrounding Christ and assimilated to him to form the unrepeatable foundation of the Church as the Body of Christ, are no longer prominent, for their unique revelatory function is fulfilled in what came to be handed on as the New Testament. Certainly the living Lord continues to heal and to forgive sins in the midst of his Church, and that is no less a miraculous activity than what he manifested before his ascension, but now in on-going history his healing and for-giving work is normally mediated through the Holy Sacra-ments which are given to the historical Church to accompany the proclamation of the Gospel and to seal its enactment in the lives of the faithful. This does not mean that it may not please God throughout history to answer the prayer of his people for direct miraculous healing, but it does mean that with the withdrawal of the resurrected body of Christ from visible and physical contact with us in the world, there is no appointed *programme* of anything like 'faith healing' or mira-culous activity of a kindred sort. The ascension means that Christ holds back the physical transformation of the creation to the day when he will return to make *all things new*, and that meantime he sends the Church to live and work in the form of a servant within the measures and limits of the on-going world of space and time. He calls it to follow his own example, who when he was on earth, as we have seen, in the midst of our hunger in the wilderness did not call in the miraculous power belonging to him as Son of God in order to make bread out of stones. Although he wrought miracles as signs of the Kingdom, as part of his revelation in act and word, he did not call in supernature to help himself, but lived and worked within the nature, weakness and limitations of the creature, to the very end. Even on the Cross when the temptation came, 'If you are the Son of God, come down from the Cross' (Matt.

27: 40; cf. Mark 15: 31f.; Luke 23: 35, 39), he resisted it and suffered patiently – and by his weakness and passion overcame all the powers of darkness.

However in his life-time Jesus did institute the Sacraments. Taking over Baptism from the Baptist he transformed it through submitting to it and made himself its real content. He instituted the Holy Supper by reconstructing the Passover with reference to his own body and blood in the New Covenant. Then with his resurrection and ascension these sacraments were constituted by the power and presence of the Spirit the 'miraculous signs' of the Church's forgiveness and healing, of its crucifixion and resurrection with Christ, to be used perpetually throughout the course of its historical existence. There are, Calvin once said, two kinds of miracles: one in which a miraculous act takes place in a supernatural form, such as a miracle of healing, and one in which a miraculous event takes place under a natural form – Sacraments are of the second kind, and they are the greater kind of miracle.[8] The two Sacraments of the Gospel enshrine together the two essential 'moments' of our participation in the new creation, while we are still implicated in the space and time of this passing world. Baptism is the Sacrament of our once and for all participation in Christ, and may be spoken of as the Sacrament of Justification, which is not to be repeated. The Eucharist is the Sacrament of our continuous participation in Christ and may be spoken of as the Sacrament of Sanctification, which is regularly to be repeated, until Christ comes again. They thus express in their togetherness the core of the ontological and eschatological relation which we have within the crucified, risen and ascended Lord.

3. Eschatological Relation to the Ascended and Advent Jesus Christ

By *eschatological* is meant here what is directed toward the end or the consummation in the final *parousia*, what is related to the *eschaton*, the last Word and final Act of God in Christ.[9] The

[8] John Calvin, *Commentary on Isaiah*, 7: 13.
[9] Cf. E. Hoskyns, *Cambridge Sermons*, 1938, pp. 2–38; and also H. R. Mackintosh's discussion of the eschatology of Jesus and of the apostlic age, *Immortality and the Future*, 1915, pp. 39ff., 60ff., which is still very relevant.

Word and Act of God to which we refer in eschatology, however, must be understood as *God's* Word and Act *within our
world of space and time*, even though it means at the end its
transformation. This is quite different from the meaning of
'eschatological' in the thought of Rudolf Bultmann, who speaks
of the act of God at the end of the world, where the world
ends or ceases. This is in line with Bultmann's radical disjunction between this world and the other world of God, and
his rejection of any interaction between God and this world
which he holds to be a closed continuum of cause and effect.
God's 'acts' are related to this world only in a tangential
fashion, and are not acts within this cosmos. This is similar to
Heidegger's idea of the boundary between being and non-
being where we must leap beyond the boundary of being in
order to open out the source of being – although how that is
possible when it is a leap into nothing is a puzzle.[10] At any
rate, that seems to be what Bultmann means by the end of the
world, or the boundary of being where we have to take the
existentialist leap of decision. But when he speaks of this as
eschatological event, it would appear to be the antithesis of what
the New Testament means, for in it, eschatology is constituted
by the act of the eternal within the temporal, by the acts of God
within our world of space and time. On this Biblical view the
eschatological acts of God run throughout time to their end at
the consummation of time; they are teleological as well as eschatological, for they are not just abrupt acts abrogating or ter-
minating time, but rather acts that gather up time in the
fulfilling of the divine purpose. In this sense then we may speak
of *eschatological* as related to the final Act of God but which (in
the on-going world) is still in arears so far as our experience
and understanding of it are concerned; or as related to the
ultimate reality of divine fulfilment and completion which will
be manifested within our world only at the last day. Yet by
eschatology we refer not so much to the *eschaton* as to the
Eschatos, that is, to Christ himself who is the last (*Eschatos*) as
well as the First (*Protos*), and who is the Last because he is the
First, for he who has already come and accomplished his work

[10] See my review of M. Heidegger, *Being and Time* (tr. by John Macquarrie and Edward Robinson), *Journal of Theological Studies*, 1964, vol.
XV. 2, pp. 471–86.

of salvation in our midst will bring it to its final manifestation and consummation at his coming again. Since the ascension his eschatological operations are veiled from our sight, by the fact that we live within the time-form of this world, and communicate with the new creation only through the Spirit in Word and Sacrament. The final *parousia* of Christ will be more the apocalypse or unveiling of the perfected reality of what Christ has done than the consummating of what till then is an incomplete reality. It will be the unveiling of the finished work of Christ. He will come again in the fullness of his humanity and deity to judge and renew his creation, but that will not be another work in addition to his finished work on the Cross or in the resurrection, so much as the gathering together of what the cross and resurrection have already worked throughout the whole of creation and the unveiling of it for all to see, and therefore an unfolding and actualization of it from our point of view.[11]

The difficulty about the eschatological relation as set forth in the New Testament is that it involves a two-fold relation: (*a*) *a relation here and now between the old and the new*, as through the Spirit we partake already of the new creation in the risen Christ; and (*b*) *a relation between the present (including the past) and the future*, as through the Spirit we are united to the ascended Christ who is still to come again.[12] Because of the ascension there has been introduced, as we have seen, into the midst of the one whole *parousia* of Christ an eschatological pause, so that in all our relations with Christ there is an eschatological reserve or eschatological time-lag. That applies to both relations but in different ways. In the here and now relation to Christ what stands between us is the *veil of sense*, so that although we communicate with him immediately through the Spirit, he is mediated to us in our sense experience only through the sacramental elements. In the relation between the present and the

[11] It would be a serious mistake, however, as Oscar Cullmann has contended rightly, to interpret this to mean that there is *nothing new* to be manifested at the end. *Salvation in History*, pp. 177ff.

[12] On the role of the Holy Spirit in this eschatological relation, see Oscar Cullmann, *Christ and Time. The Primitive Christian Conception of Time and History*, Eng. tr. 1951, pp. 72ff.; and also Neil Q. Hamilton, *The Holy Spirit and Eschatology in Paul, Scottish Journal of Theology, Occasional Papers*, No. 6, 1957, especially chs. II and III, pp. 17ff., and 26ff.

future what stands in between us is the *veil of time*, so that although we communicate with him immediately through the Spirit, he is mediated to us only through temporal and spatial acts of sacramental communion in the midst of the Church until he comes. The Church has its life and mission within the time and space of this world, but because of the ascension of Christ and the pouring out of his Spirit upon it, the Church is constituted throughout history as the place of meeting and worship under the vaulted arch of the one indivisible *parousia* of Jesus Christ which spans the first and second advents. Since there through the Spirit we are united to the risen, ascended and advent Christ, he is immediately present to us, and every time we have communion with him we have contact with him in his *parousia*, for the ascended and advent Christ impinges upon every moment of our Christian life and work in history, and the content of that impingement is none other than the historical, crucified and risen Jesus Christ. That is why the *parousia* is always and inevitably imminent, and why expectation of it in New Testament times could never give way to disillusionment but could only be constantly renewed.[13] It is failure to gasp this, and the two-fold eschatological relation to Christ which it entails, that has apparently misled scholars in unduly stressing the idea of a 'delayed advent' which allegedly forced the early Church to alter its whole eschatological outlook and to adjust its life and mission accordingly. Just as we split space and time because our eyes cannot keep track with the speed of light in the physical universe, and thereby create problems which we try to solve through artificial devices, so we tend to split the space-time of the one indivisible *parousia* when we lose track of the risen and ascended Lord, and are found creating artificial theories to account for connections which we have broken ourselves. Apart from the fact that there seems to be very little, if any, support in the writings of Christians in immediately post-New Testament times for such a thorough-going transmutation of their eschatological expectations, it can hardly be got out of the New Testament itself without a rather strained exegesis.[14] This is not to deny that

[13] Cf. Karl Barth, *Church Dogmatics*, III/1, p. 490f.

[14] This lack of evidence has been demonstrated by an extensive examination of early patristic writings by Dr. Gordon W. Martin in a dissertation

there is a relatively different emphasis, and to that extent a change, within the New Testament, for example, between the first Epistle of St. Paul to the Thessalonians and his Epistle to the Philippians, but that still falls within the 'all is present, yet all is future' orientation of the basic outlook of the New Testament. The eschatology of the New Testament is neither simply a 'realized eschatology' nor simply a 'futurist eschatology', but one in which both realized and futurist elements are woven together all the time *in Christ*.[15] It is when those elements are artificially torn apart in the minds of the interpreters that the idea of a delayed *parousia* is begotten, and then projected back into early Christianity. When the one indivisible *parousia* suffers refraction like that, the end is detached from the beginning, and it seems inevitable to hold that the arrival of the end has been delayed or put off. Regarded in this light the idea of 'the delay of the *parousia*' looks rather like a legend of the critics! But it is as true for us nearly two thousand years later as it was for St. Paul, that 'salvation is nearer to us now than when we first believed' (Rom. 13: 11).[16]

We may now seek to interpret this eschatological relation to Christ more fully in its cosmic, corporate and individual aspects.

(a) *The cosmic range of eschatology.* The eschatological relation has the same cosmic range as the incarnation and the atonement. He who was made flesh is the Creator Logos by whom all things were made and in whom all things are upheld. When he became incarnate, and divine and human natures were united in his one person, his humanity was brought into an ontological relation with all creation. So far as our humanity

---

for the University of Edinburgh, 'Eschatology in the Early Church with special reference to the theses of C. H. Dodd and Martin Werner', 4 vols. 1970. Cf. also J. E. Fison, *The Christian Hope*, 1954, ch. 6, in which he shows that in the pattern of development, while the futurist elements remained strongly in force, they were modified by *mystical* elements in a 'realized' direction.

[15] See the contribution of William Manson to *Eschatology*, *Scottish Journal of Theology*, *Occasional Papers*, No. 2, 1953, 2nd edit. 1957, pp. 1–16, and also *Jesus and the Christian*, part III, pp. 163–226.

[16] And also, John Burnaby, *The Belief of Christendom*, 1959, pp. 178ff. We require here 'a more theological understanding of what is meant by the nearness of the End'. C. E. B. Cranfield, *op. cit.*, p. 408.

is concerned that means that all men are upheld, whether they know it or not, in their humanity by Jesus Christ the true and proper man, upheld by the fulfilment and establishment of true humanity in him, but also through his work in the cross and resurrection in which he overcame the degenerating forces of evil and raised up our human nature out of death and perdition. But the range of Christ's mighty acts in incarnation, reconciliation and resurrection apply to the whole universe of things, visible and invisible. The whole of creation falls within the range of his Lordship, as he works out his purpose by bringing redemption together with creation, and actualizing the holy will of the Father in everything.[17] Eschatology has here a teleological relation to the whole realm of created existence, and leads into the doctrine of 'the new heaven and the new earth'.[18] God does not abandon his creation when he has saved man, for all creation, together with man, will be renewed when Christ comes again. Since he is the first-born of the new creation, the head in whom all things, visible and invisible, are reconciled and gathered up, the resurrection of Christ in *body* becomes the pledge that the whole physical universe will be renewed, for in a fundamental sense it has already been resurrected in Christ. It is understandable, therefore, that for classical Greek theology it was the resurrection, supervening upon the incarnation, that revealed the final cosmic range of God's redeeming purpose.[19]

[17] Cf. Oscar Cullmann, *Christ and Time*, pp. 185ff.; *The Early Church*, pp. 105ff.; *Salvation in History*, pp. 171ff.

[18] Properly expounded this must take fully into account an adequate doctrine of creation and its continuous preservation under the Lordship of Christ. See Barth, *Church Dogmatics*, III/3, section 49.

[19] See for example, Athanasius, *De Incarnatione*, 29ff., or Maximus, *Capita gnostica*, MPG 90, 1108. The contrast between East and West, Greek and Latin theology is very great at this point, for Western eschatology (apart from the Irenaean tradition), as dominated by the North African theology of Tertullian and Augustine (and even of Donatus!), is essentially 'world-denying' in character, whereas Eastern eschatology is basically 'world-affirming' in the risen Christ. Much the same contrast is found between Luther's eschatological outlook, which is basically Augustinian, and Calvin's, which is basically Athanasian. See *Kingdom and Church. A Study in the Theology of the Reformation*, for a development of this contrast between the eschatology of faith (Luther) and the eschatology of hope (Calvin), especially pp. 139ff. where the differences are spelt out.

(b) *The corporate aspect of eschatology.* Here we are concerned with the relation between Christ and the Church which is his Body. The Church is not only the Body of the crucified and risen Christ, but the Body of the ascended and advent Christ, and therefore through union with him is necessarily thrust urgently forward through history to meet its coming Lord. Here we have to take into account what we have already discussed about the Church as the Body of the risen Christ in which its relation to him is determined by the immediate *koinonia* of the Spirit, but now we must think of the relation of the Church to Christ as governed also by the *distance* of the ascension and the *nearness* of the advent. This is the 'eschatological reserve' in the union between Christ and his Church, in which the Church is sent to carry out its work in the world, in a sense, 'on its own', and for which it must give an account to Christ when he comes again. The Church is thus given a measure of freedom for its life and operations in the world, for it lives and fulfils its mission within the ambiguities of history, society, politics, world events, etc. Although it is already one Body with Christ through the Spirit, it is yet to become One Body with him, but meantime in the world and history the Church is a mixed body, with good and evil, true and false, wheat and tares in its midst. It is still characterized by sin and evil and partakes of the decay and corruption of the world of which it is a part, so that it is not yet what it shall be, and not yet wholly in itself what it is already in Christ.[20] In this eschatological reserve and deep teleological ambiguity the Church lives and works under judgment as well as grace, so that it must constantly put off the 'image of the old man' that passes away and put on 'the image of the new man' who is renewed in the likeness of Christ. The New Testament expresses this relation of union and distance be-

---

[20] In this respect the function of the ascension is to point upwards and forwards, unlike the empty tomb which points backwards and downwards, Karl Barth, *Church Dogmatics*, III/1, p. 453. Hence, the theological content of that pointing can be expressed in the Pauline word: 'If you are raised together with Christ, seek the things that are above, where Christ is seated at the right hand of God. Set your mind on things above, not on things that are upon the earth. For you died, and your life is hid with Christ in God. When Christ, who is our life, shall be manifested, then shall you also with him be manifested in glory' (Col. 3: 1–4).

tween the Church and Christ in terms of the two-fold figure of the *Bride* of Christ and the *Body* of Christ – the Church waits for the consummation of the mystery of its union with the Saviour who will present the Church when he comes again to himself, no longer spotted and wrinkled like an ageing lady but 'without spot or wrinkle as a chaste virgin'. This means that the Church is constantly summoned to look beyond its historical forms to the fullness and perfection that will be disclosed at the *parousia* and must never identify the structures it acquires and must acquire in the nomistic forms of this-worldly historical existence with the essential forms of its new being in Christ himself.

(*c*) *The individual aspect of eschatology.* Here we are concerned with the personal union of the believer with Christ. What the New Testament has to say about being *in Christ* and about *Christ in us* may well be primarily corporate, but the individual is certainly given his full and integral place within that corporate union of Christ with his Church. The believer finds his reality and truth not in himself but in Jesus Christ risen and ascended, and therefore coming again. It does not yet appear what he will be, but when Christ comes he will see him and be changed, transformed into his likeness. This implies the resurrection of the body, but in the nature of the case it is an actualization in the body of the saving acts of Christ finally only when that takes place within the whole of creation and in the whole body of the redeemed. Hence the individual believer also lives in the eschatological reserve created by the ascension in the midst of the whole *parousia* of Christ. He must therefore learn to live and work 'on his own', as it were, for he is sent to occupy himself with the talents the Lord has given him, and will have to render account of what he has done with them when Christ comes again to judge the quick and the dead.

Like the Church the individual Christian will not be able to escape the deep ambiguities of this-worldly existence whether in its cultural, social, political or other aspects, and he too will inevitably be a mixture of good and evil, with a compromised life, so that he can only live eschatologically in the judgment and mercy of God, putting off the old man and putting on Christ anew each day, always aware that even when he has done all that it is his duty to do he remains an unprofitable

servant, but summoned to look away from himself to Christ,
remembering that he is dead through the cross of Christ but
alive and risen in him. His true being is hid with Christ in
God. The whole focus of his vision and the whole perspective
of his life in Christ's name will be directed to the unveiling of
that reality of his new being at the *parousia*, but meantime he
lives day by day out of the Word and Sacraments. As one
baptized into Christ he is told by God's Word that his sins are
already forgiven and forgotten by God, that he has been justified once and for all, and that he does not belong to himself
but to Christ who loved him and gave himself for him. As one
summoned to the Holy Table he is commanded by the Word
of God to live only in such a way that he feeds upon Christ,
not in such a way that he feeds upon his own activities or lives
out of his own capital of alleged spirituality. He lives from week
to week, by drawing his life and strength from the bread and
wine of the Lord's Supper, nourished by the body and blood
of Christ, and in the strength of that communion he must live
and work until Christ comes again. As often as he partakes of
the Eucharist he partakes of the self-consecration of Jesus
Christ who sanctified himself for our sakes that we might be
sanctified in reality and be presented to the Father as those
whom he has redeemed and perfected (or consecrated) together with himself in one. Here he is called to lift up his heart
to the ascended Lord, and to look forward to that day when
this same Lord Jesus will come again, and when the full
reality of his new being in Christ will be unveiled, making
Scripture and Sacrament no longer necessary.

CHAPTER 8

THE LORD OF SPACE AND TIME

The last of the canonical books of the New Testament begins with the words, *The Revelation of Jesus Christ*. What that means is indicated in the opening chapter in which St. John 'the divine' (*ho theologos*), as he was called in the early Church, tells us of an experience he had on the Lord's Day, the day of the resurrection, when, as it seems probable, he was engaged in celebrating the Eucharist.[1] There broke in upon him the vision of 'one like unto the Son of Man' ineffably transfigured in the very heart of divine majesty and power, but one whom he recognized as none other than *Jesus*, although he was glorified (as the Fourth Gospel would have said) with the glory which the Son had with the Father before the world was, that is, glorified with the very glory that resides in the inner self of the Godhead (John 17: 5). St. John recounts that when he saw him he fell at his feet as though dead, but Jesus laid his right hand upon him saying, 'Fear not, I am the first and the last, and the living one; I died and behold I am alive for evermore, and I have the keys of death and hades' (Rev. 1: 17f.). And again, at the end of the book, 'I am the Alpha and the Omega, the first and the last, the beginning and the end . . . I Jesus. . .' (Rev. 22: 12, 16). That is to say, Jesus identified himself to St. John with words out of the mouth of God, ' "I am the Alpha and Omega", says the Lord God, who is, who was and who is to come, the Almighty' (Rev. 1: 8).[2] This is significantly similar to the word of Jesus in his self-identification before the high priest and the Sanhedrin prior to his

[1] See 'Liturgy and Apocalypse', *Church Service Society Annual*, 1944, No. 24, pp. 1–18.

[2] 'I am he who is' is a citation from Exod. 3: 14, 'I am who I am' – the self-identification of God to Moses. These words are amplified in Rev. 1: 8 by 'who was and who is to come', while in Rev. 1: 17, 'who is' is replaced by 'who lives' or 'the living one'. Cf. Hebrews 13: 8.

crucifixion: 'I am, and you shall see the Son of Man sitting on the right hand of power, and coming in the clouds of heaven' (Mark 14: 62; cf. Matt. 26: 64; Luke 21: 27; Acts 7: 56) in which he was undoubtedly understood to be identifying himself as Son of God and equal to God (Mark 14: 61f.; Matt. 26: 63f.; Luke 22: 67ff.), and was accepted as such by the Evangelists, although in their remarkably faithful reporting of this they did it in such a way as to point back through the hesitancy and ambiguity among the disciples to the indirect identification of Jesus as Son of God in the spontaneous reaction of people, even of his opponents, to him.[3] Their own direct identification of Christ as Son of God, like that of the disciples, follows from the resurrection, and it is indeed in the light of the startling unveiling of who Jesus Christ really was in and through the resurrection that they finally present all their reporting of Jesus: they now allow his *Self*, in the majestic *I am* of the risen Lord, regnant and triumphant over all the forces of darkness, to provide inward enlightenment and objective depth to the evangelical report of the words and deeds of Jesus in such a way that their account of the life and mission of Jesus has a unifying intra-structure deriving from, and forced upon the witnesses and disciples, from the intrinsic nature of the Son of Man himself.[4] That is the truth or reality of the matter which they cannot but attest, for they themselves have fallen under its objective control and transformation of their religious consciousness. Now they are able to present Jesus Christ in

[3] See Matt. 2: 15; 4: 3, 6; 8: 29; 14: 33; 16: 16; 27: 40, 43, 54; Mark 1: 1, 11; 3: 11; 5: 7; 9: 7; 15: 39; Luke 1: 32, 35; 3: 22; 4: 3, 9, 41; 8: 28; 9: 35.

[4] See William Manson, *Jesus the Messiah*, 5ff., 12ff., 94ff., 103ff., 156ff.; *Jesus and the Christian*, 67ff., 174ff. See also Bultmann's long discussion and analysis of the '*I*' *sayings*, *The History of the Synoptic Tradition*, tr. by J. Marsh, 1963, pp. 150–66, which Manson has in mind throughout. I am not at all convinced by Bultmann's arguments as I am, for the most part, by Manson's. Bultmann's phenomenalist method (rooted in the familiar Marburg Neo-Kantianism) compels him to be concerned only with a regrouping or mapping of phenomena, to the exclusion of any objective reference to things in themselves, from which it follows that the '*I*' *sayings* are robbed of any objective rooting in Christ himself and can be considered only on the relatively superficial level of their phenomenal and literary forms. Moreover, confidence in his 'results' is considerably lessened by the invalid epicheirematic pattern of argument of which he makes such frequent use.

accordance with his essential nature and reality, whereas before that they were only able to offer a fragmentary and relatively superficial account of him as a disturbing and enigmatic manifestation, in which they encountered a divine authority (*exousia*) before which the disciples and opponents of Jesus were alike turned inside out. They recognize that in all that he said about God and did in the name of God, Jesus confronted them in his own person in such a way that they were in fact face to face with *the ultimate exousia* of God himself. In claiming that authority as his own, Jesus was in fact putting himself in God's place.[5] And so all the Evangelists themselves have to say of Jesus Christ, even of his life and teaching before the crucifixion, is shot through and through with deep Christological significance. In Jesus God himself has directly and personally intervened in the existence and plight of humanity, in accordance with the creative and redeeming intention of his love, cherished and adumbrated throughout the long history of Israel but now at last unveiled in its finality and universality.

In order to make this movement of the understanding from the risen to the historical Jesus clear, let us perform a thought-experiment. Project back through time and space a modern reporter and give him as a special assignment 'Jesus of Nazareth' in the three years from his emerging to be baptized by John the Baptist to his resurrecting from the tomb of Joseph of Arimathea – and we shall have to suppose within the conditions of the experiment that he knows nothing whatsoever about Jesus before he begins but can cope quite adequately with the language or languages involved. How does he act? He makes a great effort to maintain close contact with Jesus, following him in his travels back and forth between Galilee and Judaea, so that he can keep him under direct observation over lengthy periods and listen to his teaching as he repeated it to different groups of people and adapted it to different situations, doubtless many hundreds of times. Above all he studies Jesus himself, in his treatment of the common people, his encounter with the authorities, his behaviour in the synagogue and in the temple, his arguments with lawyers, his conflict with the priests, his exposure of the hypocrites, his association with outcasts, his

[5] See here the discussion of W. Pannenberg, *Jesus–God and Man*, Eng. tr. 1968, pp. 53ff.

treatment of Samaritans and aliens, his compassion for the
poor, the sick, the crippled and the blind, his welcome to little
children; and all the time he seeks to penetrate into the inner
intention of Jesus in an attempt to understand him from
within his own life and mission. Note-book after note-book is
filled with 'data', and as he reads them over and reflects upon
them he looks for a way of putting it all together. Of course he
has to select what he thinks to be particularly significant, giving
full play to recurring and revealing features, and he must
organize his material round events of evidently salient importance. The gaps between the data he selects for use have to
be bridged, and some sort of framework must be introduced
into it if he is to build up a coherent account of Jesus; but he
makes a special point of being as accurate as he can in putting
down the facts as they are and narrating the events as they really
happened. Nevertheless he finds himself more and more
puzzled. It is not simply the incredible things Jesus does – and
he is forced to conclude after relentless sifting of the circumstances again and again that no trickery or sorcery is involved.
Nor is it merely his quite unaccountable power over the lives
and physical existence of human beings, even at a distance,
and even over nature. Nor is it just the complete mastery he
reveals in difficult situations in which with a gentle magisterial
ease he turns the tables on his critics and opponents in such a
way that they find themselves under question at the bar of
the Almighty – although that is certainly a part of it. It has
more to do with his astonishing insight into the minds of
others and the uncanny way in which his very presence searches
the innermost recesses of their hearts, shames them, and brings
to light secret thoughts and motives hidden even from themselves; and then with the fact that through a word of forgiveness, spoken with a breath-taking prerogative, he sets people
free from the fetters of their guilt and their past. It has to do
also with the sheer holiness of the man, his translucent purity
and simplicity, the unsullied truth of his being, the utter
selflessness of his compassion, his complete lack of guile, in-
sincerity or pretension – there is no inward darkness in Jesus
but rather something like an excess of light. And not least there
is the towering authority of his self-consciousness as to the
critical centrality of his own person and mission in the Kingdom

of God which he proclaims, and the paradoxical combination of his calling for unreserved self-renunciation and an absolute relation toward himself from his followers together with an unbelievable meekness and lowliness, all without a vestige of arrogance, making it impossible for any sincere charge of megalomania to be levelled against him – although some of the Jews who were his bitterest critics kept on saying he was usurping divine prerogatives and making himself out to be equal with God.

In the last analysis, however, what baffles our reporter is Jesus himself. He does not seem to fit into any conceivable mould; he breaks through every ordinary conceptual system; he resists being subsumed in any general scheme of things or even being brought into a connected relation with other understandable possibilities and conditions, for his nature somehow transcends all the criteria that he can think of on the basis of hitherto recorded experience. Of one thing at least our reporter seems certain: in spite of all his direct experience, the carefully tested observation, the objectively established data, and his assiduous first-hand study, he is still very far from understanding Jesus. There are too many unanswered questions (and vast questions at that) to permit anything like an adequate or coherent account of him: all he is finally left with is a collection of fragmented reports, without a proper structure to hold them consistently together, for he is now convinced that the concepts he feels himself being forced to use for this purpose are alien to Jesus, and are blinding him as to the real clues. And what is more, this makes him doubt the validity even of his 'objectively established data', for evidently he does not really know how properly to *see* what he is observing, far less assess and conceptualize the 'raw facts' he has been trying to ascertain with such care. There must be some standpoint or frame of meaning, from which all this would make sense, but if so it must be one altogether different from what he can imagine, with a quite different way for understanding, integrating and describing all that he has observed and heard and still observes and hears.

Such are the thoughts, we may suppose, of our reporter as he enters the last passover season in his association with Jesus, when events move quickly and startlingly to their terrible climax on the cross. Looking back, he remembers particularly the fixed gaze of Jesus as he set his face for the ascent to Jerusalem in a way that stunned and struck fear into the disciples; then the awesome passover meal in which Jesus anticipated his passion and transformed the rite in such a way as to invest his death with the significance of a covenant sacrifice; the response of Jesus to the question of the high priest, 'Art thou the Christ, the Son of the Blessed?': 'I am: and you shall see the Son of Man sitting on the right hand of power and coming in the clouds of heaven!' (Mark 14: 61–62); then the cry from the cross, 'My God, my God, why hast thou forsaken me?'; and finally the word of the Roman centurion as Jesus cried out and gave up his spirit, 'Truly this was the Son of God' (Mark 15: 34, 39). All his most acute problems and difficulties are shatteringly confirmed by those contradictory events and words. Right up to the very end, and then most of all, everything about Jesus is so paradoxical that it is impossible to fit it all consistently into a single picture – it is like a fascinating jig-saw puzzle in tantalizing disarray, while some of the pieces which here and there evidently fit into one another actually seem to belong to a very different puzzle.

This is the state of affairs upon which the resurrection of Jesus supervenes, once more turning everything upside down in the thoughts of our reporter, or rather, as it transpires, right side up. Like the disciple Thomas he is very sceptical at first, but as soon as he and the others are convinced of the truth of the resurrection and the physical identity of the risen Jesus, his whole approach to Jesus is lifted with a single stroke on to an altogether higher level of reality. The resurrection imposes upon all that has taken place hitherto an entirely different aspect, so that things begin to fall into place and steadily to take on a depth of meaning and consistency impossible to conceive before. Here at last is the key to the bewildering enigma of Jesus, for it provides it with a structure consistent with the whole sequence of events leading up to and beyond the crucifixion, or rather it discloses embedded in those events their own dynamic structure of significance, one that rises naturally out of the very ground of Jesus' being and life, one in which the supreme intention of God is seen to be built into the life and not least the very passion of Jesus. This is not an interpretation externally imposed upon the facts but one inherent in them, belonging to their inner 'necessity': 'Was it not necessary that the Christ should suffer these things and enter into his glory?' (Luke 24: 27).[6] It is now clear that the facts themselves are controlled by the power of the redemptive purpose they embody which, despite all the violence of men, does not originate with men but with the foreknowledge of God himself. This transcendent and victorious Jesus is none other than the very Son of God. And what does that mean for our understanding of God? the reporter asks himself. The very foundations of the universe seem to rock at the thought of the answer that forces itself upon him.

After the ascension of Jesus the reporter takes out his note-books and goes over them carefully, for he knows that every-thing must be corrected and recast now that he is able really to *see* and understand what he observed. His 'careful' account of the events in the life of Jesus as they actually happened is, he is forced to admit, seriously distorting, for it abstracts their appearance, their phenomenal or literary surface, from its objective structure in Jesus Christ himself and thereby de-prives the events of their underlying ontological integration; while 'the objectively established data' are quite evidently organized through concepts which, in considerable measure, derive from himself rather than from Jesus, and thereby betray his own subjective bias. Regarded in the penetrating light of the resurrection 'the observational facts' about Jesus now assume a conceptual organization in accordance with their own intrinsic significance and are found to be inter-preting themselves in terms of a natural vectorial coherence of their own. Thus an astonishing thing about the resurrection is that instead of cutting Jesus off from his historical and earthly existence before the cross it takes it all up and confirms its concrete factuality by allowing it to be integrated on its own controlling ground, and therefore enables it to be understood in its own objective meaning. Far from being 'violated' the

---

[6] Cf. Arnold Ehrhardt, 'The Disciples of Emmaus' (*New Testament Studies*, vol. 10, 1964, p. 185). 'Already a Father as early as Origen stressed the fact that the manifestation of the risen Lord to the disciples of Emmaus aimed at showing that Jesus after the resurrection still instructed his dis-ciples how they should give witness to him'.

historical Jesus comes to his own within the dimension of the risen Jesus, and the risen Jesus is discerned to have no other fabric than that in the life and mission of the historical Jesus. It is the resurrection that really discovers and gives access to the historical Jesus, for it enables one to understand him in terms of his own intrinsic *logos*, and appreciate him in the light of his own true nature as he really was – and is and ever will be.[7]

One or two further points striking our reporter must be noted. As he reflects upon his memoranda, corrects and re-organizes what he had written, he finds himself recalling other sayings and incidents in the life of Jesus, together with the reactions of other people to him, which had been tucked away in the back of his mind because they seemed to have no particular significance. Now, however, they force themselves upon his thoughts in a new and exciting way, for they are lit up with inherent meaning; and so he struggles hard to recall them more accurately. Then gradually as the material begins to take shape under his pen in a remarkable inherence of words and events, he is aware that under the creative impact of the resurrection something like a *new literary form* is struggling to come into being. His reporting has to take on a new character to do justice to its subject-matter, and yet that is precisely what it cannot really do: it has to be shaped in such a way that it indicates and bears witness to more than it can formally express.

In this thought-experiment we projected our reporter back into the last three years of Jesus' life before his ascension, so that it does not enable us to reflect upon the oral tradition or the layered memory of the primitive Church in which the apostolic reflection and reorganization of witness to Jesus Christ had such a distinctive function to fulfill (cf. Acts 6: 2–4). We would have to extend our thought-experiment beyond the point where we broke it off, to help us think out some of the problems there, and perhaps also project another reporter back several decades later. But what does the thought-experiment we have undertaken show? To use the analogy of stereoscopic

---

[7] It is in the light of the resurrection that the disturbing disparities in the sayings of Jesus using the *present* and the *future* tense (for example in respect of 'the Son of man' sayings) fade away, for the indirect self-revelation of Jesus, in which he held back his revelation in word so that it could keep pace with his revelation in deed, now merges with the direct revelation.

viewing, it shows that only when the two separate pictures of the historical Jesus and the risen Jesus are fused into one image of spatio-temporal depth are we really able to see and understand Jesus Christ as he is *in reality*. But it is precisely the *disparities*, the *conflicting differences*, of the pictures when viewed apart which, when viewed together to yield a conjoint significance, make such a knowledge of Jesus Christ in a dimension of ontological depth possible. Here we have an objective self-disclosure of Jesus Christ which is not to be read off the literary form, no matter how 'appropriate' that may be, is not to be found in the separate 'appearances' themselves, and is not to be derived by historico-critical analysis of, or through, some process of historical deduction from, the 'observational facts', but only through a process of creative integration deriving from the intrinsic significance or *logos* of the living Christ himself. It is an intelligible revelation which requires 'depth-exegesis', and listening, intelligent and indeed committed participation. As the Jesus of the Fourth Gospel expressed it, if we are unable to understand his language (*lalia*), it is because we cannot (or, perhaps, cannot bear to) understand his *logos* (John 8: 43).[8] That is, I take it, the very *logos* to which the apostles were said to devote themselves, when they appointed the first 'seven' to undertake a local ministry in the Church (Acts 6: 2-4). And it was evidently out of that devotion that the apostolic tradition took shape which we have handed on to us in the canonical New Testament. It was a *logos*, however, in which the decisive deeds of Christ in his passion and in his resurrection were incorporated, a *logos* which God sent forth through the Apostles in the light and in the power of the resurrection.

If we attempt to abstract from the New Testament the dimension of the resurrection, the actual picture of the historical Jesus Christ it presents disintegrates, for not only do we erase the basic clues on which we rely in apprehending Christ in his objective reality, but we remove the dynamic Christological structure which makes it cohere significantly together on its own proper ground. There is a two-fold problem here: at the level of our interpretation of the Gospels, and at the level on which the Gospels themselves were composed. Once we have understood the message or *logos* of the Gospels in the

[8] See R. Bultmann, *The Gospel of John*, Eng. tr. 1971, p. 316f.

revealing and integrating light of the risen Lord and apprehended the witness to Christ in its objective depth, so that our
attention is focused on the living reality of Christ, we .are
unable to return to the Gospels and read them in such a way
as to obliterate from our minds the understanding and the
conviction which have already been mediated to us – it would
be rather like trying to fit together a second or a third time the
scattered pieces of a jig-saw puzzle in pretended ignorance of
the picture disclosed when we completed it the first time. But
further, since the Gospels themselves were composed in the
light of the resurrection and its unveiling of who Jesus Christ
really is, which has decisively moulded their writing (as well as
the tradition out of which it grew), it is impossible by digging
beneath the evangelical presentation of Jesus Christ to get at
the so-called 'raw facts' upon which it relies and which are
indissolubly assimilated into its account, for those 'raw facts',
dirempted from their original frame in the dynamic reciprocity
between Jesus and his disciples and therefore from the Christological structure embedded in the tradition, inevitably take on
a distorted and fragmented character, with the all-significant
clues eradicated, and become something quite different (in
fact something that never really existed). This is rather like
what happens when we take twin pictures out of a stereo-
scope so that we may examine them separately and analyse
their integrating clues, only to discover that the clues have been
cancelled out and that the three-dimensional image has
vanished. Reductive analysis of this kind always results in
semantic disintegration of the picture into relatively meaningless fragments, when the interpreter is tempted to impose upon
them some artificial framework in order to restore coherence,
and then, failing to grasp the proper significance of the resulting disparities, he is tempted further to tamper with the evidence, tailoring the data, to fit his theory – surely the one un-
forgiveable sin in any kind of scientific procedure – as, for
example, those scholars appear to do who are determined to
make out that St. Mark's Gospel was not composed under the
impact of the resurrection![9] All this is not to decry the place
for historico-critical analysis of the Gospels, but rather to

[9] See, in contrast, C. E. B. Cranfield, *The Gospel according to St. Mark*,
pp. 78, 128, 188f., 278f., 288, 295ff., 429.

warn that it has only a limited validity, beyond which it can only lead to the destruction of meaning, and that in any case it cannot be fulfilled properly even in its limited way apart from theological interpretation, for that would mean tearing empirical and theoretical components in the New Testament witness artificially apart and the inevitable imposition of the interpreter's own subjective bias upon the witness. Historico-critical analysis of the New Testament material is really helpful only in so far as we correlate it with the objective ground from which it is shaped and controlled, just as inter-pretation of the text is meaningful only in so far as we follow through its semantic references and understand it in the light of the reality it signifies. One of the supreme lessons we gain from the study of rigorous scientific method is that the splitting apart of empirical and theoretical components in any field of inquiry and knowledge inevitably disintegrates the funda-mental epistemic structure and therefore brings about the alienation of meaning. That applies no less in the field of biblical inquiry than in any other.

We may now return to the point that the whole life of Jesus Christ from his birth to his resurrection and beyond is an in-divisible continuum, in which the historical Jesus is con-sistently and indissolubly one with the life of the risen Jesus, so that now after the resurrection the historical Jesus confronts us only as suffused with the light of the risen Lord, but this is a continuum after the resurrection in which the life of the risen Jesus takes up the life of the historical Jesus into itself as its permanent material content so that the risen Lord meets us only on the actual ground of the historical Jesus, in his birth, life and passion. That is the truth of the matter which is brought out with such clarity and force in the Gospel according to St. John. There, precisely where Jesus is presented to us in his earthly and fleshly reality – and no Gospel more than the Fourth Gospel stresses the humanity of Jesus so much – the eternal *I am* of the living God is irresistibly evident in Jesus' self-consciousness and self-disclosure, above all at those points where he stands forth as the Lord of life and death, dispensing the creative power of the resurrection. 'My Father works hitherto, and I work. . . . As the Father raises the dead and gives them life, so also the Son gives life to whom he will. . . .

He has granted the Son to have life in himself, and has given him authority to execute judgment, because he is the Son of Man' (John 5: 17, 21, 26, 27). 'I and my Father are one' (John 10: 30). 'I am the resurrection and the life: he who believes in me, though he were dead, yet shall he live' (John 11: 25). 'I am the way, the truth and the life; no man comes to the Father, but by me. . . . He who has seen me has seen the Father. . . . I am in the Father and the Father is in me' (John 14: 6, 9, 11). Thus regarded, even the human life of Jesus, the incarnate Son, falls within the life of God himself, and is as such the source of eternal life to us. Our sharing in the life of Jesus is, as the First Epistle of John also teaches, a sharing in the life which the Son had with the Father preceding the creation (1 John 1: 1f.). How far this account of Jesus in the Fourth Gospel has been suffused with the life of the risen Lord, inconsistently with the historical Jesus, is a question for scholars, but it seems evident to me that essentially the same teaching is found in the Synoptic Gospels.[10] Thus Jesus, clearly speaking of himself, can say on the one hand that the Son of Man came eating and drinking, does not know where to lay his head, must suffer and be rejected and be slain, etc. (Luke 7: 34; 9: 58; Mark 8: 31), and can say on the other hand that the Son of Man must rise again, will come again in clouds and with great glory, will be seen sitting at the right hand of power, etc. (Mark 8: 31; 13: 26; 14: 62), capped by the significant *I am* (Mark 14: 61, etc.).[11] Such is 'the tremendous Christology' mediated to us through the Synoptics (whether from the common source or its editors is ultimately theologically immaterial), and surely there can be little doubt in the mind of a reasonable interpreter that although it is found here in a lower key, it is essentially of the same tissue as that found in the Pauline, Petrine, Johannine and other material of the New Testament: *Jesus Christ stands revealed by the resurrection as the manifestation of God in the flesh.*[12] The manifestation *in the flesh* must be stressed.

[10] As Karl Barth has pointed out even the Synoptic statement that 'the kingdom of God is at hand' is materially identical with the Johannine 'I am', *Church Dogmatics*, IV/3, p. 180f.

[11] See here Jeremias' discussion of 'the emphatic *ego*', *New Testament Theology*, Eng. tr., vol. 1, pp. 250ff.

[12] See Francis Noel Davey, *The Word of Testimony*, 1951, pp. 17ff.

This is the perspective within which we can speak meaningfully of the incarnation and the passion of the Son of God. It is in the light of the resurrection of Jesus in body, in which he is revealed as the transcendent Lord within and over our mortal existence and as the creative source of our life and being, that we have reason to speak of God become man, that is, not simply of God in man but of God come among us in the flesh as himself man, while nevertheless remaining God Almighty, the Creator of the universe. And it is in this light also that we can grasp the significance of the humiliation and crucifixion of Christ, even of the terrible cry of dereliction from the cross, for, far from being the despairing end of Jesus of Nazareth and all his eschatological expectations, this is precisely what God has deliberately undertaken on our behalf, when he came to take our lost condition upon himself and thereby to effect our redemption from perdition and our reconciliation with himself. Apart from the resurrection the death of Christ on the cross could not take on any sacrificial or vicarious significance. Here in the resurrection, therefore, as Wolfhart Pannenberg has expressed it, 'we have to do with the sustaining foundation of the Christian faith. If this collapses, so does everything else which the Christian faith acknowledges'.[13] But the obverse is also true: the resurrection does not come to its real significance unless it is the resurrection of the incarnate and crucified Son of God, that is, unless there is included in the full material content of the resurrection the concrete historical actuality of Jesus Christ in the whole sequence of his vicarious human life and passion, for what we have to do with here in the risen Lord is 'the whole Christ', Christ clothed with his Gospel of saving deeds. The resurrection is the fulfilment of the incarnate mission of the Son of God who has taken up our worldly existence and history into himself and remains regnant over all space and time. While the resurrection, like the incarnation, took place within a definite span of space and time which can be geographically and historically plotted, it is possessed of a finality and universality whereby it transcends all mere localization or temporal transience, yet in such a way that far from infringing the space-time reality of Jesus Christ it

[13] Wolfhart Pannenberg, *The Apostles' Creed in the Light of Today's Questions*, Eng. tr. 1972, p. 97; see also, *Jesus—God and Man*, Eng. tr., 1968, p. 73.

establishes it for ever. As such the resurrection constitutes in
all times and places the one avenue of real access to the historical Jesus Christ who was born of the Virgin Mary, suffered
under Pontius Pilate and rose again from the tomb of Joseph
of Arimathea.

Two aspects of the resurrection regarded in this way require
further elucidation: the nature of its objectivity and the interrelation of redemption and creation which it involves.

(a) The objectivity of the resurrection is to be understood,
on the one hand, in relation to the historical Jesus Christ in
whom God has made himself the object of our knowledge,
within the subject-object structures of our human existence in
the world, and, on the other hand, in relation to his own
transcendent reality as the Lord God Almighty – and it is the
concept of the towering authority (*exousia*) of Jesus Christ, to
which all the Gospels bear witness, that supplies us with the
link between them. In Jesus Christ the self-revelation of God
took place within the restraints of a concrete limited historical
happening in space and time, and since it is with this self-
revelation of God in Jesus that the resurrection is wholly and
inseparably bound up it stands or falls with that objective
constraint of the historical medium. That is surely why the
Fourth Gospel lays such emphasis upon the fact that Jesus
Christ is the way, the truth and the life, and there is no other
way into knowledge of God except through him (John 14: 6),
and why the doctrine of the Trinity is built round the fact that
it is through Christ that we have access by one Spirit to the
Father (Eph. 2: 16). To cut away the objective reality of the
historical Jesus Christ as the ground for our knowledge of
God, or to allow the Christian message to become detached
from it in some sort of transcendentalized 'Easter faith' would
disrupt the very foundations of Christianity. The objectivity of
the resurrection, therefore, cannot be detached from the space-
time structures of this world, any more than that of the historical Jesus Christ. On the other hand, the self-revelation or
self-communication of God in Jesus Christ within the limitation
of those structures is not one that falls under our control or
manipulation, for it retains its objectivity precisely by objecting
to any attempt on our part to subject it to ourselves. That is the
high significance of the *authority* of Jesus which so astonished

his contemporaries in his teaching (Mark 1: 22, 27; Matt. 7: 29; Luke 4: 32), in his forgiveness of sins (Mark 2: 10; Luke 5: 24; Matt. 9: 6) etc., for it is the authority of his *Lordship*, evident for example in his treatment of the law, the sabbath or the temple (Matt. 5: 21ff.; 12: 1ff.; 21: 12ff.; Mark 2: 23ff.; 11: 15ff.; Luke 6: 1ff.; 19: 45f.; 20: 1ff., etc.).[14] That is why, indeed, the historical Jesus cannot be known through subjecting him to our analysis and methodological control, for even though we can know him only within the concrete actualities of history which call for empirico-theoretical analysis, he cannot be netted within the mesh of our criteria, but breaks through them precisely as he broke through entombment by his resurrection.

Here we have an objectivity that is both irrevocable and invincible. It is irrevocable, for it is bound up once and for all with the incarnate reality of God in Jesus Christ – even he does not, cannot, go back on it; and it is invincible because it has a depth and range which we are unable to overtake or transcend, for it is grounded in the transcendent reality of the Lord God himself. It is important to see that this is the kind of objectivity we have already in the historical Jesus Christ who, though he meets us within the subject-object structures of our space and time which we share as human creatures, nevertheless cannot be known in the same way in which we know natural objects or creaturely events which in being known have to be known.[15] This is not altogether true of persons who are more than natural objects like their bodies; they are *voluntary* objects who may be known only in so far as they freely reveal themselves to us within the constraints of their physical existence – they do not therefore have to be known in being known by us, for they retain in their own authority the capacity to reveal themselves without which they may not really be known. How much truer that is of God! When he *gives* himself to be known by us, he does so in pure grace, in his own sovereign authority and freedom, and not in such a way that he resigns himself to the control of our knowing. He remains not only our Lord but the Lord of our knowing of him, who certainly

---

[14] Cf. again J. Jeremias, *New Testament Theology*, vol. 1, pp. 250ff.
[15] See the discussion of this point by Karl Barth, *Church Dogmatics*, II/1, pp. 204ff.

gives himself as the object of our knowledge yet in such a way that the gift is a continuous self-giving in which the gift and the Giver are identical, and therefore in such a way that he *retains his objectivity*, so that he may be known only in and through constant communion with him and ever fresh appropriation of his self-revelation. That is the way in which God revealed himself in and through Jesus to his contemporaries, with a sovereign freedom and lordly authority even in Jesus' earthly life which evoked such awe and wonder from his contemporaries. This is the character of his self-revelation which is so ascendent in the risen Jesus who is recognized to be invested with all authority in heaven and earth (Matt. 28: 18). As the risen and exalted Lord, Jesus occupies a place of finality and universality in the Godhead. It is nevertheless precisely *Jesus* with whom we have to do here, that is, the historical reality of Jesus resurrected in his human integrity in such a way that the risen Lord remains in indissoluble unity and continuity with the incarnation in space and time, the same yesterday, today and for ever.

In view of this we have some reason to speak of the resurrection in terms of a double objectivity, for the concrete objectivity of Jesus in space and time is bound up with the transcendent objectivity of God, so that he meets us even as this same Jesus in the ultimate authority and irreducible Lordship of the Godhead. On the one hand, this gives the objectivity of the historical Jesus in and through the resurrection an invincible constancy and persistence such as we do not meet with anywhere else. He is so profoundly objective that no culture, no philosophy, no church has ever been able to subject him to its own framework of thought or action. On the other hand, in the resurrection there is conferred upon that objectivity an open indeterminate quality through correlation with the limitless reality of God himself, making it an objectivity with an infinite depth of intrinsic significance and therefore with an inexhaustible power of self-revelation beyond all our expectations in the future. This is why knowledge of the risen Jesus Christ is so powerfully eschatological in character: not only because in him we come up against the ultimate Judge of the quick and the dead and are face to face with the final things of God, which have broken through into the present,

but because in him we have to do with one whose self-revelation ranges throughout and beyond all space and time
and which as such may be known only in terms of the vectorial or predictive character which it cannot but take on
when mediated to us at any point within on-going space and
time. There is far more to it than is expressible or knowable at
any time, so that the self-revelation of Christ keeps on out-
running the Church's knowledge of him in history. Hence, the
kind of objectivity manifested in the resurrection of Jesus Christ
is one which, on the ground of the once and for all historical
self-revelation of God in the incarnation, increasingly accredits
itself as ultimately real and meaningful as it continues to disclose an infinite depth of intelligibility. It is so infinitely real
that it is greater than anything we can conceive in terms of
what we already know, and may apprehend (as far as it can
be) only in proportion to the measure in which we ourselves
participate in its eschatological and teleological movement
through space and time, in eager hope and expectation of the
day when we shall know as we are known.

(b) The second aspect of the resurrection that we have to
consider further is the profound interrelation between redemption and creation which it involves. As we have seen, the
resurrection would have no material content apart from its
inner connection with the incarnation, apart, that is, from the
entry of the Creator himself into his creation in order to effect
its redemption. It is in the resurrection of Jesus from the grave
that that incarnational movement is both consummated and
unveiled in its fundamental significance: the intersection of the
order of creation by the order of redemption in such a way
that it is set upon a wholly new basis. The resurrection of
Jesus was not to a state of affairs in the old order of things
but to a new state of affairs entailing the redemptive transformation of the old order. While here redemption has made
contact with the very foundations of creation the basic structure of what emerges in the Easter event is absolutely new: a
reality which is not only entirely unknown to us but entirely
unknowable in terms of what we already know or think we
know, and only knowable through a radical reconstruction
of our prior knowledge.

A resurrection of this kind inevitably contradicts the shape of things in the old order and is naturally stubbornly resisted by the old order. That is after all something intrinsic to the inseparable interconnection between the crucifixion and the resurrection. This is very evident in the conception of the resurrection as the act of God raising up and installing Jesus with power in his messianic office. When we put that together with the fact that Judaism had no idea of a resurrection as a decisive event in history, it is clear how profoundly this conception of messiahship conflicts with the notions of it current among the contemporaries of Jesus. A good case can be made out for the claim that, historically speaking, Jesus was crucified because he would have nothing to do with the image of a political messiah, and would not allow himself to be manoeuvered into a position where he could be cast in that kind of role. Moreover the proclamation of the apostles that Jesus is the Christ of God enthroned in office and power through the resurrection, could not but have been heard as a shattering contradiction of a conservative and recalcitrant Judaism. But this holds good also for the clash between the resurrection and the whole world of things in space and time as we know it in our daily life, and not least our this-worldly conceptual frameworks – by its very nature the resurrection of the crucified is inevitably controversial, for not only does it create upset and challenge collision in itself, it sanctifies the crucifixion as the one way into the world to come in which all things will be made new. This is something which we may gloss over only at the expense of defusing it of its critical and explosive significance.

It is this externally contradictory character of the resurrection that helps to account for its elusiveness, the fact that we are unable, as it were, to pin it down and speak about it in precise terms or enclose it in a web of controlled inferences. This elusiveness, or indeterminate nature, of the resurrection, however, is not due to any deficiency in reality but, quite the reverse, to an excess in reality over the mundane actualities of our perishable existence. The resurrection of Jesus is so real that it cannot be tamed and tied up in our conceptual formalizations, for its reality transcends anything we can say about it, and thus retains a depth of objective intelligibility which does not allow itself to be 'objectified' by us. Its elusive-

ness is due to its sheer excess of genuine objectivity over the
kind of reified objectivity which is the result of our own
'objectifying' operations and the massive subjectivity they
embody.

There is of course another side to all this. Since the resurrection is the redemption of the old order of things, and is
already the irruption of the new creation into the midst of the
old, it brings with it the capacity to create in us new conceptions and new categories of thought with which to apprehend
and speak appropriately and therefore objectively about it.
This also belongs to its elusiveness, the fact that we can think
and speak about it truly only in strange and unfamiliar ways,
but once again this is totally in keeping with the nature of its
reality: it is so absolutely new that it may be apprehended only
in accordance with that newness and not in any other way. In
seeking to grasp the message of the resurrection, therefore, we
must allow for a yawning disparity between it and our own
habits of thought, but allow also for a movement on the part
of the risen Lord whereby he discovers himself to us in the
sovereign freedom and authority of his own independent
reality, summoning us to renounce ourselves, take up the cross
and follow him, but enabling us to know him beyond any
capacity we have in ourselves through the power of his own
resurrection. To know Jesus Christ in this way is to experience
the redemptive and recreative impact of the resurrection in our
minds and lives. That happens only as we allow the resurrection to break through the normal patterns of our knowledge
and to constitute itself the ultimate, and ultimately indefinable,
ground on which it is to be understood and at the same time
to transform our thoughts of it in such a way that they are
properly matched to that ground and its inherent intelligibility, in the risen Lord himself.

Since the whole fact of Jesus Christ from his birth to his
resurrection is indivisibly and identifiably the same, in which
the historical Jesus is consistently and indissolubly one with
the risen Jesus, it must be said that the risen Jesus Christ has
essentially the same kind of objectivity and elusiveness as the
historical Jesus Christ, and the same kind of persistent reality
in space and time which will not be dissolved by reductive
analysis or explanatory reinterpretation into some spaceless and

timeless event (*Ereignis* as the German scholars love to speak
of it). On the contrary, it insists on being understood and interpreted in its own intrinsic significance within the context of
meaning which the incarnation has created for mankind within
the history and religion of Israel among the nations of the
earth and within the sphere of human existence and thought.
The ultimate fact with which we have to do here is the coming
of God himself within the contingent structures of space and
time, which could not but affect the very foundations of our
relations with God and of our knowledge of him in the world.
It is a coming specifically to be one with us through the
psycho-physical totality and reality of Jesus Christ, even
within the conditions of the perceptuality and conceptuality
of the created universe, which he has made his own in order to
reveal himself to us and reconcile us to himself. Jesus Christ
does not represent some tangential, or timeless and spaceless
mathematical point where somehow the totally other world of
transcendental deity impinges on our space and time existence.
On the contrary, God has not come in Jesus Christ to operate
above the world or over our heads, even when acting savingly
on our behalf; he has entered into our human and physical
existence in order to operate within its limits and measures,
within its created order and intelligibility, and there to establish relations with us in an intimate reciprocity in which he
communicates himself to us and takes us into communion
with himself, and since we are not bodiless spirits but psycho-
physical beings, these relations which God has established
with us in Jesus Christ necessarily take in our whole body-and-
soul reality and it is within that reality that his work on our
behalf is brought to its consummation through the concrete
spatio-temporal events of the crucifixion and resurrection of
Jesus – otherwise God would not have established relations
with *us*, and the Gospel would have no relevance at all for
men and women of flesh and blood. Hence nothing that Jesus
Christ was, taught and did is to be understood and interpreted
through any kind of abstraction from the spatio-temporal
structures and conditions of concrete human existence. Cut
away from Jesus Christ the fact of the incarnation of the Son
of God in this world, and everything becomes fragmented, and
paradoxical, and empty of decisive significance. This applies

above all to the resurrection of Jesus Christ from the dead, for
it would be quite unintelligible and nonsensical if the consummation of God's work in space and time were not of the same
tissue as all the rest of it. However difficult it may be for us,
the message of the resurrection is inseparably bound up with
the objective structures of the space and time of the created
cosmos, but the fundamental reality inherent in it all, which
the resurrection itself unveiled, is that in Jesus Christ God himself has come in person into our world and manifested himself
in the body, in the wholeness and undiminished integrity of
human being, yet in such a way as to redeem and transform
what he has assumed through the birth, life, passion and resurrection of Jesus. 'Without controversy great is the mystery of
godliness: he was manifested in the flesh, justified in the
spirit, seen of angels, preached among the nations, believed on
in the world, received up in glory'. (I Tim. 3: 16).

*   *   *

What are we to make of such a conception of the resurrection
in the intelligibilities of the space-time structures which
theological science shares with the other sciences, natural or
human? It will not do to hold our theological conceptions and
our natural scientific conceptions apart in entirely disparate
realms. Certainly they are divergent, for natural science is
concerned only with the universe in its natural, contingent
processes, whereas theological science is concerned with *the
acts of God* which in *creation* brought those processes into being
out of nothing and established them in their utter contingency,
and which in *incarnation* accepted and established the reality of
contingent processes and their intelligibility. Neither the
doctrine of creation nor the doctrine of the incarnation will
allow theology to detach itself from, far less despise, natural or
human science in which man is set by God to the task of exploring, and bringing to word, the order and harmony of the
universe and all that takes place within it, for the universe is
the sphere in which the believer glorifies and praises God the
Creator, as well as the medium in and through which God
makes himself known to man. Thus regarded science itself is

part of man's religious duty, for it is part of his faithful response to the Creator and Sustainer of the cosmos.

Theological and natural science, Christian beliefs and the beliefs of natural science, inevitably overlap with one another within the structures of space and time which are the bearers of rational order within the created universe, and are therefore intelligibly interconnected. But they also inevitably diverge from one another within that area of overlap and interconnection, for the vectorial movements of theological and natural science run in different directions: one inquiring into the transcendent source and ground, and the other into the contingent nature and pattern, of all created order. Theological inquiry is not to be conceived as having only an asymptotic bearing in relation to natural science, for there are significant points of intersection: evident in the all-important empirical correlates of theological statements about God's revealing and saving operations within our spatio-temporal existence, and also evident in the open or indeterminate nature of scientific concepts and propositions which, if they are consistent, cannot be completely formalized within closed systems, for their contingent intelligibility by its very nature requires to be completed beyond itself, that is by meta-theoretical relation to ever higher and wider systems of understanding. Because of this overlap, and these significant points of intersection, theological science, in sheer faithfulness to its proper task, must enter into dialogue with the natural and human sciences and their understanding of the created universe, for it is within that created universe and not in abstraction from it that it seeks to understand and interpret God's revealing and saving operations.

A relationship of this kind between theological and natural science cannot be pursued on the assumption of any kind of *dualism*, theological or scientific. So far as theology is concerned, a dualism forces upon it a deistic disjunction between God and the universe, in which God is not conceived of as acting objectively within space and time, with the result that theological and natural science are kept entirely apart. So far as natural science is concerned, a dualism forces upon it a mechanistic conception of the universe as a closed gravitational system of bodies in motion which are externally connected through cause and effect, in which the idea of God has no place at all, with the result that theology tends to be secularized out of the scientific and academic realm as an anachronistic irrelevance. Whether the dualism concerned is epistemological or cosmological or both (which is usually the case), there results a conception of reality and a frame of mind which automatically and indeed dogmatically excludes any idea of miracle or of resurrection,[16] or of any such objective act of God within the concrete structures of the world, as 'an interference in the laws of nature', and therefore as 'scientifically inconceivable'. The basic problems here, however, are not theological, so that it is impossible to argue with such a position merely on theological grounds. They are rooted in an obsolete positivist conception of science and the kind of closed mind which it regularly throws up, which have been just as inimical to non-mechanistic ideas in biology, for example, or even in physics, not to mention psychology, as in theology. If rational argument is to take place, it will have to take the form of a critical questioning and a logical reconstruction of the very foundations of knowledge, the development of an understanding of reality more in accordance with its rich variability and indeterminate scope of possibility, together with a more adequate and open conception of science in accordance with the nature of things as it is progressively disclosed in the course of actual inquiry. Such a view of science would not dogmatically exclude from the start any possibility before ever it had been given reasonable consideration on its own evidential grounds, so that it would be open to genuine and rational cooperation with disciplined inquiry in every area of knowledge.

While these problems are not theological, as has been said, they are nevertheless found among theologians and also among historians today only too frequently. This is a complaint that Pannenberg makes in connection with the resurrection, which

---

[16] R. R. Niebuhr criticizes A. M. Ramsey's designation of the resurrection of Christ as a 'miracle' as misleading, on the ground that it perpetuates the false understanding of the resurrection as an event that is discontinuous with the rest of history. Apart from a failure to appreciate Ramsey's understanding of the resurrection as a recreative act of God within history, this comment on Niebuhr's part seems to indicate that he is still tied to a dualistic outlook of the obsolete positivist kind. *Op. cit.*, p. 177.

he expounds as 'unique break-in of the reality of the end-time'. 'Why should the historian', he asks, 'not in fact be able to reckon with something like this in his critical investigation of the past? If the ideas of an end to all things and a resurrection of the dead be otherwise justified as meaningful, why should they not be capable of finding a place in the historian's knowledge of reality, just as much as the facts of physics, biology, sociology and psychology?' Then he adds: 'One often hears the objection that a historian who reckoned with possibilities of this kind would come into conflict with the natural sciences. Curiously enough this objection is seldom raised by scientists nowadays, and least of all by physicists; it is most often heard on the lips of theologians, or even historians. In these quarters a dogmatic view of the natural sciences is evidently still widespread which is no longer held by the sciences themselves'.[17] Unfortunately, this is only too true. Theologians, historians and sociologists are often found still trapped within the cultural split between the sciences and the arts thrown up by the nineteenth century ambivalent reaction to the mechanistic universe,[18] and still operating in the backwater of dualist ideas long since left behind in the advance of the pure sciences. This has disastrous effects upon their own academic and scientific pursuits, for the closed character of the ideas in which they have been stuck for so long has prevented them from thinking out adequately and rigorously enough how they are to develop their own inquiries properly in accordance with the distinctive nature of the matter they are committed to investigate, and to do that in such a way that they allow themselves to be tested through the critical questions directed to them from other areas of knowledge where the advance has taken place from a dualist to a unitary outlook upon the universe of observable and non-observable realities. Here where the old cultural split is being steadily overcome and the whole horizon of human inquiry is profoundly altered, the greatest benefits

[17] W. Pannenberg, *The Apostles' Creed in the Light of Today's Questions*, 1972, Eng. tr., p. 110.
[18] This is particularly evident in the 'secessionist movement' of history from natural science – Cf. R. G. Collingwood, *The Idea of History*, pp. 165ff. He has in mind especially the Germans, Windelband, Rickert, Simmel, and Dilthey.

appear to derive from inter-disciplinary activity. There is no reason why theological science which had to do with the whole relation of God to the universe should not benefit most.

Certainly one of the benefits which theology today derives from dialogue with the natural sciences, within the radically transformed outlook upon the universe which they have brought about, is the discovery that the non-theological problems which have troubled so many theologians and historians in the last two centuries are now being discounted by scientists themselves as pseudo-problems for the grounds that gave rise to them, e.g. a closed mechanistic universe, have largely disappeared. The effect of this upon biological science has been enormous, for the liberation from the tyranny of mechanistic concepts which it has entailed has allowed biology to develop organismic concepts and methods in accordance with the nature of its own fields of inquiry, concepts and methods which a positivist instrumentalist science had hitherto denigrated as scientifically unacceptable. Historians and sociologists are still largely bemused by nineteenth century habits of thought, but the effect upon theology is increasingly to throw it back upon its own proper ground where alone it can pursue its inquiries in a rigorously scientific way, but where nevertheless, in accordance with the radical transformation of human thought in the shift from a dualist to a unitary understanding of the universe (resulting largely from relativity theory), it is scientifically incumbent upon theology, precisely as theological science, to engage in cross-questioning with other sciences, since it must operate with them within the same intelligible structures of space and time in the universe which God has created. Since that kind of inter-disciplinary thought will not allow us to detach our understanding of the resurrection from the framework of space and time, for that would make it unintelligible and meaningless, not only for scientists but even for theologians, as theologians we are rationally obliged to clarify for ourselves the area of intersection between theological and natural science within which we must offer an account of the resurrection on its own proper ground while letting ourselves be questioned by the understanding of the same framework by natural science. This does not mean that once again theology looks for a way of making its understanding of the

Gospel conform to the concepts of natural science, for in that context it must take primary account of the way in which theological thought *diverges* from that of all the other sciences – otherwise it cannot remain scientifically faithful to its own distinctive subject-matter and character as *theology*, as 'science of *God*'. Nor can it be faithful to that subject-matter if it does not include within it the universe which God has made and with which he interacts in establishing communion with us, and if it does not try therefore to understand the universe in the contingent nature and contingent intelligibility which God has conferred upon it in creation and which are the ground upon which all natural science rests.

This opens up a field of inquiry far beyond the limited scope of this book, but it may be sufficient here, by way of concluding this discussion, to consider several aspects of the new scientific outlook upon the universe which have a bearing upon the way in which a scientific theology may make its own proper understanding of the resurrection intelligible within the rational structures which it shares with the other sciences.[19]

(1) Perhaps the first point to note is the basic change in the *concept of reality*. This has to do with the transition from the earlier concept of reality, which since the days of Galileo and and Newton was identified with what is causally necessary and quantifiable, the world of 'real, mathematical time and space', as Newton called it, in contrast to 'the apparent and relative time and space' of our ordinary experience, to a new concept of reality in which that kind of dichotomy is transcended and in which structure and matter, or the theoretical and empirical components of knowledge, are inseparably one. The older view of reality was one in which its analysed particulars (atoms, particles, etc.) were conceived of as being externally and invariably connected in terms of *causes*. In actual fact this reduced itself to a conception of a rigid uniformity of all natural processes which by definition excluded as 'real' any event which did not conform to its 'system'. Such a

---

[19] The reader is here referred to the forthcoming book, *Integration and Interpretation in Natural and in Theological Science*; see meantime, 'Newton, Einstein and Scientific Theology', *Religious Studies*; and 'The Integration of Form in Natural and in Theological Science', *Science, Medicine and Man* (now *Social Science and Medicine*), vol. 1, 1973, no. 3, pp. 143–72.

view, however, began to shatter itself against the actual 'fact'
of the electro-magnetic field which could not be explained in
such a mechanistic way, and since the emergence of relativity
theory has had to give way to a profounder and more differential view of reality in which energy and matter, intelligible
structure and material content, exist in mutual interaction and
interdetermination. This is a dynamic view of the world as a
continuous integrated manifold of fields of force in which
relations between bodies are just as ontologically real as the
bodies themselves, for it is in their interrelations and transformations that things are found to be what and as and when
they are. They are to be investigated and understood not by
reference to a uniformity of causal patterns abstracted from the
actual fields of force in which they exist, but in accordance with
their immanent relatedness in the universe and in terms of their
own inherent dynamic order. In such a universe in which form
and being and movement are inseparably fused together,
things and events are to be explained and interpreted in terms
of their ontological *reasons*, that is by penetrating into what
they are in themselves in their interior relations in which they
exhibit an intrinsic intelligibility independent of our perceiving
and conceiving of them, and thereby discriminate themselves
from our scientific constructs and formulations about them.
The effect of all this is very far-reaching. It emancipates us
from the narrow-minded and cramped way of thinking in which
we impose our own abstract patterns upon the universe and rule
out of court all possibilities which transgress the prescriptive
conditions we have laid down for what is conceivable or real.
At the same time it gives rise to a powerful ontology in which the
fatal gap between empirical and theoretical concepts is
transcended, and in which being is found to be essentially
open, requiring open concepts and open structures of thought
for its understanding. And it also lays the foundation for an
integration of thought which affects the whole range of human
knowledge, and thereby provides ground from the side of the
natural and human sciences for much closer relations with
theological science. Here, then, we have a radical change in the
whole horizon of thought which is consistent with the implications of the Christian doctrines of creation and incarnation,
and within which theologians should have little difficulty in

offering an intelligible account of the intrinsic significance of the resurrection, without being tempted into devious interpretations of it in conformity to pseudo-scientific ideas.

(2) Another aspect of the new scientific outlook upon the universe which is relevant to our theme is the *relational concept of space and time*, which we have already had several occasions to discuss. This involves the rejection of receptacle or container notions, along with the dualist cosmologies with which they are bound up, which held sway in the eras of classical and mediaeval science and of modern Newtonian science, and the development of an understanding of space and time as inherent in the contingent processes of nature.[20] This way of thinking is not new to Christianity, for it was early developed by Greek Patristic theology as it sought to think out the interrelation between the incarnation and the creation, or the activity of God within space and time and his creative transcendence over all space and time. In the course of this development classical Christian theology had to reconstruct the foundations of knowledge in Greek philosophy and science, and then in the sixth/seventh century through John Philoponos it translated this teaching into physics with remarkable anticipations of twentieth century scientific thought. While these conceptions were denigrated by Byzantine and Western thought as 'monophysite' and were lost after being rather swamped by a massive revival of Neoplatonic philosophy and Ptolemaic cosmology, they nevertheless remain bound up with the foundations of classical Nicene theology. Hence it is not surprising that this kind of thinking finds itself very much at home today in the post-Einstein era of scientific and cosmological thought.[21] What is new to Christian theology, however, is the concept of space-time, and of the space-time metrical field understood as controlling and regulating the orderly patterns of all observable, and indeed of non-observable, processes and events in the universe. Since space-time is a four-dimensional continuum inseparable from the constituent

[20] See *Space, Time and Incarnation*, pp. 22ff.
[21] See 'The Relation of the Incarnation to Space in Nicene Theology', in *The Ecumenical World of Orthodox Civilization, Russia and Orthodoxy*, vol. III, *Essays in honor of Georges Florovsky* (ed. by A. Blane and T. E. Bird, 1974), pp. 43–70.

matter and energy of the universe it constitutes a profoundly objective dynamic structure; but since it is bound up with the speed of light which is of such a velocity that our senses cannot cope with it, the space-time continuum is necessarily invisible. This means that we must penetrate beyond the immediate and crude observation of things into the inherently non-observable structure of the space-time framework of the universe, if we are to grasp reality in its own objective depth. The fact that space-time, which embraces all our human experiences, is essentially an imperceptible, intangible magnitude, helps to prevent us from restricting the nature and range of experience to crude and limiting conceptions of it such as we tend to acquire under the pressure of a materialist outlook upon the universe. 'The discovery that space-time plays such a regulative role not only in the structure of the universe but in our ordinary experience, serves to disclose that knowledge at all levels arises on grounds that are not always or completely identifiable, and that there is much in the activities of our minds in their correlation to the intelligibility of the world around us that transcends our ability to track it down. This is why wonder must be accorded an important place in scientific inquiry, for it keeps our minds open to an indefinite range of possibility, not least when something novel in our experience conflicts with forms of thought that are already stereotyped in our minds'.[22] Such a way of thinking is of particular significance in theology where we are so often concerned not only with what transcends our powers of observation, but with unique and decisive events – and where more than in the case of the resurrection of Jesus? – which are not fully explicable through being brought into connection with anything else we can experience or conceive in the physical universe. However, we must not be misled into thinking that such an event as the resurrection may be 'explained' or made 'intelligible' simply in terms of the invisible structures of space-time, for what we are concerned with here is the interaction of *God* with the structures of space-time, but it should help us nevertheless to realize that although they are invisible, those structures have a

[22] 'The Integration of Form in Natural and in Theological Science', *op. cit.*, p. 154.

depth of objectivity in this world which we cannot explain away in terms of 'appearance'.

(3) A third aspect of modern thought which has a helpful bearing upon the interrelation between theological and other scientific inquiry is what is sometimes called the multi-levelled structure of human knowledge, upon which Einstein and Polanyi in particular have laid such stress.[23] This has to do not only with the fact that each science reveals a stratified structure of at least three layers or levels, in addition to that of pre-scientific experience and thought, the physical, the theoretical and the meta-theoretical (which has been Einstein's principal interest), but with the fact that the various sciences themselves), ranging from physics and chemistry to the humanities and theology can be regarded as constituting a hierarchical structure of levels of inquiry which are open upwards into wider and more comprehensive systems of knowledge but are not reducible downwards (which has been of special interest to Polanyi). The significance of this can be indicated in various ways. For example, in our investigation of nature we frequently come across a set of circumstances or events which do not seem to make sense for we are unable to bring them into any coherent relation with one another, but then our understanding of them is radically altered when we consider them from a different level, for from that point of view they are discerned to form a distinct, intelligible pattern. This can happen when an additional factor is included at the original level which helps us solve the puzzle, but often the all-important additional factor must be introduced from a higher level, which means that the coherent pattern of the circumstances or events we are studying is reached only through a dimension of depth involving cross-level reference. That is precisely the kind of objective thought that obtains in the application of four-dimensional geometries to our understanding of events in space and time, or rather, as it turns out to be, in space-time. Further, in genuinely objective knowledge of this kind, there is an intrinsic and necessary element of openness or indeterminacy at all levels of consistent thought, for, as the famous theorems of Kurt Gödel established, it is impossible to produce

[23] See, for example, A. Einstein, *Physics and Reality*, 1, *Out of My Later Years*, pp. 62ff.; or M. Polanyi. *The Tacit Dimension*, pp. 34ff., 40ff., 45ff.

a formalized system of thought which is both consistent and complete at the same time; to be consistent it requires to be completed from a level beyond itself.[24] There are then in our various levels of inquiry or layers of knowledge certain 'boundary conditions' (to use Einstein's expression) where each one is coordinated with a higher system, in terms of which it becomes explicable and intelligible. It is in this way that the various sciences are coordinated with each other through functioning conjunctively on different levels at the same time. While each science is governed by its own distinctive laws, these leave undefined a number of boundary conditions which may be controlled by the operations of a science governed by its own distinctive laws on a higher level. While such a science on a higher level relies on the laws governing the science on a lower level, without infringing them, for the fulfilment of its own operations, these operations are not explainable in terms of the laws governing the science on the lower level. Thus, if we take chemistry and biology as our examples, chemistry may be coordinated with biology through boundary conditions where its own laws are left indeterminate or open to biology, and biology is coordinated with chemistry in such a way that it relies on the laws of chemistry for the fulfilment of its own multivariable organismic operations which nevertheless cannot be explained through reductive analysis in terms of the principles of chemistry. The broad effect of this is to get rid of the kind of segregation that arises between branches of human knowledge when each science, or group of sciences, is regarded as constituting a closed and exclusive system on its own, and to reveal the lines of an inner semantic structure which coordinates and holds together all levels and areas of knowledge within the one universe of human inquiry. Such an integration of knowledge implies, however, what Michael Polanyi has called the principle of boundary or dual control.[25] Applied to the interrelation between science and theology with respect to the resurrection, this would mean that the only acceptable account of the resurrection would be one which took seriously

[24] K. Gödel, *On Formally undecidable Propositions in Principia Mathematica and Related Systems*, Eng. tr. 1962, pp. 37ff., 41, 62ff., 70f.

[25] M. Polanyi, *Knowing and Being*, pp. 153ff., 216ff., 225ff., etc. The argument here is deeply indebted to Polanyi.

empirical correlates in space and time, such as the empty tomb, which would be open to testing and critical control on a level or levels 'lower' than the theological, yet in such a way that the event of the resurrection is not subject to reductive specification or explanation in terms of the principles of such a level or levels of knowledge; but also one which took seriously its distinctive nature as act of God within the structures of space and time and which as such is open to testing and critical control in terms of the intrinsic principles of theological science. Engineering operations rely upon and do not infringe but transcend the principles of physics and chemistry; instead of being explainable in terms of them, engineering operations exercise control over them through the boundary conditions where they are left undefined, in such a way that patterns, artefacts, happenings, etc., are imposed upon nature beyond anything that nature is capable of producing merely in accordance with its own laws. It is the introduction of an entirely *new* factor, or set of factors, which brings about such astonishing transformations within nature as we have, for example, in an aeroplane.

This provides us at least with an intelligible analogy in helping us to understand the resurrection within the space-time structures of our world – although like all significant analogies it comprises many more elements of dissimilarity than of similarity. In fulfilment of his eternal design God has acted in the resurrection of Jesus Christ from the dead in such a way that, far from setting aside or infringing or interfering with the spatio-temporal order of the universe which he created (and which we try to formulate in what we call 'laws of nature'), he accepts and affirms its reality, but he introduces into the situation a transcendently new factor which brings about an utterly astonishing transformation of it which is quite inexplicable in terms of anything we are able to conceive merely within the intelligible structures of the world, or in accordance with our scientific formulations of them. And it is supremely in accordance with this new factor, and the intrinsic significance which it imports, that the resurrection of Jesus Christ is to be understood and interpreted. Any other way of understanding and interpreting it would be, to say the least, scientifically unacceptable, for it would not be a way of understanding and interpreting the resurrection according to its own distinctive nature.

(4) The last aspect of the new scientific outlook upon the universe which we are to consider is one upon which we have already encroached in discussing the multi-levelled structure of knowledge. It is that the universe itself is a stratified structure, for we have to do not only with levels of knowledge but with different levels of existence or reality.[26] Lying in the background here is the older familiar idea of a hierarchy of being, reaching from inanimate, merely physical things like stones through vegetative and animal existence to human being and so upward to God as the supreme Being. While this idea has its problems, it is not to be discounted altogether, but it seems better to approach the matter in another way. All created things have a significance of their own which invites inquiry, but this is a significance which we find to intensify the higher up the scale of existence we move. As the universe becomes progressively disclosed to our scientific inquiries it is found to be characterized by an intrinsic intelligibility of an ever deepening dimension which far outranges our powers of comprehension, invoking from us awe and wonder. Moreover, we become aware of being confronted in and behind it all with a transcendent reality over which we have no control but which, while utterly independent of our minds, has an indefinite capacity for revealing itself to them in quite unanticipated ways. It is indeed in response to this transcendent reality that our minds develop their own powers of comprehension and in recognition of it that they derive their primary thrust in passionate search for understanding and truth.[27] What we are concerned with here, however, is the place occupied by the human mind in the correlation between the different levels of knowledge and the different levels of reality and intrinsic significance in the universe itself.

We have already noted that each science tends to develop its own stratified structure, comprising primary, secondary and tertiary layers, as Einstein called them.[28] This is inevitable, for

---

[26] Cf. especially M. Polanyi, *The Study of Man*, 1959, pp. 71–99.

[27] These are ideas brilliantly developed by Michael Polanyi in a number of his works, but see especially here, *Science, Faith and Society*, new edition, 1964.

[28] A. Einstein, *Physics and Reality*, op. cit., pp. 62ff.

just as in pre-scientific activity we operate with at least two levels, that of the field or object we are investigating and that of ourselves the investigators or observers, so we cannot have a science without having a level above our basic activity on which we reflect on our investigations, the so-called meta-theoretical level, and indeed a higher level still, the meta-meta-theoretical, on which we test our reflections with reference to what Einstein used to speak of as an ultimate logical economy or simplicity. In such a stratified structure we the observers and thinkers occupy a level 'higher' than that which we investigate, which makes some form of anthropocentrism probably inevitable even in the most rigorously controlled scientific activity. However, the more intensively we probe into the inherent profundity of the universe, the deeper the dimension in which its objectivity and intelligibility become disclosed to us, the more we find our epistemic relation to it being reversed: we are up against a reality that towers above our intelligence, which we cannot know or reflect about by trying to occupy some epistemic stance 'above' it. This is the kind of reality which we may know by inquiring into it from 'below', as it were, by submitting our minds to the authority of what it actually is and seeking to apprehend it by allowing our understanding to fall under the power of its intrinsic but transcendent intelligibility, but this is to embark upon a course of humble discipline in which our minds will be stretched beyond our capacities which they may claim to have in themselves. As Polanyi has argued, this is the kind of experience we have even in the study of some great historical personality where 'we need reverence to perceive greatness, even as we need a telescope to observe spiral nebulae'.[29] He goes on, 'Clearly, when arrived here, we can no longer think of ourselves as observers occupying, as such, a logical level above that of our object. If we can still distinguish two levels we are now looking *up* to our object, not down'.[30] We have already noted, at the outset of our discussions, the kind of situation into which we are put when we come up against *ultimates* in human knowledge. But *the* ultimate with which we are concerned in the Christian message is the Lord God, whose

[29] M. Polanyi, *The Study of Man*, p. 96.
[30] *Ibid.*, p. 97.

saving acts we cannot hope to apprehend, far less God himself, by occupying a logical level above his reality. If God really is God we cannot know him except in recognition of his absolute priority and actuality, and therefore not by stealing knowledge of him behind his back, as it were, nor by climbing up to some vantage point above him, but only through reverent submission of our minds to his uncreated Light and Majesty. Only the mind which surrenders in awe and wonder to the transcendent reality of God himself will be able to approach the resurrection in a way appropriate to its intrinsic significance, worshipping the risen Jesus Christ as the Lord of space and time.

INDEX OF NAMES

Anderson, G. W., 29
Anselm, 20
Athanasius, 6, 75f, 96, 155
Athenagoras, 79ff
Augustine, 75, 82, 140, 155

Barth, Karl, ixff, 22, 32, 54, 59, 66f, 73, 80, 82f, 95f, 98, 105, 120, 123, 129, 141, 146, 153, 155f, 170, 173
Basilides, 72
Beasley-Murray, G. R., 19
Best, E., 118
Bird, T. E., 126, 186
Black, Matthew, 34, 41, 109
Blane, A., 126, 186
Bornkamm, G., 4
Brunner, Emil, 83, 88, 95, 102
Bultmann, Rudolf, 4, 9, 17ff, 39, 45, 66, 82, 84, 89, 95, 151, 160, 167
Burnaby, J., 154

Calvin, John, 63, 103, 124, 128, 132, 146, 150, 155
Celsus, 38
Clement of Alexandria, 142
Clement of Rome, 27, (72), 120f
Collingwood, R. G., 9, 182
Cranfield, C. E. B., 41, 66, 83, 87, 146, 154, 168
Cullmann, Oscar, 19, 41, 54, 88, 119, 148, 152, 155
Cyril of Alexandria, 21, 32, 78, 84

Danby, H., 29
Dante Alighieri, 140
Davey, F. N., 14, 170

Denney, James, 36, 39, 46, 82
Descartes, R., xii, 40
Diem, H., 119
Dilthey, W., 9, 182
Dodd, C. H., 41, 95, 154
Donatus, 155

Ehrhardt, A., 165
Einstein, Albert, ix, xi, 10f, 22, 184, 186, 188f, 191f
Ernst, C., 87
Euripides, 72

Ferré, N., 55
Fison, J. E., 154
Florovsky, G., 126, 186

Galileo Galilei, xii, 180
Gödel, Kurt, 15, 188f
Gregory of Nazianzus, 29
Gregory of Nyssa, 35

Hamilton, N. Q., 152
Harnack, A. von, 18, 39
Harris, Horton, 43
Harvey, W. W., 122, 142
Heidegger, M., 151
Hermas of Rome, 72, 101
Herrmann, W., 9
Hilary of Poitiers, 6, 48, 53
Hippolytus, 144
Hoskyns, Sir Edwin, 14, 150
Hunter, A. M., 4, 65f

Ignatius of Antioch, 72, 142
Irenaeus of Lyons, 20, 72, 75, 123, 133, 141, 155

Jeremias, J., 4, 30, 41, 75, 104, 113, 170, 173
John of Damascus, 20, 84, 96

John Philoponos, 186
Johnston, W. B., 128
Jüngel, E., 43
Justin Martyr, 19f, 72, 144
Justinian, 140

Kähler, M., 9
Kant, I., ix, xii, 40
Künneth, W., 39, 57, 66, 73f, 83, 90

Lampe, G. W. H., 65, 68
Lombard, Peter, 6
Luther, Martin, ix, 125, 155

McKinnon, A., 16
MacKinnon, D. M., 59, 65, 68, 90
Mackintosh, H. R., 56, 105, 143, 150
Macmurray, John, 42
MacQuarrie, John, 151
Mansi, G. D., 140
Manson, William, 4f, 14, 34, 41, 63, 68, 111, 113, 154, 160
Marcion, 64
Marsh, J., 160
Martin, Gordon W., 153f
Maximus the Confessor, 155
Meltzer, B., 15
Methodios of Olympus, 136
Milligan, William, 37, 52, 82, 112, 116f, 123
Minucius Felix, 27
Morrison, A. A., 146
Mowinckel, S., 29

Newbigin, Lesslie, 57
Newton, Sir Isaac, ix, xii, 8, 184, 186
Niebuhr, Reinhold, 95
Niebuhr, Richard R., 3f, 14, 181

Ogden, S. M., 4
Origen of Alexandria, 38, 110, 136, 140, 165

Pannenberg, W., 34f, 161, 171, 181f
Parker, T. H. L., 128
Philo Judaeus, 112f
Plato, 6, 140
Polanyi, Michael, 11, 14f, 22, 38, 188ff, 191ff
Purcell, W. E., 59, 65
Pusey, E. B., 32

Quick, O. C., 5, 38, 46

Rahner, Karl, 87, 129
Ramsey, A. M., 31, 48, 181
Ratzinger, J., 130
Rickert, H., 182
Robinson, E., 151
Roth, C., 29

Schmitt, F. S., 20
Scholz, Heinrich, ixf
Schweitzer, A., 104
Serapion of Thmuis, 142
Simmell, G., 182
Stewart, J. S., vii, xiii, 28, 32, 58, 64, 100, 148
Strauss, D. F., 45

Tatian, 27
Temple, William, 126
Tertullian, 25, 72, 75, 82, 155
Teselle, E., 140
Theophilus, 27

Vogel, Heinrich, 53, 59, 110

Werner, Martin, 154
Wilkinson, John, 60
Windelband, W., 182